OAKTON COMM
3 3211 0016

D1572744

New Transport Architecture

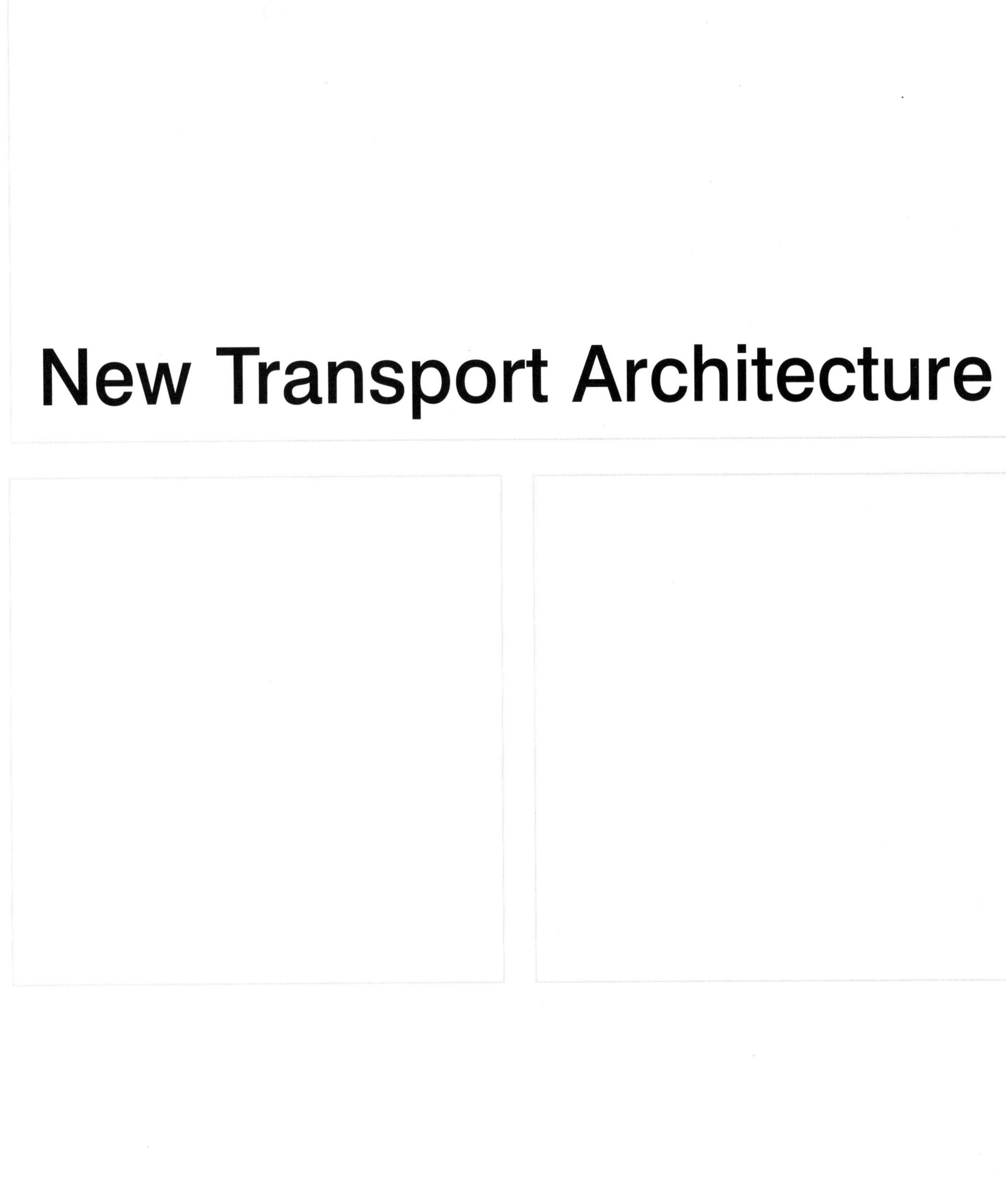

New Transport Architecture

Will Jones

MITCHELL BEAZLEY

Contents

6 Foreword
by Ivan Harbour of Richard Rogers Partnership
8 Introduction
12 Adding Retail Value to Airports by David Holm

1 Air

20 **Barajas Airport** Spain Richard Rogers Partnership
28 **Beijing Capital International Airport** China Foster and Partners
32 **International Terminal, Philadelphia Airport** USA Kohn Pedersen Fox
38 **Virgin Atlantic Upper Class Lounge** USA ShoP
42 **Bangkok International Airport** Thailand Murphy Jahn
48 **Tianjin Binhai International Airport** China Kohn Pedersen Fox
52 **Ben Gurion International Airport** Israel Moshe Safdie & Associates
58 The Politics of Public Transport by Yoichi Shimatsu & Stephen S Y Lau

2 Road

66 **Vauxhall Cross Interchange** UK Arup Associates
74 **Carpark Burda Media Park** Germany Ingenhoven Architekten
80 **The Whale Jaw** Netherlands NIO Architecten
88 **Cycle Parking Garage** Netherlands VMX Architects
94 **Border Station** USA Ross Barney + Jankowski Architects
100 **Sound Barrier and Cockpit** Netherlands ONL
108 **Central Bus Station** Germany Auer & Weber Architekten
112 **Underground Parking Garage** Austria Szyszkowitz & Kowalski
118 **Mölndal Commuter Station** Sweden Wingardh Arkitektkontor
124 **Box Hill Transport Interchange** Australia McGauran Soon Architects
128 **Cycle Station** UK Fourth Door Research and the Architecture Ensemble
132 Engineering in Transport Architecture by Richard Prust

3 Water

140 **Yokohama International Port Terminal** Japan Foreign Office Architects
148 **Naviduct Lock Complex** Belgium Zwarts & Jansma Architects
152 **DFDS Terminal** Denmark 3X Nielsen
158 **Maritime Terminal** Italy Zaha Hadid
162 **Leith Ferry Terminal** UK Jessam al Jawad
170 **Ferry Landing Stage** Netherlands DAAD Architecten
174 **Falkirk Wheel** UK RMJM
182 **St George Ferry Terminal** US Hellmuth, Obata + Kassabaum
190 **Whitehall Ferry Terminal** US Frederic Schwartz Architects
196 Water-based Transport Architecture by Kenneth Drucker & Eve Michel

4 Rail

204 **Three Kinds of Flow** Japan Makoto Sei Watanabe
212 **Moscow City Transport Terminal** Russia Behnisch Behnisch & Partner
216 **King's Cross Station** UK John McAslan + Partners
224 **Leuven Train Station** Belgium Samyn and Partners
230 **Stuttgart Central Station** Germany Ingenhoven Architekten
234 **Worb Station** Switzerland Smarch
242 **Central Station** Germany BRT Architekten
248 **Fulton Street Transit Center** USA Nicholas Grimshaw & Partners
254 **Stratford International Station** UK Rail Link Engineering
260 Environmental Rail Building Design by Oliver Lowenstein

264 Contact Details
267 Bibliography
268 Index
272 Acknowledgments

To my Dad, for instilling all the best values in me and for setting a lackadaisical 16-year-old on a winding journey that has led from building sites to books and a profession that I love, thank you

New Transport Architecture
First published in Great Britain in 2006
by Mitchell Beazley an imprint of
Octopus Publishing Group Ltd,
2–4 Heron Quays, London E14 4JP

ISBN 13: 978 1 845332 18 1
ISBN 10: 1 84533 218 0

A CIP catalogue copy of this book is available from the British Library

Commissioning Editor Hannah Barnes-Murphy
Project editor Catherine Emslie, Peter Taylor
Executive Art Editor Yasia Williams-Leedham
Design John Round Design
Copy editor Virginia McLeod
Proofreader Francis Sandham
Indexer Sue Farr
Production Gary Hayes

Set in Swiss 721

Colour by Sang Choy International Pte Ltd
Printed and bound in China
by Toppan Printing Company

Previous image: Mölndal Commuter Station Sweden
Opposite image: King's Cross Station, London
Overleaf image: Barajas airport, Madrid

Foreword

by Ivan Harbour
Director, Richard Rogers Partnership

Transport architecture is a manifestation of extremes of scale and complexity. At one extreme, it is represented by a huge airport hub covering more than one million square metres (10,763,910 square feet), processing 40 million people every year and costing hundreds of millions of dollars to construct and maintain. At the other end of the scale, it can be a simple bus shelter serving the needs of a few hundred people every day, but still playing an important role in the life of a local community.

Transport architecture deals with constant and often rapid changes in capacity, technology, and process. It is an architecture that may need to work within a tight city context, contributing to the quality of a city's public realm. Alternatively, it can be an architecture that stands alone, connected to urban areas via roads, railways, runways or waterways. It is the architecture of the "loose overcoat", rather than a tight fitting garment. The architecture accepts change, while the constants of space, light and acoustics remain in place throughout a building's lifespan to give users a strong sense of the excitement of travel.

However, in spite of this diversity of scale and type, transport architecture fundamentally creates spaces where we wait for our chosen mode of travel and start or finish our journeys. But this does not detract from its importance. A transport node or interchange is a place of mixed emotions – excitement tinged with anxiety, happiness at greeting loved ones and sadness when they depart, comings and goings, the beginning and end of a good night out. In urbanized societies, these spaces are often our principal meeting places.

In turn, buildings associated with transport – arguably the most public of all architectural typologies – take on a role as indicators of renewal, of modern and forward thinking. The organizations that encourage and promote transport-related buildings demand that they act as "gateways" or symbols, for example, for the wider regeneration of an area or to evoke civic pride. At the same time, these organizations have to balance this demand with the delivery of buildings that are efficient, offer value for money, and compete effectively with other modes of transport – for example, short-haul air travel versus high-speed, international rail services. So while lingering between embarkation or transfer, having to endure delays and security checks, we are bombarded by advertising and presented with retail offers.

Despite the often huge technical complexities, transport architecture has a fundamentally simple job – to process individual users from one transport source to another. From foot to bus, bus to aeroplane, plane to train, train to ship, plane to plane, and so on. The scale of the buildings required is a direct reflection of the movement of users or passengers, multiplied by the maximum predicted capacity for any given timescale.

When an architect is faced with a commission for a transport development, the briefing document can often be extremely short and succinct. In the case of the New Area Terminal at Barajas airport, Madrid (illustrated opposite) the brief to Richard Rogers Partnership was initially simply a requirement to process a specified number of passengers per annum. The size, organization, and disposition of functions were determined from this simple requirement, through the involvement of a huge, multi-disciplinary design team. These are buildings about process.

So what makes good transport architecture? Clearly, there are many examples of transport hubs that manage to process individuals in a relatively uninspiring way – just think of the unappealing experience of passing through an old-style airport terminal that lacks natural illumination. In addition, others have been unable to evolve and adapt to the impact of new technologies and requirements and are, at the same time, faced with having to deal with the demands of significant increases in passenger numbers – for example, the rail network in the southern and eastern regions of the UK in the past decade.

Good transport architecture is an architecture that celebrates the intrinsically mundane processes governing transport hubs, such as that of the environments in which we wait and through which we move from one transport process to another. This is uplifted by the spatial experience of the building – its clarity, volume and scale. It is an architecture that fully exploits these aspects of design to make way-finding clear, to make the process of dealing with users obvious, and helping to reduce stress and anxiety among the travelling public.

Colours, materials, acoustics, daylight, and artificial illumination – these are the constants that lend relief to a process often obscured by the conflicting demands of retail, advertising and security. Well-executed architecture effects a fine balance between these varying demands.

This book contains examples of buildings and spaces of all scales that deal with many types of transport. From car parks to airports, bus stops to ferry terminals, all impact upon our lives. What they have in common is a delight in celebrating the role of transport architecture in our lives.

Introduction

Travel is now, more than at any time in the past century, an emotive subject. While 200 years ago, the only voices heard preached of the great advancements being made in public and personal transport, today opinions are being raised both in support of our right and ability to go farther and faster, and against the proliferation of transport in the global society.

Low cost airlines offer flights across the Atlantic for the price of a pair of designer running shoes, greater global wealth is fuelling a massive boom in automobile sales throughout the Third World, and scientists are investigating sending humans to Mars. This is good, isn't it?

Fuel emissions of nearly all forms of powered transport, especially the air industry, are pumping vast amounts of pollution into the atmosphere, causing stifling smog in large conurbations. Obesity is one of the biggest killers in the western world. Why? Because we have no need to stretch our legs when we can hop into the car. And, global terrorism is a new anomaly brought about by our ability to travel anywhere at any time.

These things taken into consideration, the human race is driven by a compulsion to further itself in all aspects of life and travel – transportation – will not be left behind. Before we think of the future, let us dip back into the history books and remind ourselves about how, quite literally, we got where we are today.

Making history

The remains of sleds used by hunter-gatherer clans in northern Europe have been found in excavations dating back to 7000 BC. Evidence of the wheel dates back to 3000 BC. It was first discovered somewhere near what is now Zurich, Switzerland. Within 1000 years its use had spread from northern Europe to western Persia and Mesopotamia.

In subsequent centuries, up until fairly recent times, advancements in transportation were based almost solely around water-borne travel. In the sixth century BC the Persian emperor Darius I built canals to transport goods throughout Mesopotamia, and, between 520 and 510 BC his forces built a canal in Egypt, linking the Nile with the Red Sea. Its access to the sea was near the modern Ismailia, which would much later become the terminus of the Suez Canal.

Some 300 years later in the second century BC, the Romans took on the pioneering mantle and over a period of 400 years built a vast arterial road system totalling some 50,000 miles across Europe. However, these new thoroughfares were primarily for communication and troop movement on foot or by horse: their resulting straightness and scant regard for contours made the steep hills almost impassable for heavily laden carts.

With the Roman roads came one of the first forms of transport architecture, the post house. This ancient service

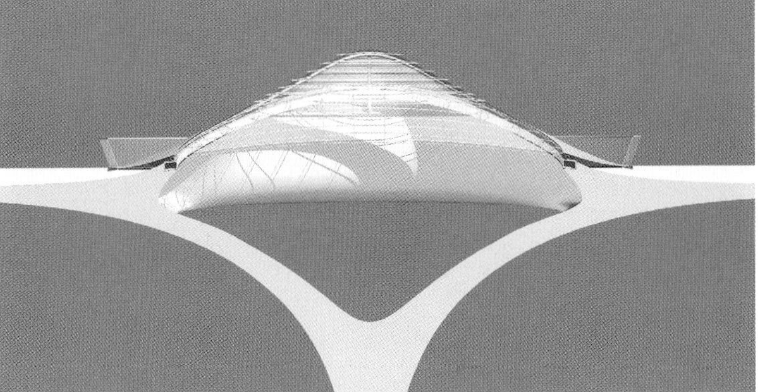

station, located at approximately ten-mile intervals along the roads, housed fresh horses and accommodation for travellers.

However, while transport architecture didn't really become a large-scale requirement until the 19th century and the Industrial Revolution, engineers have been at the forefront of our desire to travel since the very dawn of transport. Locks transformed travel on canals – the invention of the Pound Lock for the great Chinese canal system in the 10th century AD is credited to Chiao Wei-yo. Leonardo da Vinci refined the design by combining it with mitred gates on a project in Milan in 1500. What da Vinci built over 500 years ago is essentially what is still in use on canals today.

Roads and canals sufficed for many years. Neither the invention of the hot air and hydrogen balloons in the 1780s by Joseph Montgolfier and Jacques Alexandre Cesar Charles respectively, nor Thomas Telford and John McAdam's new road building techniques in the early 1800s, had any real impact on everyday transportation.

Then, with the invention of the steam engine, transportation took its next great step. In 1825 George Stephenson's Rocket locomotive began pulling passengers on the Stockton & Darlington Railway and the rail transport was born. Five years later, the Tom Thumb, designed by

Far left Whale Jaw bus station, by NIO Architecten, Hoofddorp, The Netherlands

Centre St George Ferry Terminal, NYC by HOK

Above top Stuttgart Central Station, Germany, by Ingenhoven Architecten

Above lower Ben Gurion International Airport, Israel, by Moshe Safdie & Associates and TRA Architects

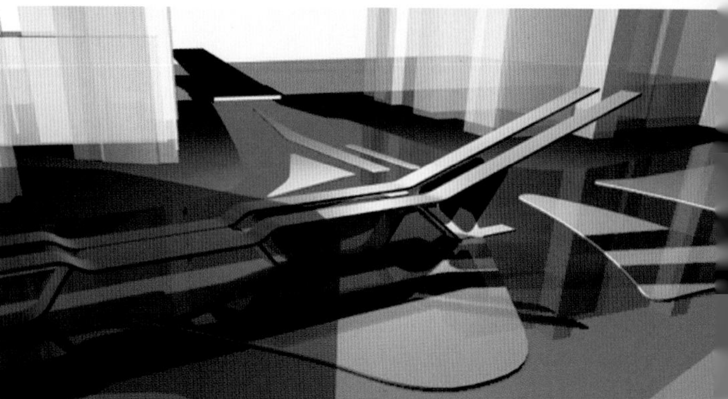

Peter Cooper, was the first American-built steam locomotive to operate as a common-carrier railroad. By the 1860s long distance railroads linked most cities and train travel ruled.

Stations sprang up at all main terminuses, with small shelters at stops in between. Liverpool Road, credited as the first real station, opened in 1830 and is preserved as part of the Museum of Science and Industry in Manchester, England. It resembles a row of Georgian houses. Many existing stations date from the 19th century and reflect the architecture of the time. The Gothic stations of St Pancras in London, designed by George Gilbert Scott and William Henry Barlow (1865–77), and the Chhatrapati Shivaji Terminus, or Victoria Station, in Mumbai, by Fredrick Stevens (1887) are fine examples.

Steam was also used to power road-going vehicles including small carriage buses. However in 1859, the double acting spark ignition engine was invented by J J Etienne Lenoir and by the 1880s motorized transport was first seen. The bicycle appeared at about the same time too, and within 20 years it had advanced to a form, complete with pneumatic tyres, similar to modern day models.

Man's last great transport hurdle was the air, and, on 17 December 1903, the Wright brothers made their historic 12-second flight. By the latter part of the First World War bi-planes were battling it out over the skies of Europe and in 1919 the British pilots Captain John Alcock and Lieutenant Arthur Whitten Brown made the first non-stop aerial crossing of the Atlantic, taking sixteen hours and twenty-seven minutes.

The century spanning 1830 to 1930 was the dawn of real transportation architecture. Grand rail stations were the pride of every city and in the 1920s "air stations" as they were initially known were built at Croydon in the UK, at Konigsburg and Tempelhof in Germany, and in a host of cities in the USA.

The 1930s saw airport designers expanding existing airports and designing new ones on a much larger scale. Tempelhof's large expansion was commissioned by Hitler's chief architect Albert Speer and designed by Ernst Sagebiel, while Gatwick Airport, by Hoar Marlow & Lovett, was completed in 1936 outside London. Across the Atlantic, La Guardia Airport, or North Beach as it was called on its 1937 opening in Queens, New York, got a new marine terminal for flying boats, by Delano & Aldrich, in addition to its land plane terminal.

Many of the airports that we experience today, with their central terminals and radiating departure gates, derive from designs first muted in the 1950s as "pier finger" or star terminals. And, while vehicle technology has advanced, both it and the design of the buildings that accompany it, have changed only to a limited degree in the last 50 years, mainly to facilitate use by larger numbers of people.

Building the future

Current research in both automotive and aeronautical transport is now attempting to marry our desire to travel to the ends of the earth with the need to find less polluting methods of getting there. People are beginning to realise the destruction that we are reaping on our planet and there is a growing consensus that we must learn to forego private travel modes in favour of saving energy, the environment, and our health by once again using greener means and public transport.

Transportation architecture is advancing in much the same direction. The foremost requirements for these most public of buildings are efficiency in the processing of travellers, legibility and ease of use, safety and security, and the minimization of environmental impact (energy and location). But the architect's job is not a purely functional one. The airport, train station, bus or ferry terminal must also be engaging, enlivening and even iconic. This is a tall order but a necessary one and it is something that the projects in this book achieve on a multitude of differerent levels.

Far left Ferry landing stage in Vlieland, The Netherlands, by DAAD Architecten

Centre top Whitehall Ferry Terminal, New York City, by Frederic Schwartz Architects

Centre below Vauxhall Cross Interchange, London, by Arup Associates

Above International terminal, Philadelphia Airport, by KPF

Adding Retail Value to Airports

David Holm
Is an architect and design principal for Woodhead International in Australia. An architect for 20 years, he is enthused by the interaction of education, design philosophies, and practical constraints, employing collaborative communication to balance complex design solutions.

Airports worldwide are increasingly aware of the impact and value of retail – as a source of revenue, to reinforce brand identity, and to cater to passenger needs. But how do airport operators best incorporate retail into their terminals? What design principles should be applied to add value and how can these principles be applied to airports of all different shapes, sizes, locations, cultures and passenger types? Outlined in the following text are some of the fundamental issues faced by airports when integrating commercial initiatives into a process driven environment, including design principles that may be implemented into an airport's planning strategy to add value to both the earning potential and the positive passenger experience.

Originally, airports were designed for the sole purpose of facilitating incoming and outgoing passengers: terminals were rated according to their processing efficiency, through-put and capacity. As the demand for global air travel increases, especially into the growing middle classes and Third World countries, passenger needs are more varied and passengers themselves are much more discerning. The contemporary airport operator is searching for new ways to optimize income production and service in order to meet these expectations and remain competitive in the airport marketplace.

Retail Planning

Retail planning is at its worst considered peripheral to airport design and conducted in isolation to stakeholder groups. Terminal architecture, engineering and facilities planning issues are often decided upon prior to consultation with the commercial and retail managers. However, much of the skill in airport retail design is in the coordination and understanding of the critical requirements of each user group and stakeholder in a cohesive, collaborative and integrated sense.

The use of a cohesive project masterplan is fundamental to the success of any new or existing retail environment and must begin with a collaborative, balanced approach. A masterplan requires the right team in place and needs to be undertaken with strong collaboration and regular consultation with the airport and the many relevant stakeholders. Key points that should be addressed within a masterplan are:

Vision – the collective airport management team holds this key to the success of the airport's future.

Brief – the formation of a clear and detailed brief is vital. A good brief will develop with collaborative input from airport stakeholders.

Collaboration – good design cannot be implemented in isolation.

Reliable information – local and global information is essential as well as a clear understanding of the region's growth, culture and profile, and best practice procedures.

Regional understanding – a masterplan for an Indian airport may face different challenges than a masterplan for an Australian airport, as well as a very different "sense of place".
Team – a balance of commercial and operational requirements is the key, and both commercial and operational stakeholders require sound representation.

A robust, collaborative masterplan at the project's inception is critical for the successful implementation of commercial initiatives, processing initiatives and the establishment of a spatial environment that creates a lasting positive impression upon passengers. Remember the romance of travel?

Revenue Creation

The challenge to all retailers remains "how to get people to spend?" Good shop design and clever marketing will only go part of the way. The balance between good customer service, value and ease of movement through an airport are crucial for enticing passengers to spend.

A study by Omar & Kent (2001) at Gatwick Airport using a sample of airport users showed that "impulsive shopping at the airport is induced and, or, encouraged by both marketing and airport environment. It revealed that 35 per cent of airport users are converted purchasers; however a total of 65 per cent of users do not visit the shop or browse with no intention of buying." Indeed, in times where we all claim to be time poor, the airport's captive nature provides an ideal place to dwell, enjoy and spend.

Way finding

Retail design that is vibrant and enticing should never be in conflict with clear passenger way-finding. Passengers should not be overloaded with too much information. Confusion and anxiety are minimized by using effective signage in conjunction with clear sight lines. Passengers who shop within airports are more often "on a mission" and are influenced by lack of time, premeditation, rapid impulse decision-making and sensitivity to occupant volumes. Interestingly enough, they are either unmotivated or less conscious of price point. The clarity, visibility and accessibility of the retail product are therefore essential in creating a successful and legible retail environment.

Sense of Place

As part of the vision of the airport, a sense of place or unique memorable travel experience may be reinforced. Retail area themeing, with integrated advertising and public art, reinforce the identity of the airport while creating a vibrant shopping precinct. The design should be iconic and identifiable with the airport's location.

Examples of this may be seen in the refurbishment of Australia's Sydney Airport prior to the 2000 Olympic Games, designed to be an expression of vibrant Sydney. Vancouver Airport's use of indigenous artworks expresses a cultural sense of place and Hong Kong Airport's recent retail upgrade engages a vibrant abstraction of the Nathan Road, Kowloon experience. In Sydney, the design solutions include the use of local materials – natural timbers for building details, colours that are reminiscent of the outdoor lifestyle, and themed or precinct-focussed retail hubs. The ongoing success of Sydney Airport's retail offer is seen in the 13.1 per cent increase in retail revenues in the first six months to 31 December 2004.

Comfort

Above all, the passenger's comfort and amenity is primary, especially to alleviate anxiety, increase comfort, and maximize the propensity to spend. As such, the design should focus around the experiences and facilities that a passenger will require when moving through the facility. Diverse facilities such as toilets, baby change rooms, quiet areas, and entertainment, must be clearly defined, convenient and integrated with the overall design concept. General seating areas should be close to, and compatible with, retail. The retail experience should support passenger way-finding with clear and logical signage balancing both way-finding and retail needs.

Design

Airport commercial zones are becoming more integrated, more akin to a contemporary urban marketplace or streetscape modelled on the proven forms of mixed use piazzas or traditional streets. Passengers cannot be expected to hunt for retail or refreshment – it must be placed where it will not be missed, ready, and legible. Retail tenancies need to interact, take part in, and invigorate the overall design environment of the passenger. A common retail theory is to pack stock wall to wall in the hope to increase sales. This unfortunately leads to blockages to the product on display and restricts circulation into the shop. With this in mind, the retail plan should accommodate appropriate levels of storage, in close proximity to the point of sale, and allocate sufficient circulation zones within the retail environment. This strategy reduces clutter, opens space and reduces the required retail floor areas.

Optimizing the existing architecture

A retail layout that best suits the requirements of the commercial brief will often misalign with the terminal architecture and reveal a number of volumetric challenges. Higher space is best suited to main thoroughfares and retail while lower spaces suit more intimate seating and hospitality zones. The commercial solution for Chek Lap Kok Airport's East Hall retail remodelling necessitated a total revision of the high and low space ideology within the terminal in order to optimize the use of the existing spaces. High spaces were filled with design icons, which reinforced branding and advertising, and enhanced the way finding within the multi-level terminal.

Natural light is desirable for circulation and dwelling zones wherever possible; however, retail is better served by artificial lighting and more often resents natural lighting. The lighting in airports often lacks the intensity and contrast needed to separate commercial areas from other activities. This reduces clarity and adds to passenger confusion. Increasing the lux levels at shop fronts to over 1000 lux can ensure the retail offer stands out and contrasts with the adjacent environments.

Views to the airfield are precious and are critical "dwell anchors", as people are attracted to, and love looking at, the "theatre of aeroplanes". Food and beverage tenants are well suited to these areas, and should be integrated as attractions into the retail precinct. Access to views can dramatically increase commercial activity especially on landside food and beverage operations and appropriately placed viewing decks.

Outdoor spaces offer additional viewing platforms, as well as a refuge for smokers and transit passengers, and should be integrated with the retail experience. Changi Terminal 1 in Singapore has an open-air cactus garden with an iconic bar and is a classic example of an external integrated retail space and tropical experience. It is unique, memorable and popular.

Many terminals may in fact already have great assets that only require minor upgrading. Commercial teams must be sensitive to what the market expects and recognize that some of the "quirks" may not follow the latest directions but add diversity and texture to an environment. More retail space is not necessarily better retail space.

Retail Design

Traditionally the shop front has been a device to keep the weather out, create protection from theft, and showcase the product inside the shop to an optimum level. Airport terminals are amongst the most secure environments in the world. Due to this increased security, some of the traditional barriers such as windows and doors may be manipulated or removed all together, especially in scenarios of 24 hour operations or multi-concession ownership. There is an emerging trend for primary circulation paths to be integrated within retail concessions. This provides 100 per cent footfall and increases passenger exposure to the retail offer. This is occurring worldwide especially in duty free environments where the passenger is immersed in a totally integrated retail space. These "walk through duty free" stores have proven a bonus in experiential terms and also revenue increases.

Shop front materials must be durable and often of a design that allows individual retail expression. Tenancy fit-out guides must clearly outline acceptable finishes and materials to ensure a level of quality that will withstand the rigours of the retail environment. Most modern terminals will co-ordinate both hard and soft floor finishes. Hard finishes, such as granite or reconstituted stone, are often best suited in high wear areas such as shop fronts, concourses and baggage areas (check in and baggage reclaim). These finishes can be of a reflective finish to provide higher light intensity in these areas. Softer or warmer finishes, such as carpet and timber, are well placed in quieter zones such as gate lounges and food and beverage areas as these finishes absorb sound and light, making them appropriate for the often more intimate dwelling zones.

It is critical to get shop front lighting correct. This zone can be split into two main areas – the primary shop front zone and the tenant zone. The primary shop front zone can help unify the shop edge with a light and signage portal. The tenant zone lighting reflects the personality and needs of the retailer. Seating, food and beverage, and concourses may have less intense lighting, which highlights only features, kiosks and way-finding opportunities. Empirical models indicate that a good lighting design, often simply more than less light, will enhance retail sales.

Large Terminals

Typical retail design issues to be faced in larger passenger terminal environments include:

High throughput – areas can be big and impersonal so that retail tends to be passed by in the process, if not correctly designed.

Large spaces – designers are always looking for new ways to retail for example to do without a ceiling, or to place objects within large spaces.

Creating interest in multiple locations – rigorous management programmes must ensure that all areas are

performing at their best. Promotional and entertainment zones with a good food and beverage mix help connect a larger terminal.
Way-finding – long travel distances increase passengers' speed through the terminal. Building layouts should be clear and signage available to stop passengers getting lost.
Longer busy hours – this can be tuned for higher exposure for longer times.
Complex processing – passengers are often trapped in queues rather than shopping.
Staging issues – upgrades and refurbishment can take extended periods of time due to the size of the terminal. Retail outlets need to remain fully functional throughout the construction period.
High costs – maintenance, operations complexities, and high staff numbers.

Successful retail design ensures an increase in passenger footfall and dwelling times with a correspondent increase in spending. The most successful airport retail revenue environments in the world are condensed in format, with approximately 0.7 to 1.5 square metres (7.5 to 16 square feet) of retail per 1000 passengers. Any airport seeking to improve their retail return should be aspiring to maximize gross sales per passenger, retail income per passenger, gross sales per square metre average, and retail income per square metre. "Precinctualization" is an important consideration, whereby retail is co-located with the food and beverage provisions. Food and beverage acts as an anchor for retailing to cluster around, with seating designed to allow people to eat food within the shopping precinct – the resultant increase in dwelling times in retail precincts can add 5 per cent to sales.

Some basic retail design principles can be applied. The food and beverage should constitute 30–35 per cent of the retail floor space, duty free 25 per cent of the retail floor space, and the remainder consisting of specialty stores and currency exchange facilities. The retail offer should cover all market segments, for example sell low cost beers as well as premium beers. The product mix should include the usual airport goods with a focus upon high information intensity and high margin products that are retailed in an exciting environment.

Small Terminals

Typical retail design issues encountered in smaller passenger terminal environments include:
Low or fluctuating throughput – challenging for retailers during quiet times.
Small spaces – often concessions need to be smaller and the offer can be cramped.
Small retail mix – often a smaller range of products.
Smaller sustainable tenants – can be difficult to attract larger brands.
Multi-brand shops – necessary for survival.
Gift shop mentality – cluttered multi-product souvenir shops. These are popular in many tourist destinations. Offerings can be low on sophistication and service – a single operator may control two or all of the outlets, which are often over stretched and at worst under serviced.
Long quiet times – closed roller grilles give any terminal a closed down feel.

In conclusion, the primary issues to be considered when adding retail value to an airport are:
Maximum exposure is to be focused in the high payoff post security and immigration retail areas;
Maximise retail areas in centralized passenger zones;
The integration of retail, food and beverage, and passenger facilities to create a vibrant mixed use environment;
The creation of legible spaces;
Integrate clear way-finding principles within retail environments;
Clear and improved sight lines;
Minimize multi-level retail environments;
Ensure effective queue strategies and processing before and after retailing.

The successful integration of retail into an airport will enhance the passenger journey experience and differentiate the airport from its competitors, with the constant reinforcement of a desired brand identity and sense of place. All areas of the airport, from kerb side to departure, should focus upon passenger comfort, ease of use, and resonate with local colours, textures, icons, artworks, and images. The successful addition of "retail value" to an airport comes from the balance of meeting passenger processing and facility needs whilst reinforcing positive travel experiences and simultaneously generating revenue.

1
U·S AIRWAYS
Welcome To
elphia Intl Airport

Air

20 Madrid Barajas Airport
28 Beijing Capital Airport
32 International Terminal Philadelphia Airport
38 Virgin Atlantic Upper Class Lounge
42 Bangkok International Airport
48 Tianjin International Binhai Airport
52 Ben Gurion International Airport

Air

Flight epitomizes the glamour of travel. While trains and ships offer many delights, both seem limited and somehow crude when compared to the ability to soar into the sky, to go almost anywhere unhindered by the barriers so prevalent on the surface of the planet. And the airport is the portal to this exciting adventure or the welcoming gateway back to a reassuring *terra-firma*. It is a place of transition but also the punctuation at the beginning or end of a journey that takes us high above all we are used to, and as such, it is the most significant and somehow romantic of all transport architecture.

Airport designers did not take long to grasp this idea. Following a relatively short period of ad hoc airfield construction, the first true airports were built in the 1930s. Tempelhof Airport in Berlin, Germany, is indicative of the grandeur we associate with these dramatic changes in travel. Initially a neat Modernist building, designed and constructed in 1926–9 by Paul and Klaus Engler, it was soon expanded and rebuilt under the instruction of the Third Reich, by architect Ernst Sagebiel. The new building, a stripped classical design boasted an immense arrivals hall – a grand entrance into Germany – and but for the Second World War, the building would have featured an grand rooftop viewing platform for thousands of aviation enthusiasts.

In the 1960s Eero Saarinen took the architectural world by storm with the completion of two airport terminals in the USA, the TWA Terminal in New York (1962) and Dulles Airport, Washington (1963). The latter is credited as being the first airport of the jet age – and both airports reinforced in concrete the romance of the passenger air industry with sculptural forms that evoked wings, birds, even flight itself.

The 1970s saw a more pragmatic approach to airport design as the numbers of planes and people using the buildings multiplied dramatically. The star-shaped terminal design, first seen in the 1950s, was still favoured. Paul Andreu's Roissy Terminal One at Charles De Gaulle Airport in Paris developed it further into a rotunda for passengers to arrive and depart via cars, around which satellite mini-terminals are situated with multiple flight gates.

Much of the romanticism of air travel was laid to rest in the mid 1970s and early 80s. International terrorism led to tighter security at airports and deregulation produced profit-driven terminals that saw retail outlets as their cash cow. Stanstead Airport in the UK, by Foster and Partners, is an example of the uneasy alliance of iconic airport architecture and necessary retail units. The spacious departures hall, designed in Foster's high-tech style, is both a check-in area and a holding bay for the bottleneck of travelers waiting to go through security checks. In order to capitalize on this captive audience, revenue generating boxes containing book stores, cafes, and other retail outlets litter the floor space, detracting from Foster's pure architectural vision.

Far Left Beijing Capital International Airport, by Foster & Partners

Middle Departures hall, International terminal Philadelphia Airport, by KPF

Left top The Virgin Atlantic Upper Class Lounge bar at JFK Airport, New York, designed by SHoP

Left lower Arrivals ramp at Ben Gurion International Airport Israel, by Moshe Safdie + Associates and TRA Architects

However unsettling cultural and commercial progress is to the architectural eye, it drives our desire to build. Thankfully architects now embrace elements such as the passenger lounge to create exciting features within airports. The striking new Virgin Atlantic Upper Class Lounge at JFK Airport, New York, by Sharples Holden Pasquarelli (page 38) is a sculptural addition that recreates the glamour of air travel – a waterfall, feature bar and secluded relaxation areas add a glossy chic to the airport experience.

Design rules

Modern airport design follows the general rule, "always build in the ability to expand". As such, most new airports follow the similar pattern of a large departures and arrivals hall containing all necessary security and passenger amenities. Off of this extend long narrow wings (corridors) that are punctuated by a plethora of flight gates. These wings are always extendable if more plane parking space is required.

However, the ability to adapt and extend an airport is not only dependent upon its form but also its location. Berlin's Tempelhof is a good historic example of failure in this respect. Extended soon after it was built, the terminal was large enough to cater for the foreseeable future and planned to be open until 2000. It managed this but only because a relatively small number of business passengers enjoy short flights around Europe. In reality Tempelhof's location within Berlin means that there is no room to expand the runways to cope with larger planes and so it has lost out on international flights to the larger Tegel Airport located outside of the city.

The same problem is apparent at London's Heathrow Airport. One of the busiest in the world, it was built in the 1950s far outside of the city's boundaries, so far in fact that some doubted its success. Today however, the new Terminal Five could be the last expansion of Heathrow and economic analysts are already forecasting business trends based on it no longer being the city's primary air transport link.

Another factor to add to the equation is the next generation of aircraft. Unveiled late in 2005, the gigantic Airbus A380 is a jet capable of carrying up to 840 passengers. The length of runway required by this plane is only available at a few international airports around the world. Others are frantically expanding to allow for the new aircraft.

The airport designs for tomorrow, such as Foster's Beijing Capital International Airport (page 28) or Murphy Jahn's Bangkok International Airport (page 42), need to look to the future before they are even built. They must second-guess global passenger trends and accommodate aircraft that are not yet operational. This is architecture for the romantic, the aspirational, and the pragmatic rolled into one.

Madrid Barajas Airport

DESIGN RICHARD ROGERS PARTNERSHIP
LOCATION MADRID, SPAIN

With a total floor area of 120,000 m² (1,291,200 square feet), the Richard Rogers Partnership's addition to Spanish aviation architecture is a considerable one. Costing over £440 million, Barajas Airport Terminal is the largest in Spain and will serve 35 million passengers annually.

The terminal's design exudes a simplicity that is born out of immensely complicated planning. Each repetition of the undulating winged roof familiarizes visitors with the structure and excites them about the travel experience, while Rogers' trademark use of colour, applied to the main structural members, draws them through the building as it morphs column by column, shade by shade, from yellow through to red.

The main terminal includes four buildings in all, connected via light canyons. The first is open-air and incorporates rail, metro, coach, taxi, and drop-off arrivals functions. The second is the check-in hall, with the arrivals hall in the space below, between it and the drop-off building. The third building is security, with the baggage hall below, which spreads into the light canyons either side; the forth is the 1.2 kilometre (0.7 mile) long pier and gates.

The passenger route emphasizes the buildings' forms by providing spectacular side-on views down their length and by creating a route that leads across the three-storey light canyons on wide bridges. The international satellite building is located some 2 kilometres (1.2 miles) away and connected to the main terminal via a transit system, after passport control.

Structurally, the three-storey strips are supported along their centre lines on pairs of concrete columns. At third floor level these columns split to become radiating steel arms which support the swooping roof structure. At the roof extremities canted steel columns rise and divide to support two wing tips each.

Internally, Rogers' penchant for glass and colour is fully realized. The interior has a spacious and airy feel, shaded from the harsh Spanish sun by the huge undulating roof. This is clad on its underside with bamboo; a masterstroke that challenges the hard concrete and steel and brings warmth, both materially and visually.

The finished product is a building that belies its awesome size with an elegance that is not often evident on projects of this scale. Passengers travelling through Barajas Airport will not be daunted but uplifted by invigorating spaces that are easy to navigate and a pleasure to simply be in.

View across the immigration hall in the International satellite building

End of satellite pier, departure gates with high level arrivals above

The inherent beauty of Rogers' architecture belies the sophistication of the main terminal. The building plan (far right) illustrates the building's complexity: to the top of the image is the car park (yellow) and open-air rail, metro, coach, taxi, and drop-off arrivals functions; below that is the check-in hall, with arrivals hall in the area underneath and between it and the drop-off building; third is the security building, with the baggage hall below and spreading either side; and forth are the pier and gates.

Facade of the satellite building

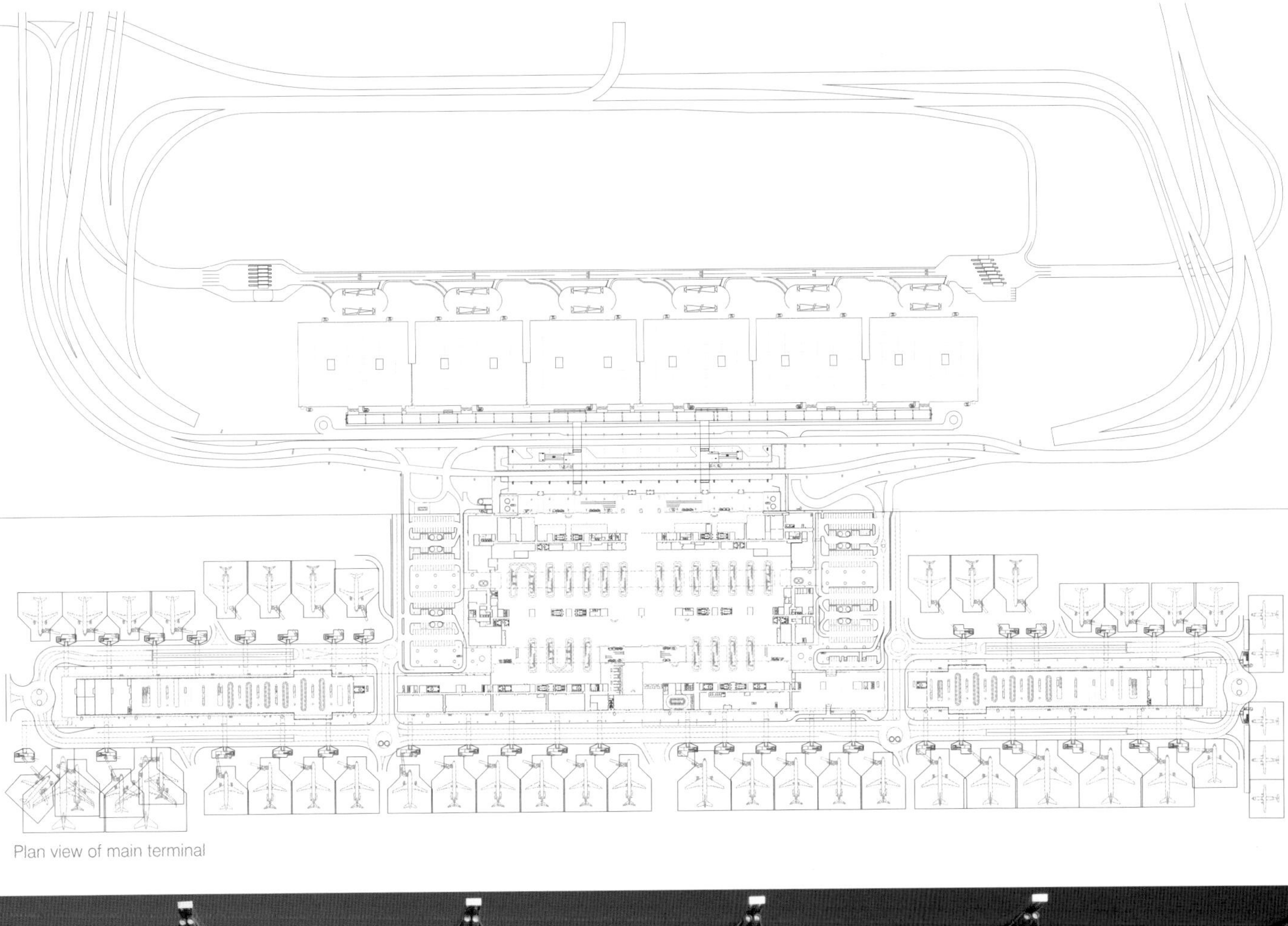

Plan view of main terminal

Terminal building: view to baggage reclaim hall (opposite page) and across departure lounge area (above)

Huge roof lights allow daylight to filter into the building without unnecessary solar glare or gain. Below is the plan of the satellite terminal used for international flights and transfers. The small building houses passport /immigration, and the long one the pier and gates. This element is more simple than the main terminal because all airport administration and main arrivals and departures activity is handled at the main terminal.

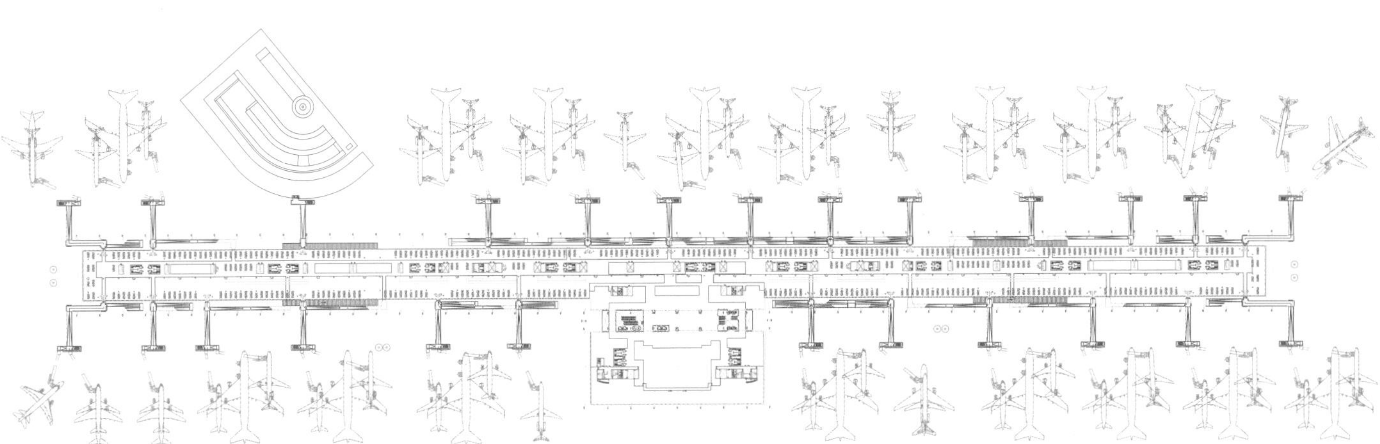

Plan of the satellite international building

View along satellite pier, high-level arrivals

The vast length of the terminal piers that connet to the gates is accentuated by the undulation of the roof. Everything about the airport buildings is eye-catching and yet functional and precise. The sparse and masterful use of primary colours hints at the world outside – hot yellow sun, red earth, and the bluest of Spanish skies – but all the while travelers are cocooned in this cool, elegant cathedral to flight.

Beijing Capital International Airport

DESIGN FOSTER AND PARTNERS
LOCATION BEIJING, CHINA

The new terminal and masterplan for Beijing Capital International Airport has been designed by Foster and Partners, the architect of Chek Lap Kok and Stansted airports in Hong Kong and the UK, respectively. With project partners, airport planner NACO and engineer Arup, the architect is creating a new US two billion gateway into China that will respond to the country's entry into the World Trade Organization and the influx of visitors for the 2008 Olympic Games.

When complete, Beijing Capital International Airport will be the largest in the world. The new terminal will combine spatial clarity and highly functional systems to process an estimated 44 million passengers per year. The soaring aerodynamic

form allows for relatively few level changes, providing easy orientation and short walking distances. This ethos takes the complexities out of modern travel, making arrival and departure efficient and comfortable through the use of invisible but highly efficient processing systems. High service standards and good integration with mass public transport systems enable quick transfer times between flights and in and out of the airport.

The reduction in storey numbers also allows everyone to enjoy the natural light that streams in through linear rooflights along the length of the terminal. These are oriented towards the south-east to maximize heat gain from the early morning sun, and so reduce the mechanical heating requirements. Another sustainable design concept is the integration of an environmental control system that minimizes energy consumption and also reduces carbon emissions.

However, the construction process adopted for the terminal is perhaps the most significant environmentally friendly operation on the project. Built in modular form, many elements of the terminal will be finished to factory standards off-site, before being delivered and installed quickly and efficiently, ensuring a fast-track construction programme and minimal material and energy wastage.

Built between the existing runway and a future third runway, the terminal design has been dubbed a "people's palace" by the architect: its soaring aerodynamic roof evoking a celebration of flight and dragon-like forms. Using colours and symbolism that figure heavily in Chinese tradition, the airport is designed to enliven those who pass through it and become an icon and visitor attraction in itself, something that so many international airports fail to achieve.

Computer visualization of aerial view of terminal

Dual level set-down and pick-up areas

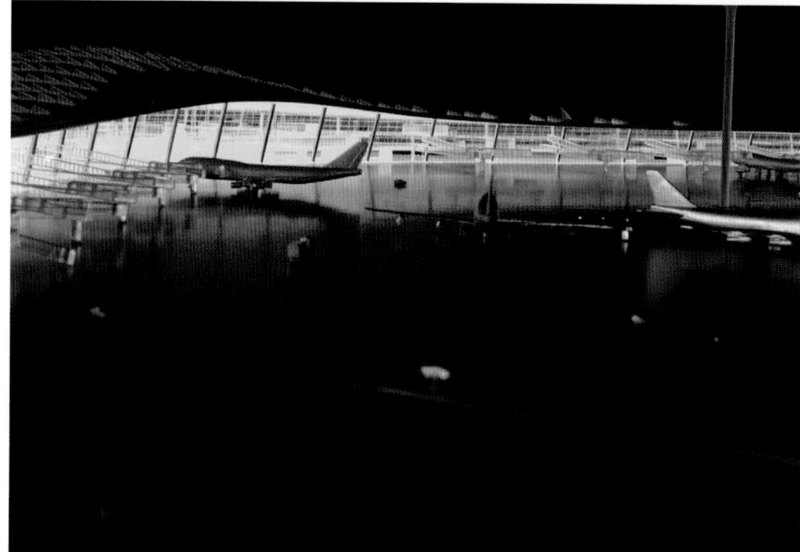

Multiple gates lit from within

The scale-like roof lights

The vast sweeping facade of Foster and Partners' new Beijing Terminal provides a dramatic introduction to this huge airport. The architect's signature style, a combination of high-tech functionality and monumental form, is best expressed in this size of project. From all angles the design is aesthetically pleasing. Foster has excelled in emphasizing the rooftop features, giving the added dimension of aerial views, which will be the first sighting that many visitors have of the airport. The elegant fish-tail design is more than purely aesthetic: internally, the spatial layout is cleverly designed to reduce walking distances from entrance to flight gates for the 44 million passengers currently expected to use the airport, and the expected expansion to between 53 and 60 million passengers by 2015.

International Terminal, Philadelphia Airport

DESIGN KOHN PEDERSEN FOX
LOCATION PHILADELPHIA, PENNSYLVANIA, USA

Philadelphia International Airport serves as the principal gateway for the fifth largest metropolitan population in the United States. Kohn Pedersen Fox (KPF) has designed what it sees as an inverted, and as such, an inspirational airport building for travellers leaving and arriving at the city on international flights.

In order to accommodate complex programmatic requirements, the terminal spans 60 metres (197 feet) on a suspended truss over the airport approach road. The space beneath serves as a weather-protected drop-off for departing travellers, who then ascend one storey into the departure hall. All arrival functions, including baggage reclaim, a sky-lit arrivals hall, the immigration and customs federal inspection service are located higher still, above the departure hall.

This inversion of the usual airport configuration – departures on top of arrivals – is the practice's masterstroke. Most international airports give over the most dramatic space to the departure hall, while arriving passengers are shunted from one artificially lit corridor to the next, through a dingy baggage reclaim and finally subjected to customs. KPF has designed a terminal building that equally distributes the architectural drama and promotes natural light in both arrival and departure areas. It then goes further, emphasizing space and light to arriving passengers, who have recently been confined to an aircraft. As they disembark, passengers ascend along a light-filled route which increases in dramatic intensity all the way to the arrivals hall. Spaces along the "sterile" secure route change in shape and colour towards the FIS inspection and into the baggage retrieval area.

Here, high above the airport runway, baggage reclaim is situated in a vast space of curving geometry, naturally illuminated via great celestory skylights. A series of interlocking spaces, each with its own identity, is linked via the natural light to form a welcoming whole.

Departures is situated below the arrivals floor, the ticketing lobby extending upwards to form a double-height space that pushes through the arrival level, allowing natural light to permeate into the space. Throughout the building, transparent walls provide views out over the runways. This light-emitting, transparent building is turned on its head at night, when artificial lighting makes the terminal glow from within, turning the building into a beacon for the surrounding area.

Naturally lit baggage handling area

Baggage reclaim, suspended above the main entrance

Dramatic roof lines allude to flight

Plan view, including the tail fin (far left)

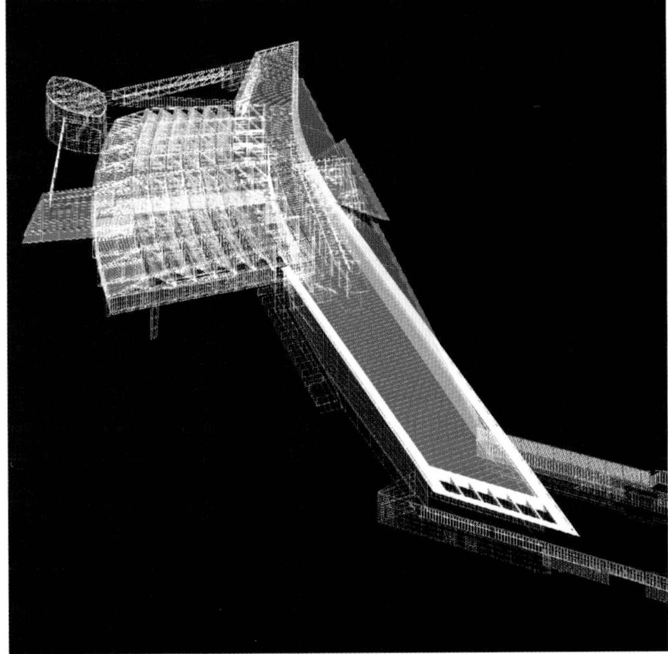

Main terminal structural elements

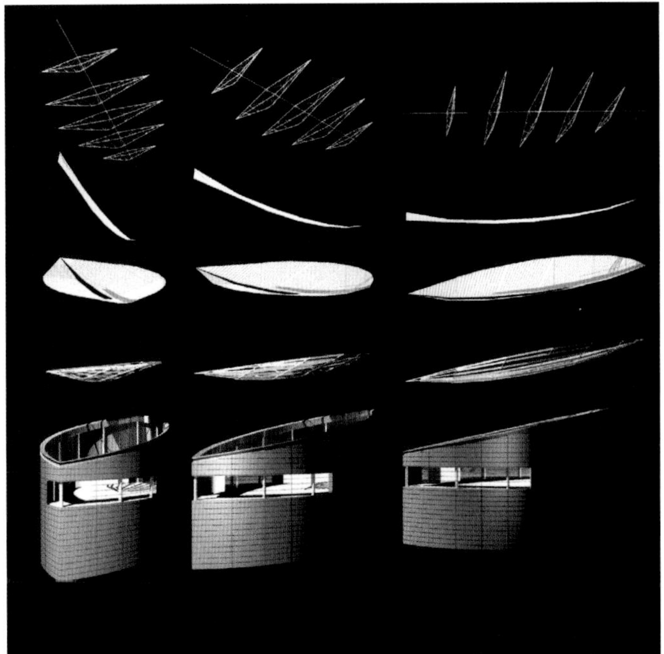

Exploded diagram of the elliptical departures hall

This is one of the first of a new breed of airport, designed to be more than functional. Both in terms of architectural drama, as in the case of the departures hall, and passenger enjoyment, the International Terminal enhances the experience of those visiting Philadelphia. Visitors enjoy good environmental comfort and expansive views from all around the terminal. The airport brings excitement back to commercial flight.

Asymmetrical design of the departures hall

This is one of the first of a new breed of airport, designed to be more than functional. Both in terms of architectural drama, as in the case of the departures hall, and passenger enjoyment, the International Terminal enhances the experience of those visiting Philadelphia. Visitors enjoy a comfortable environment and expansive views from all around the terminal. The airport brings excitement back to commercial flight.

The facade of the low-slung airport is swathed in glass

Wide perspective with road through centre

Virgin Atlantic Upper Class Lounge

DESIGN SHARPLES HOLDEN PASQUARELLI
LOCATION JFK AIRPORT, NEW YORK, US

Virgin Atlantic's new upper class lounge at JFK is described by its architect as, "an environment that celebrates both the power and possibility of New York City, and the excellence and irreverence of Virgin Atlantic Airlines". This is a strong statement considering the small scale of the project and usual rationale associated with even the upper echelons of airport interiors. However, Sharples Holden Pasquarelli (ShoP) has created something unique, making mere cargo passengers green with envy.

Entered beneath an illuminated waterfall, and bordered by a pool, the lounge is built almost entirely from layered, partially see-through 3D screens. These curving basket-like columns and walls allow views out to the main terminal and runway while defining the extent of the lounge in a form that hints at the shimmering skyscrapers of the metropolis.

Each column, wall or bar front has been designed using 3D modelling software. Individual members are cut from sheets of medium density fibre board (MDF) then joined using wooden dowels positioned according to critically calculated vertical load paths that ensure the structure's stability.

Each structure incorporates hundreds of individual pieces cut from a standard sheet of MDF. Converted from 3D to a flat form and then into AutoCad, the patterns were simply e-mailed to the fabricator who, using a Computer Numerically Controlled (CNC) router, automatically cut the pieces, drilled holes and routed indents with perfect precision. This kit of parts was then laboriously built up by hand into a 3D structure.

In daylight, when the lounge is not lit artificially, the effect is of a pristine white oriental maze. The bar and dining area, much of the latter bordering the pool, feel intimate and secluded. Computer terminals and small lounge areas are tucked away within the labyrinthine structure, allowing privacy.

At night the mood changes. Illuminated at angles by spotlights built flush into the false ceiling, as well as coloured luminaires within the structures, the lounge takes on a cosmopolitan atmosphere. What was an oriental oasis is now an exciting city bar and restaurant.

While luxury is now commonplace for the privileged traveler, both in terminals and planes, here, ShoP has brought excitement back to a small part of this historic airport, that hasn't been seen since the days when Eero Saarinen's TWA Terminal was first opened.

A waterfall (right) and moat border the restaurant

The lounge area

Work stations in the partition system

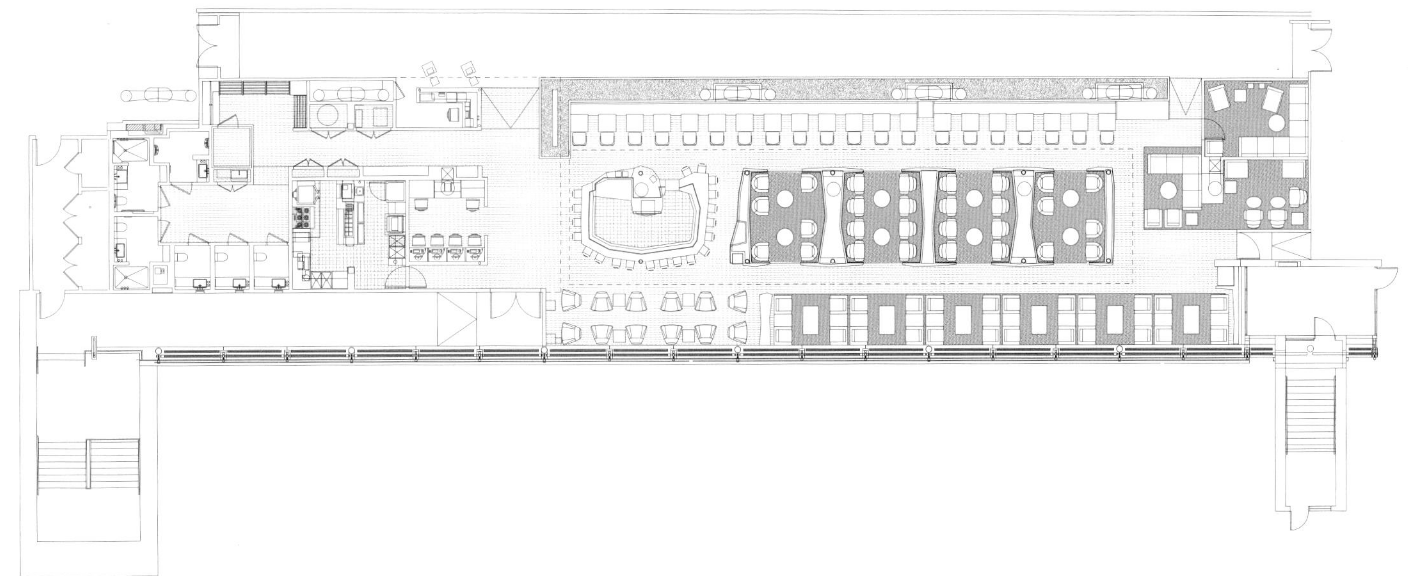

Plan with restaurant and moat at top right

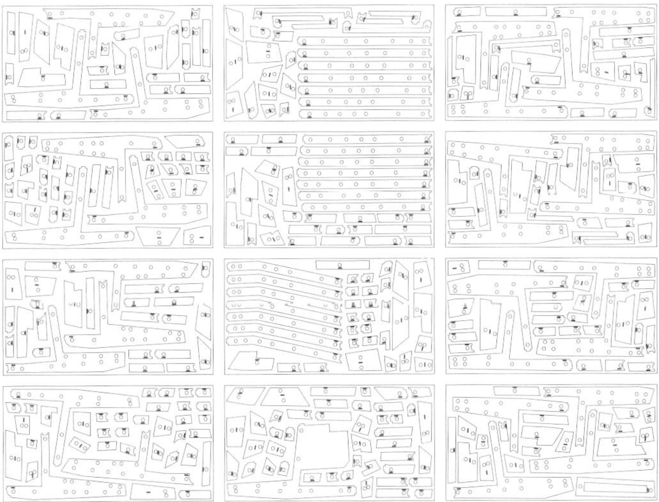

Flat patterns for the partition system

SHoP's unusual and fun design for the first class lounge features thousands of individual pieces cut out of flat sheets of medium density fibreboard. The elements are built into partitions and columns to surround the bar and semi-secluded seating areas. This area is accentuated by the lowered ceiling and features perimeter lighting. Around it, more conventional first class lounge and restaurant facilities overlook the main terminal and views of the runways.

Partially screened seating booths

Bangkok International Airport

DESIGN MURPHY JAHN ARCHITECTS
LOCATION BANGKOK, THAILAND

The new Bangkok International Airport is now nearing the completion of its first phase. This gargantuan addition to Thailand's public building programme encompasses 563,000 square metres (6,060,080 square feet) of terminal facilities, two runways and 50 flight gates, all designed to cater for around 50 million passengers per annum. On completion, the airport will include four runways and be able to cope with 100 million passengers each year.

The terminal complex is made up of a collection of separate buildings. However, to unify the scheme and to protect it from the hot sun, the entire complex is covered by a huge roof trellis. The louvred trellis allows maximum airflow across the site to provide a cooling effect, while also shading both buildings and external courtyard spaces. As a consequence, the loading and cost of air-conditioning for the internal spaces is greatly reduced.

Under this gigantic parasol, the main terminal complex has seven floors and a basement. With a materials palette of mainly concrete and glass the terminal and concourse covers an area of 182,000 square metres (1,959,030 square feet). Murphy Jahn's design concept was the prioritization of passenger circulation, over that of aircraft movement. As such, the compact design reduces the long corridors and extended walks required to flight gates that are experienced elsewhere.

Beneath the roof terrace, there is room for future expansion, however the resulting outdoor spaces are not left barren but have been designed as important part of the overall concept. While they will be filled with extra facilities as the airport expands, currently, rather than leave them empty, they are being landscaped to create external courtyards to display cultural artifacts. This simple process links the new terminal to the traditions and beliefs of the country – a replica of the "Lord Buddha's footprint" from the temple on the site is one proposed sculptural addition to the main courtyard.

However, the road to completion has been a long and rocky one. The project was initially conceived in the 1960s, so some four decades later the airport is now a reality. When open, the new Bangkok International Airport will take over all international flights from the existing Don Muang Airport, which currently serves 30 million visitors per annum. Murphy Jahn has created an enlivening new gateway into one of the most beautiful parts of the world.

Model section showing the dramatic roof trellis

Model section detailing the flight gate tunnel

View to the central courtyard

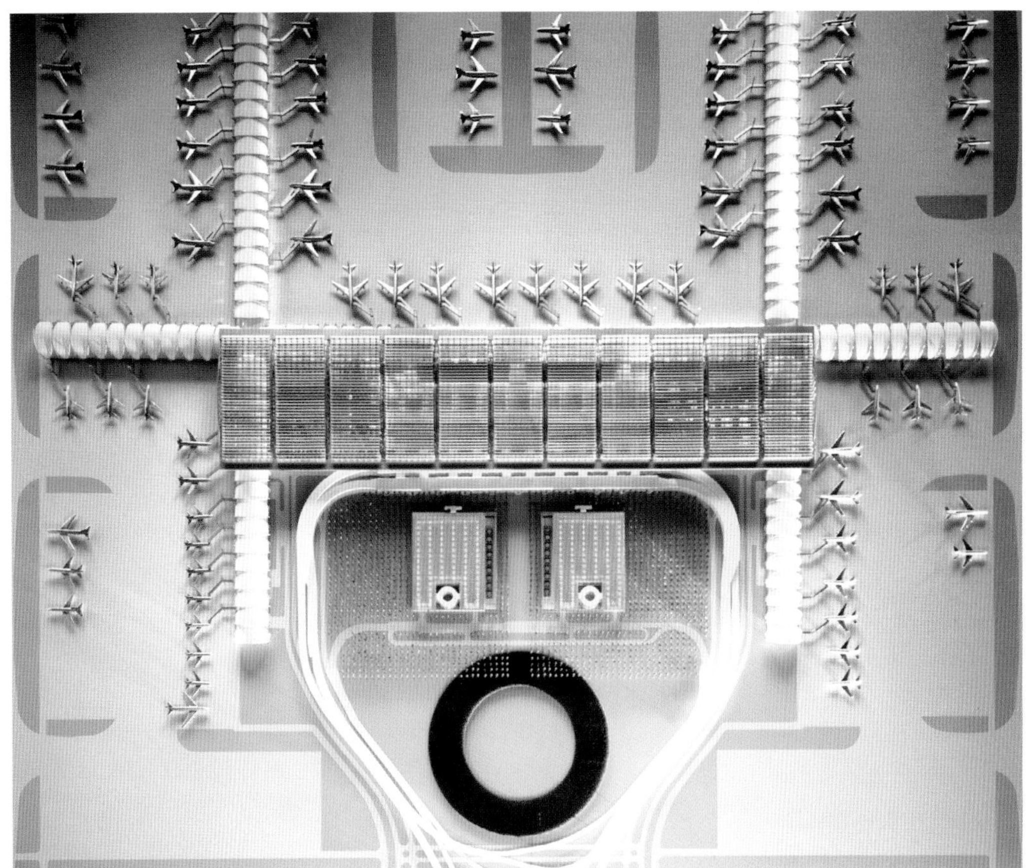
Site plan

The land for the airport was purchased in 1973 – a boggy site named Nong Ngu Hao (Cobra Swamp) – but in the same year a student uprising overthrew the government days short of the project being approved. It was not until the early 1990s that the project was revived. The functionality of this airport is immediately apparent on viewing the model. The central terminal building is flanked by flight gates located along vast elliptical tunnels projecting outwards from it at right angles. Murphy Jahn reiterates this no-nonsense approach in the structure, which is bold, angular and exposed.

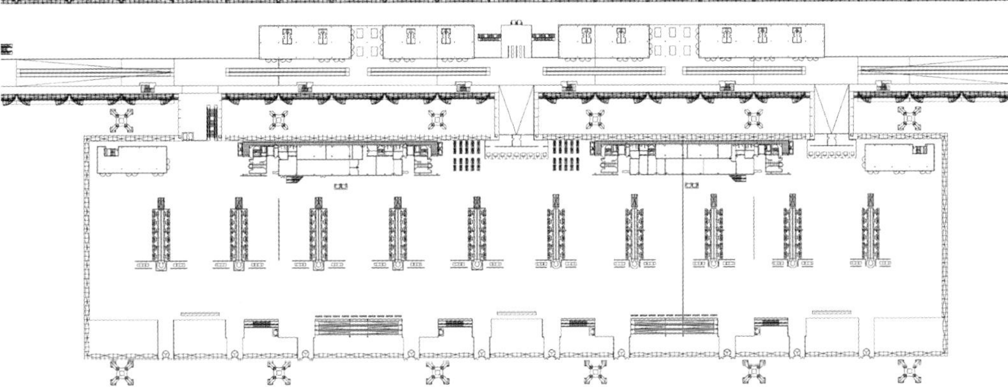
Plan showing terminal and flightgate tunnel, first floor

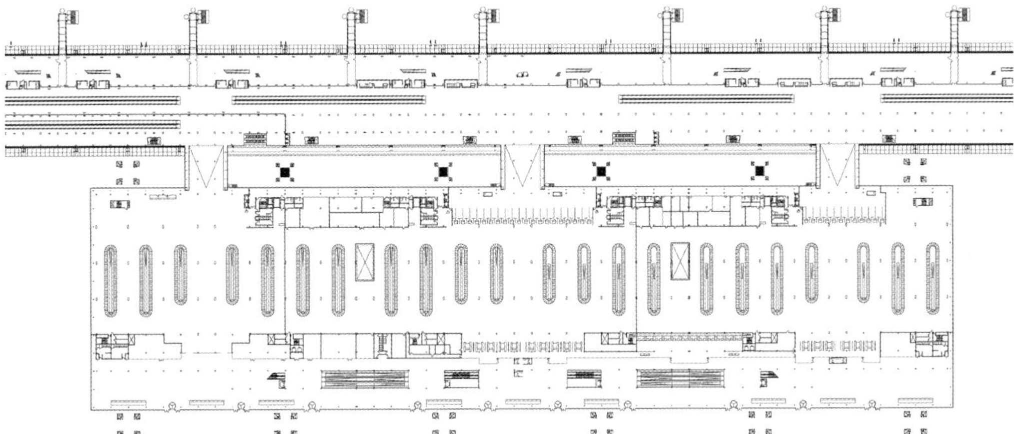
Plan showing terminal and flightgate tunnel, ground floor

The striking design features a minimal material palette of steel, glass and tensile fabric. This enables the architect to construct exciting structures that are easily replicable for initial construction and future expansion of the airport. The control tower rises above this machine-like architecture as a focal point and symbolic beacon.

View of the mesh-clad control tower

The vast flight gate tunnels

Flight gate tunnel under construction

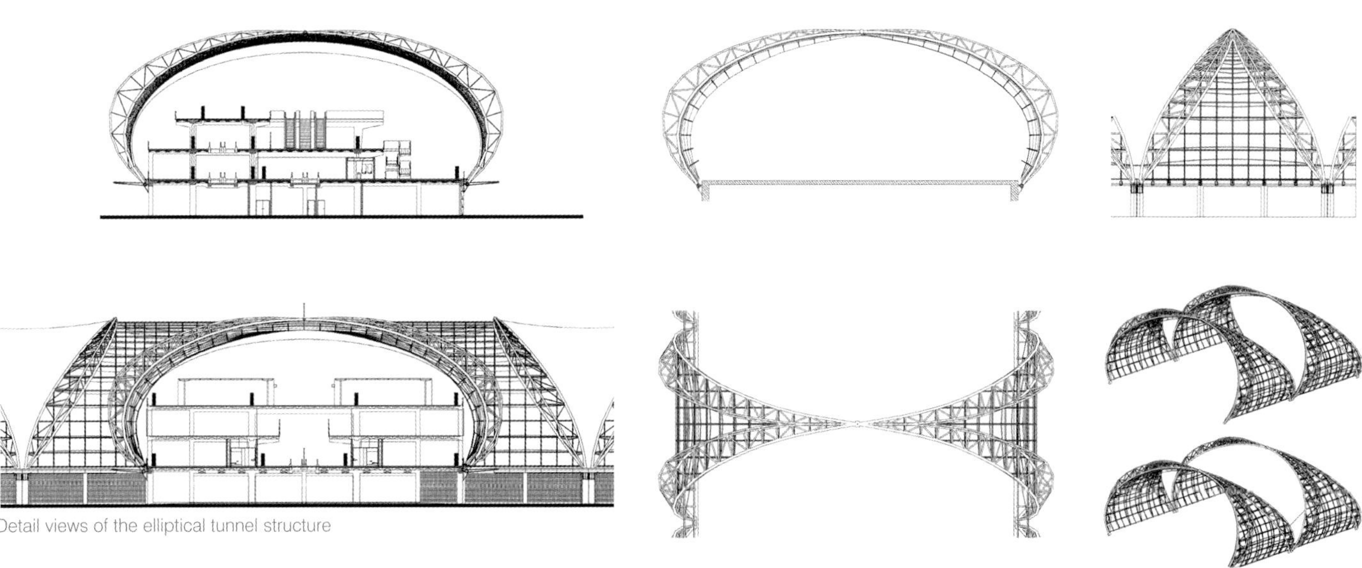

Detail views of the elliptical tunnel structure

Tianjin Binhai International Airport

DESIGN KOHN PEDERSEN FOX AND NETHERLANDS AIRPORT CONSULTANTS
LOCATION TIANJIN, CHINA

Won in international competition by Kohn Pedersen Fox (KPF) and Netherlands Airport Consultants (NACO), phase one of Tianjin Binhai International Airport is scheduled to be completed in time for the 2008 Olympic Games in Beijing. Initially the airport will cater for six million passengers per year; however, when fully complete, the airport's capacity will exceed 40 million travellers and feature 22 gates.

The KPF/NACO team has designed a scheme that integrates the existing single runway with new runways and taxiways, a new automated people-mover and a main rail connection. The project bucks the trend for the monochromatic palette and purely functionally-inspired design favoured at most western airport terminals. Instead, it celebrates oriental customs and symbolism.

The design makes strong reference to the kite. China invented kites, the very first flying machine, and Tianjin is famous for its kite-making tradition and festivals. Strong symbolic reference is found in the sweeping kite-like roof of the main airport entrance. Colour is also used extensively, which again, has cultural importance within Chinese society – most notably red for good luck. The airport is adorned with a roof featuring multiple sails, the colour of which can be changed at the touch of a button, allowing the seasons and days of importance to be marked in changing hues.

Attention to aesthetics is tempered by the need to create a building that efficiently processes vast numbers of travellers. The airport is approached from a grand park which presents views of the main entrance and gives access to the departures level. The check-in level is housed under the brightly coloured roof, offering good natural light and visual stimuli that conjures excitement at the thought of the journey to come.

From the check-in, access to the aircraft is along a simple legible route that involves no changes in level until passengers reach the gate. The gates are situated along piers that expand and contract, widening to house clusters of four passenger holding areas, and narrowing to form corridors between. Access from the gates to the aircraft is via a slowly curving ramp that swoops around to reveal a dramatic view of the aircraft through a fully glazed facade.

KPF/NACO's design combines the latter's vast experience with the former's intuitive design skills which draw on the desire to create a place more than the sum of its functions.

A kite-inspired form soars above the main entrance

Over sailing roof at main entrance

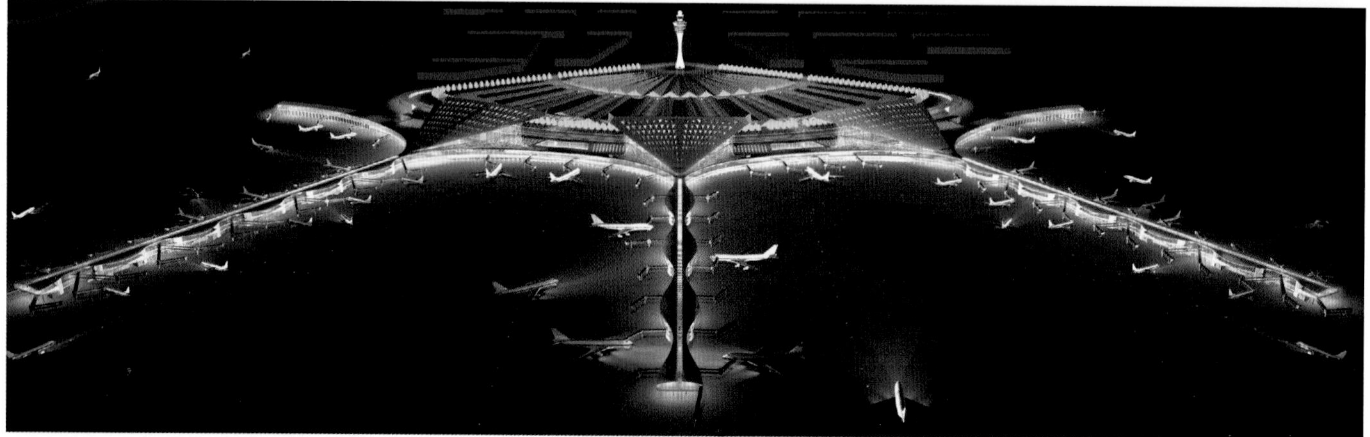

Aerial perspective from the "flight side"

Tianjin Binhai International Airport offers a new point of entry into one of the world's most interesting cultures and it will hopefully prove to be an exciting adventure in itself. This new airport is one of a number signalling the massive industrial and economic growth within China. The airport radiates out from a main terminal building on a single level. Passengers travel to flight gates situated in widened sections along the length of giant arms. This type of design is simplistic but easily replicable, an essential ingredient for a region that is already becoming a thriving industrial zone and a new travel destination for holiday-makers.

The expansive flight gates

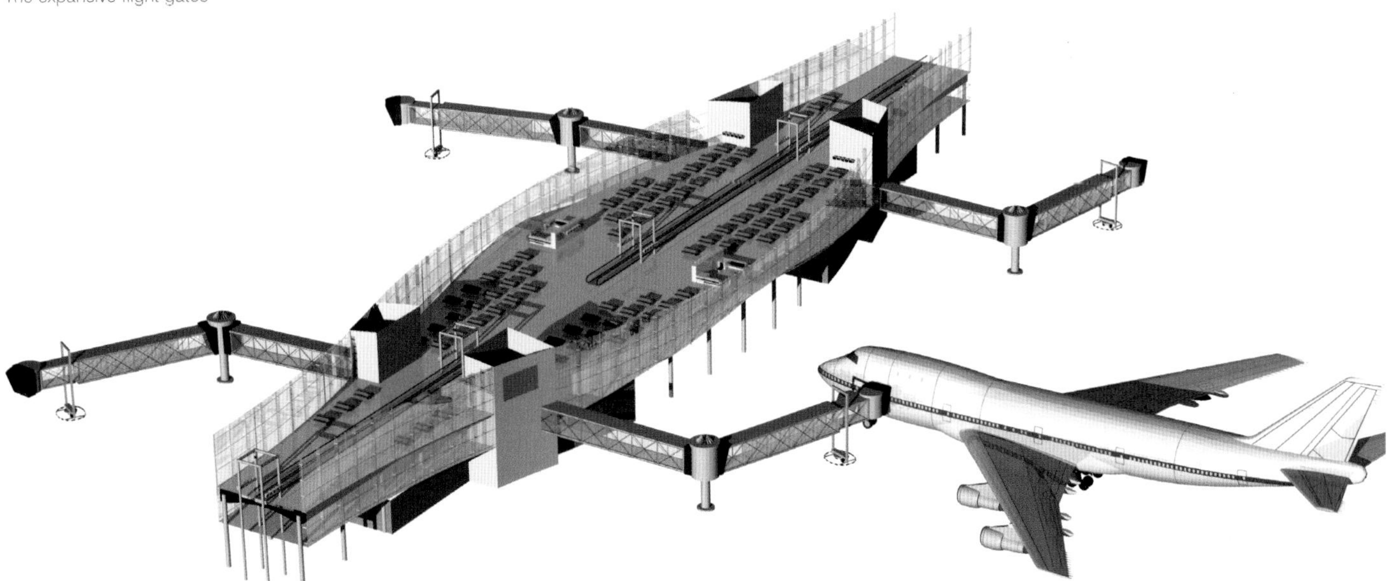

Flight gates in a bulge in the arm

Ben Gurion International Airport

DESIGN MOSHE SAFDIE & ASSOCIATES/TRA ARCHITECTS
LOCATION TEL AVIV, ISRAEL

This new terminal at Ben Gurion Airport is the culmination of a ten-year project that has created a new gateway into Israel for air passengers. Handling 16 million travellers a year, the new complex includes a landside development designed by a joint venture team of Skidmore Owings & Merrill, Karmi Architects and Lissar Eldar Architects, and an exciting airside facility designed by Moshe Safdie & Associates with TRA Architects.

While the large functional landside complex accommodates the ticketing, customs, immigration and baggage claim, the true architectural excitement for travellers flying from Tel Aviv begins on the journey to the airside Rotunda. Descending from third to first floor level via a 183 metre (600 foot) long "connector" building, outgoing passengers pass close to, but separate from, incoming travellers on two long opposing sloped ramps housed within the concrete framed glazed corridor. High glazed partitions provide ample views over the airfield, while travelators are the only internal addition to this distinctive sand-coloured graduated walkway. The architect sees this dramatic crossing space for travellers as a ceremonial portal, giving each group sight of the other as they continue their journeys.

Entering the main airside building, travellers are greeted by a waterfall descending from a massive upturned dome in the roof. Suspended on pairs of diagonal steel columns atop the concrete perimeter wall, the dome's smooth underside is naturally illuminated by celestory windows. This architectural statement catches the eye and also the rain, which is directed towards its concave centre and into the building interior through an oculus skylight to form a dramatic waterfall cascading into the centre of the waiting hall. Rainwater is supplemented by a continuous flow of pumped water in dry spells to maintain the waterfall, which assists in the cooling and humidification of the building.

The Rotunda houses all of the usual airside services including money changing facilities, retail outlets and food outlets. At equal spacing around the circular hub, five concourses radiate outwards to flight gates, each concourse serving eight gates. Below these concourses are baggage processing areas and the airline maintenance services. The flight gate concourses and the connectors are constructed of structural precast concrete columns and beams that accommodate the mechanical distribution system within them.

The dramatic upturned dish of the Rotunda

Above: Two ramps for arrivals and departures

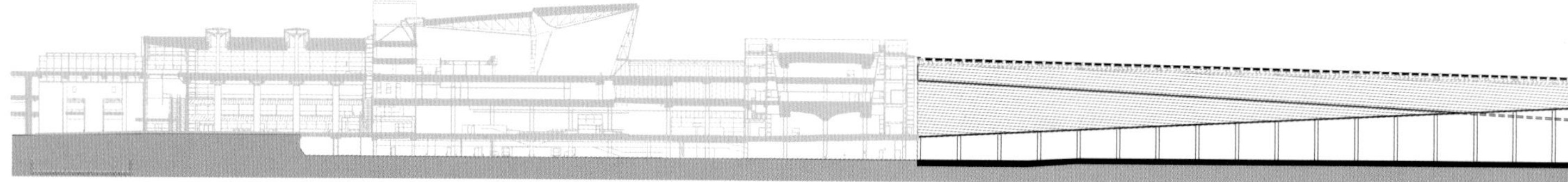

Elevation emphasizing the ground-hugging nature of the building

Built as two projects the land and air sides of this airport are distinctly different (see elevation above). Drama comes in the shape of what at first glance could be a giant satellite dish. This upturned dome dominates the architecture both externally and inside the airport, where the main departure lounge is located directly under it. Other areas, such as the departures and arrivals ramps, offer less overt design statements, while providing ample opportunity for travellers to enjoy the airport experience.

The Rotunda, complete with waterfall

Central pool feature

Circulation areas off the Rotunda

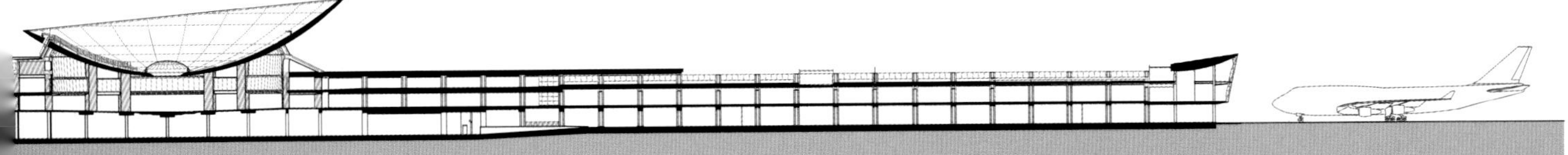

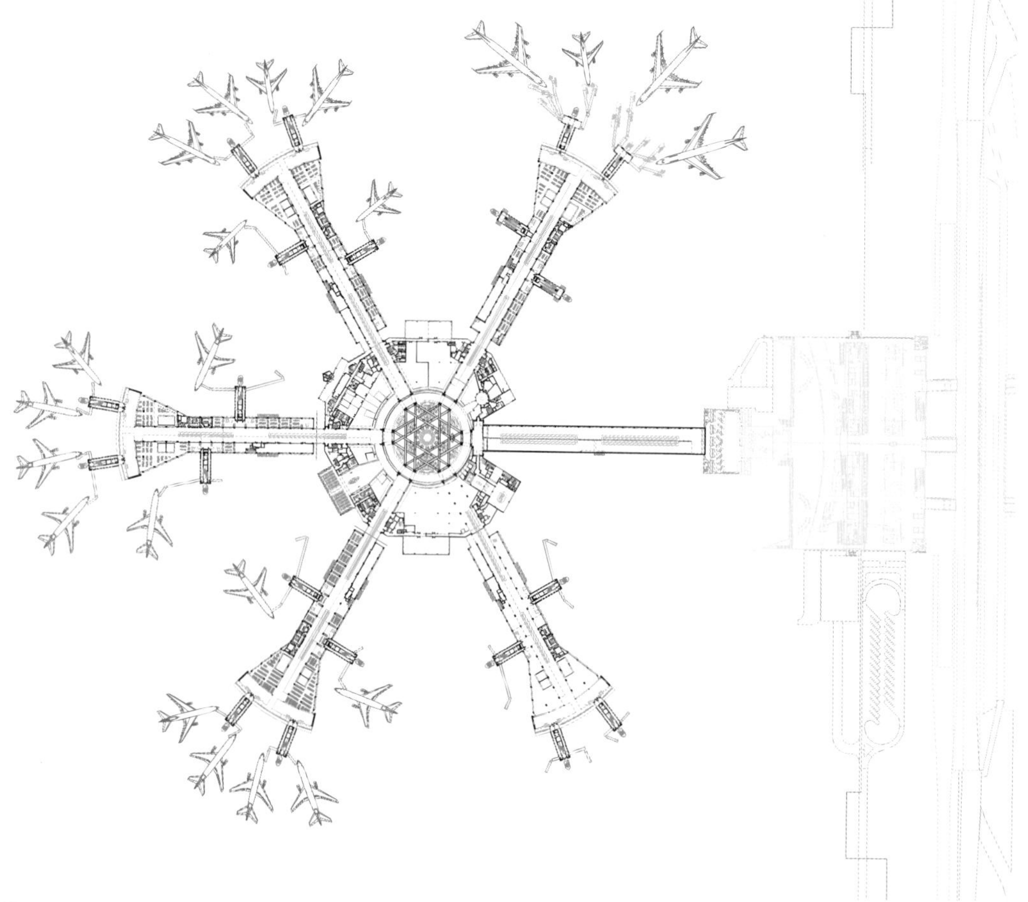

Plan view of the airside, with the Rotunda in the centre

This airport goes against current architectural fashion, being designed as a hub with radiating "satellite" gates, rather than a linear corridor with gates along its length. While Ben Gurion Airport is out of step with the norm, its design harks back to memorable aviation design including Paul Andreu's Terminal One at Charles De Gaulle Airport in Paris, completed in 1974. This circular model provides the greatest scope for statement architecture.

External view of the ramped walkway

Viewing the Rotunda from land side

The Politics of Public Transport
Bangkok case study

S.Y. Lau

S.Y. Lau teaches environmental and architectural design at the Department of Architecture at Hong Kong University. Currently, he is directing research on environmental controls and their impact on sustainable urban form with specific reference to Asian cities.

Yoichi Shimatsu

Yoichi Shimatsu is a former editor with *The Japan Times* in Tokyo and has taught journalism and critical studies in mass media at Tsinghua University in Beijing. He is managing director of the Bangkok branch of the industrial-design consultancy Asian Initiatives.

In April 2005, separatist Muslim guerrillas detonated bombs under a train in Thailand's troubled south. The guerrilla attack had little military value but was useful for sending a political message to the central government because rail systems, in war and peace, are a symbol of modern nationhood. While international airports serve this role in spectacular fashion, an older means of transport – rail – is still a keen measure of economic progress and technological prowess. Land transport is a fact on the ground that impacts everyone.

As previews of a better tomorrow, quiet-running commuter lines and their stations tend to be streamlined and futuristic. The curved steel roofs and glass walls of Bangkok's Metro entrances create a time-warp effect when juxtaposed with an ornate Buddhist temple, for example, at Wat Hualamphong. The massive concrete Skytrain stations are an understatement of modernist functionalism, seeming to float mid-air as commuters are whisked to the platform. Zooming past towers of sky-reflecting glass and over palatial gardens, the Skytrain is a Garuda – the man-eagle chimera – of this "City of Angels".

Despite this high-flying promise of prosperity, much of Bangkok remains a sea of urban poverty, where workers and clerks can afford only the cheapest of rides. The mid-level managers and tourists willing to pay the costly ticket for commuter rail barely dent the daily human traffic borne by workhorse buses, motorbikes and three-wheeled tuk-tuks. The physical disconnection between rich and poor is built into transit infrastructure. No commuter rail is directly linked to the three major bus stations at Mo Chit, Pinklao and Ekkamai (at this latter nearby station one has to haul baggage downstairs and across one block). The Hualamphong train station is met by the subway, yet other "old rail" stations remain isolated, for example, Makkasan in the east and the Mae Klong line in Thonburi. New commuter lines have yet to overcome Bangkok's fragmentation.

Commuter rail and expressways (along with the cars needed to reach them) are a political football for rival parties, serving as proof or promise of their fitness to govern. Beneath this contest are issues related to ownership, land use, urban planning and property development. A business group that supports a governing party or powerful bureaucrats expects to gain construction contracts, building permits adjoining stations, office towers in good locations, and access to new consumers. Of course, chaos would reign if every turn in the road were to depend on political intrigue. Even with rampant rumours of favouritism and corruption, budget constraints undoubtedly have a bigger impact on routing decisions.

The experience of the Hong Kong-financed Hopewell Line is a cautionary tale of global financial instability and the local encumbrances of bureaucratic indecision and political volatility. Newly arrived visitors to Thailand are immediately struck by the sight of 1560 sets of concrete pillars stretching farther than the eye can see, from Don Muang Airport to the edge of downtown. The concept of a high-speed express, obviously conceived in one of those infamous traffic jams outside the airport, must have seemed ideal on paper. The dual road-and-rail elevated line required little investment in land purchases since it could simply follow the State Railway track. Yet this best-laid plan went awry when the Asian financial crisis of 1997 gutted investment in mass transit.

City of Angels

Bangkok, a city of between 9 and 10 million inhabitants, occupies a flat expanse of 1568 square kilometres (605 square miles) slightly north of coastal swamps and prawn ponds along the Gulf of Thailand. Getting 10 million people to and from work, school and leisure activities is a Herculean task, especially in an economy hit by the Asian financial crisis of 1997–98, an avian influenza outbreak, the Indian Ocean tsunami, and an ongoing insurgency in the southlands. Despite these shocks, the Thai capital has made amazing progress against air pollution. In the 1980s Bangkok was notorious for its choking emissions pollution and standstill traffic. Since then, new diesel standards and the introduction of natural gas as fuel have dramatically improved outdoor air quality.

The metropolis's most important transport lifeline is the Chao Phraya River. Every day, ferries packed with tourists and commuters ply its cocoa-brown waters to reach the shrine of the Emerald Buddha and, on the other side, Wat Arun, the Temple of Dawn. The river splits Bangkok into two centres, the older capital Thonburi on the west bank and the dynastic seat of Krung Thep, or City of Angels, on the east. The separation of old capital and new is reflected in the many delays in extending either the Skytrain or subway across the Chao Phraya.

Warfare is the reason that Bangkok – like Edo, the predecessor of Tokyo – was built on an oppressively humid flood plain. Tropical heat and wetness conspired to create a homegrown solution – the klong, or a long watercourse, many of which serve triple duty as canal, drain channel and air-cooler. Since the capital's founding in 1782, most royal palaces and major temples, called wats, were built close to the river or along wider klongs, to take advantage of their cooling effect.

The state-owned klongs form continuous lanes through the city centre. To save on the cost of acquiring private land, rail tracks and roadways often run alongside, or are elevated over, sections of canal, for example, Krung Kasem over its namesake klong and the Skytrain section over Klong Sathorn, past the outcrops of international banks.

The klongs and riverfront support the only examples of indigenous vernacular building methods adapted from traditional Muslim coastal villages – the stilt house. Mosques and humble halal eateries are hemmed in along the klongs. The urban waterways are teeming with Muslims and ethnic Chinese minorities – whose ancestors arrived aboard boats.

Over the past century, these klong communities were replicated as squatter encampments and markets along the State Railway tracks, as can be seen in the Phaya Thai district and along the Mae Klong line. Most of the workers who migrated to Bangkok during the boom years of industrialization in the 1970s arrived by train, before highways gave the speed advantage to buses and trucks. Reflecting the close ties between the military and State Railway, most Thai train stations, including Sam Sen platform in the heart of Bangkok, are simple open structures, built of wood and fitted out with hard benches and few amenities.

Bangkok's fragmented skyline is a scattering of high-rise islands of wealth separated by low-rise arteries of poverty. Office towers and high-rise residences tend to be clustered in pockets of solid ground or landfill in places such as Asoke, Sukhumvit, and Silom, while slums and blocks of shophouses are squeezed along the waterways and other margins. Fishermen and traders who settled the river plain had a profane name for their town: Bangkok, or Plum Orchard. Today, this fertile land is still a prime source of juicy plums – for building contractors, property developers, retail malls and their political patrons.

Turf Wars

Rising above the central plain atop massive concrete pillars, the Skytrain line could have been a brutalist monstrosity imposed on a vista of temples and palaces. Instead, the absence of adornment makes the stations, erected by Siemens and the Bangkok-based Ital-Thai group, a cool neutral counterpoint to the hot cityscape of decorative Thai architecture and the mosaic of facades and billboards.

For all its glory, the Bangkok Mass Transit System (BTS) is an orphan disowned by the governing Thai Rak Thai party, a pariah set apart from the A-list of mega-projects. The ruling party has favoured instead the Metro subway, whose first section, known as the Blue Line, was inaugurated in

December 2004. Subway construction has been overseen by the Metropolitan Rapid Transit Authority (MRTA), directly under the Prime Minister's Office, and its daily operations are managed by the Bangkok Metro Company (BMCL).

The Skytrain, operated by the BTS, was rolled out in 1998, after completion under Prime Minister Chuan Leekpai, whose Democrat party fell out of power for failing to stem the regional financial crisis. An original priority of the Skytrain project was to connect with Thonburi, yet support for the link failed to materialize until Apirak Kosayodhin, an upstart Democrat maverick, pulled off a surprise victory in the Bangkok gubernatorial election of 2004.

The dispute over mass transit between the ruling Thai Rak Thai and the opposition Democrats – and between Prime Minister and Governor – hinges on two questions: which commuter rail line best serves the evolving needs of a newly industrialized economy? And, which is better positioned to carry a critical mass of passengers and raise the funds needed to pay back the loans?

Without expansion into industrial zones and bedroom communities, neither Skytrain nor Metro subway can garner enough fares for optimum profitability. Without profits, the foreign loans, mainly from Japan for construction costs, cannot be cleared. Given the chronic shortage of investment funds, the commuter line that wins the race to cross the Chao Phraya would be in the position to take control of its weaker rival. The winner-take-all rivalry is as fierce as those other most gladiatorial examples of Thai combat – kickboxing and cockfighting.

Unlike fully private lines, semi-public corporations cannot take full advantage of commercial opportunities, and in contrast to public-owned entities, they are ineligible for bailouts. The prospects of paying the debt were so remote that one deputy prime minister even suggested nationalization of the BTS and MRTA that, respectively, are responsible for building the Skytrain and Metro. Mass transit with its built-in financial constraints has become an inevitable arena for the blame game and political jockeying.

Among its campaign promises, Thai Rak Thai issued maps showing extensions of the Blue Line subway into the Thonburi side, now an industrial region with a working-class population. The planned route forms a rectangle, with tunnels under the Chao Phraya at two points, north and south. The transport ministry followed through with a timetable for groundbreaking in autumn 2006 and completion by 2012. In addition, a Purple Line linking downtown Bangkok with the north-eastern city of Nonthaburi would run parallel to the river, intersecting the Blue Line at two points.

Soon after his unexpected victory, Governor Apirak revived civic support for the Skytrain crossing into downtown Thonburi. A savvy public-relations executive, Apirak stole the populist thunder from the governing party in late October 2005 by proposing the unprecedented step of issuing a municipal bond to finance the Skytrain extension. The race to cross the Chao Phraya was on.

In grossly simplified terms, the Skytrain and the subway reflect divergent visions of Bangkok's future as projected by the Democrats and Thai Rak Thai. The opposition Democrats, with their base among management executives and intellectuals, have tended to see the metropolis as an "international city", a platform for large global corporations operating in Asia. The Skytrain, to a large degree, serves the primary nodes of elites based in foreign-owned businesses and the tourism industry, passing through the posh Sukhumvit and upscale Siam district. The Democrats also have a loyal following among urban Muslims and small shop owners, and the Ratchathewi Station in a lower-class district serves this constituency.

Thai Rak Thai, with its name that translates as "Thais love Thais", promotes itself as a populist party guided by a business coalition of Thailand-rooted manufacturers, large-store retailers and food processors. The subway route is a marriage of mass transit and mass marketing, which delivers budget shoppers and low-income residents to the central train terminus at Hualamphong, local business districts in Phahon Yothin and Lad Phrao, and importantly the megamarkets along the Ratchadaphisek corridor.

The Ratchadaphisek area was planned as part of the Sathorn Line in the original Skytrain proposal drawn up in 1979 under the government of Gen. Kriangsak Chomanand. Ratchadphisek was then seen as the logical next step for downtown expansion into the rural east. In 1994, however, parliament restricted new mass transit investment to built-up and heavily populated areas of the city core, and so the Ratchada route was downgraded in subsequent planning.

Meanwhile, suburbanites took the Ratchadaphisek roadway for speedy access to downtown, and the corridor began serving a new middle class of automobile owners. An American-style highway culture of shopping malls, car showrooms and parking lots quickly sprang up along the Ratchada strip. Massive sex spas and massage parlours (many since converted into hotels) contributed to a racy nightlife. With this fast growth, Ratchadaphisek met the qualifications for a populated core district. The north-south axis stretching from Klong Toey to Phahon Yothin became the backbone of the Blue Line subway, inaugurated in December 2004.

The Battle of Tao Pun

In the summer of 2005, within a year of the Metro's opening, a smoldering dispute erupted when residents of Tao Pun town launched protests at hearings for an elevated section of the Purple Line subway across the Bangkok–Nonthaburi gap. The community wanted the track to be put underground to prevent road congestion and pollution, as well as a ban on construction on the site of the Tao Pun outdoor market.

Tao Pun seems the unlikeliest place for a political uprising. Its broad tree-lined streets are lined by rows of shophouses retailing doorknobs, spirit houses (residential shrines resembling dollhouses), gold jewelry and gambling dens. Tucked behind this nondescript facade, narrow lanes open to an enchanting realm of Thai culture. Tao Pun and the surrounding Bangsu district are the centre of traditional woodcrafts, including the carving of masks and musical instruments.

In this techno-drama, the River Chao Phraya waits in the wings like a Godot, a silent yet outspoken character, nowhere and everywhere at the same time. Nonthaburi is the upstream terminus of the ferries that deliver tourists to the wats along either bank. Bang Pho, the dock for Tao Pun, is just one stop downstream. The northwest leg of the Blue Line is slated to pass under the riverbed at Bang Pho to Bang O on the west bank.

For Metro planners, the high cost of tunnelling is justifiable only in the high-density city centre, and Tao Pun by no means fits that description. Routing over public-owned land is always preferable to time-consuming negotiations over compensation claims for private-owned property. Under the plan released in October 2005, the Tao Pun market became the logical choice for an elevated Purple Line track to Nonthaburi and the junction with the Blue Line heading toward the Thonburi side.

Petty vendors, fearing that closure of their outdoor market was for the benefit of a nearby megastore, found a seasoned leader in retired Major Gen. Kittisak Ratthaprasert, a one-time Defence Minister and aide de camp to Democrat former Prime Minister Chuan Leekpai. Only a personage of his stature could stand up to the pressures from the Cabinet and the elders of Nonthaburi.

Faced with the prospects of a bitter showdown, the government side blinked. The compromise allows vendors to operate stalls and shops under the local station and adjoining sections of elevated track. The deal marked a break with the policy of excluding commercial venues, other than commuter services such as coffee corners and news stands. An earlier attempt by the MRTA to install an underground shopping centre inside a subway station, similar to Tokyo's subterranean malls, was blocked due to strict expropriation rules against land grabs for commercial purposes. The Tao Pun deal stands as a fragile truce amid the ongoing conflict.

In time, the fractious competition to cross the river at the heart of Bangkok will be water under the bridge – and over the tunnel – for all things must pass. Whatever the dislocations in its mass transit network, Bangkok is a most livable city, where residents and visitors enjoy mobility and convenience greater than in many advanced economies, be it river boat, skytrain, metro, or tuk tuk.

Road

66 Vauxhall Cross Interchange
74 Car Park
80 The Whale Jaw
88 Cycle Parking Garage
94 Border Station
100 Sound Barrier and Cockpit
108 Central Bus Station
112 Underground Parking Garage
118 Moindal Commuter Station
124 Box Hill Transport Interchange
128 Cycle Station

Road

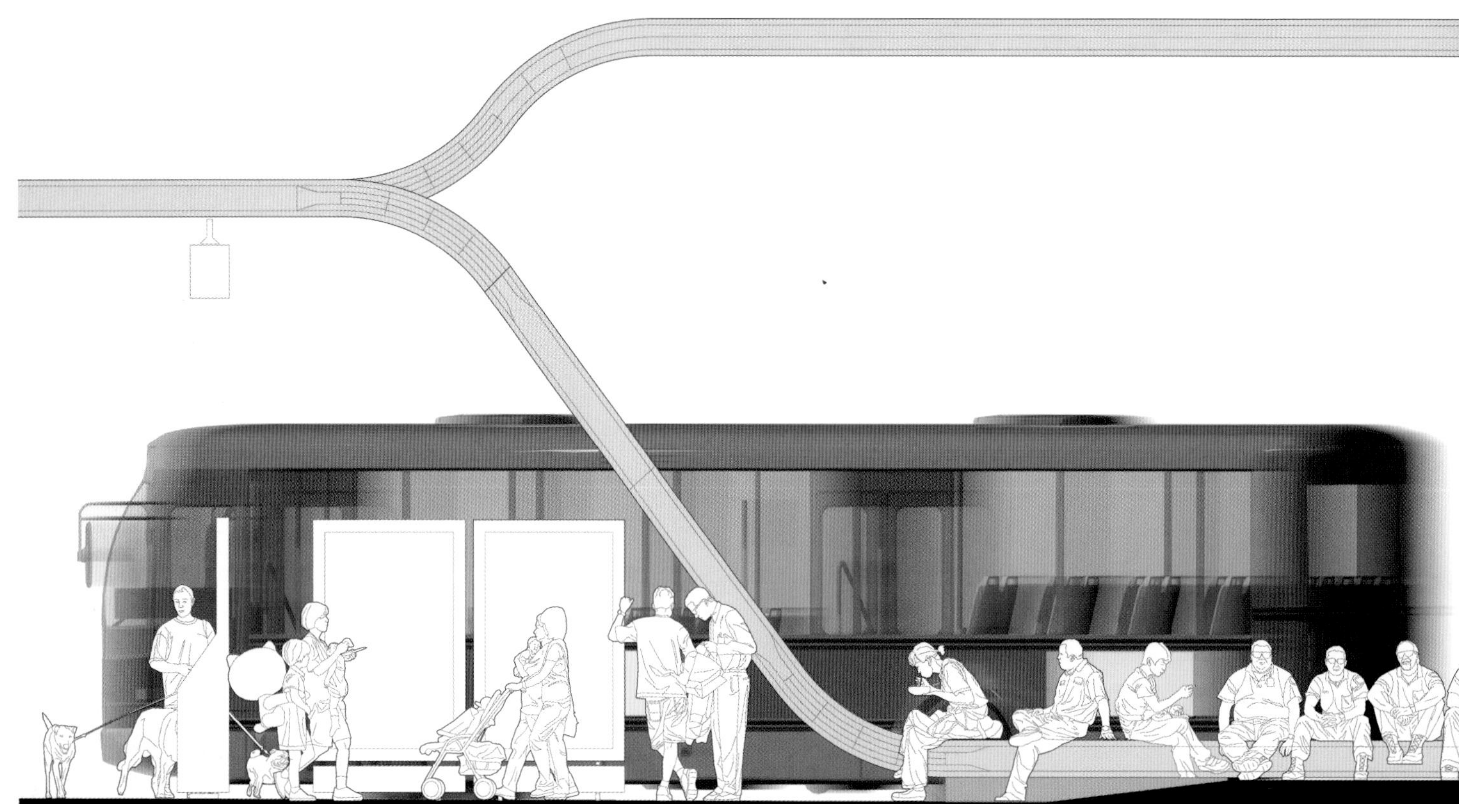

The first evidence of constructed roads dates from around 4000 BC. Stone paved streets have been found at the city of Ur in modern-day Iraq, while timber roads were discovered preserved in a swamp in Glastonbury, England. The first prolific road builders of more recent history were the Romans, who created a network of layered stone pavements stretching out some 50,000 miles from Italy.

These first highways were built with purpose and unstinting hard labour. They facilitated exploration and trade but more so they were built to conquer distant lands and people. Evidence of early roads is still easy to find today, especially the Roman roads of Europe. Many routes are still in use although they no are longer considered an empire-building necessity, more a convenience, a route from A to B.

Our necessity now is of course the car – our own moving cocoon that allows us to travel almost anywhere at any time. And it is this desire for private transport that has spawned a monstrous phenomenon that creates crippling smog and traffic gridlock in crowded cities across the world.

The power of the car, and our desire to own one, cannot be understated. Governments go soft on the issue of fuel tax in the face of global warming, and oil induces them to go to war in their clamour to protect dwindling fossil fuel reserves. This imbalance can not be sustained for ever, no matter how far global powers stick their heads in the sand.

The power shift

We know the answer: public transport. Along with the train and tram, buses are our most affordable, accessible option for local and national travel. We have spent the last 6000 years creating roads, now we should use them wisely. On a micro level the bicycle is the best option of all. In cities such as Amsterdam and various Asian urban centres the bike is king. Either by sheer weight of numbers or through intelligent urban planning, a large proportion of the population can get around most easily using pedal power. The UK is coming around to this way of thinking with its new National Cycle Network but, even with this, its roads are still predominantly the domain of the car. More dedicated routes and specialist facilities such as Oliver Lowenstein's Cycle Station (page 128) are required.

Initiatives such as the re-energizing of public transport and the National Cycle Network, both designed to attract people away from cars, are only part of the story. We also need to think imaginatively about how to best handle the huge volume of vehicles on our roads – from traffic management systems to innovative parking solutions.

Architecture can play a large part in all aspects of the assault on the motor car. Difficult spatial problems such as mass parking in cities can be solved with inspired design and engineering like that encountered at the underground parking garage by Szyszkowitz + Kowalski (page 112). Meanwhile new

Far left Vauxhall Cross Interchange, London, by Arup Associates

Centre ONL's sound barrier in Utrecht, The Netherlands

Top left Bicycle parking in Amsterdam by VMX Architects

Lower left Spiral car park ramp in Graz, Austria, by Szyszkowitz and Kowalski

public transport architecture must engage with its users, actively encouraging them to get on the bus or ride a bike.

Three main criteria – ease of access, shelter, and legibility, are the primary concerns of any public transport interchange. However, the architect of today must provide added attractions and excitement if that bus station or cycle garage is going to be a success. Projects such as the Burda Car Park (page 74) or Amsterdam Cycle Garage (page 88) do this purely with architectural form. Visitor testimony from both projects states that users actually enjoy interacting with the well-designed parking garages. Alternatively, the creation of reasons to visit, such as retail outlets and restaurants, as with the Central Bus Station in Munich (page 108) or Box Hill Transport Interchange (page 124), provides an added attraction to using what would normally be considered a bland passenger processing building.

Even with the best architectural additions to our road transport infrastructure, we are never going to eliminate the car. However, phenomena such as traffic gridlock have been happening since the 17th century, when horse-drawn carriages were first made widely available. We could, if we really wanted to, have tackled the problem years ago but our selfish desire to ride alone prevailed.

Now is our last chance to reassess our priorities and bring about change that will benefit us and generations to come. One simple step would be to designate major road traffic destinations such as city centres as car-free zones to relieve congestion, pollution and energy waste. Some people will not like this but the road transport problem will only ever be solved by compromise. This yearning for a cleaner, greener environment will always be hampered by the human race's two desires to explore and to own. We will never reach that total public transport utopia and so we have to do what we can to create a better architectural environment for the road user while trusting to science, and more worryingly government, the job of creating cleaner cars for us to drive.

Vauxhall Cross Interchange

DESIGN ARUP ASSOCIATES
LOCATION LONDON

Vauxhall Cross Interchange is a new transport hub in south London. Designed by Arup Associates, this striking ribbon-like structure undulates for 200 metres (656 feet) before reaching skywards in a dramatic statement that adds an important landmark to the contemporary architecture of the South Bank.

Commissioned by Transport for London, the £5 million project minimizes bus traffic on busy roads and integrates the new bus station with existing tube and rail services. Able to handle 45,000 people per day, the interchange is pedestrian- and environmentally friendly: photovoltaic cells on the raised cantilevers power public lighting.

The final design remains faithful to the original concept, drawn up for a limited competition in 2002. Taking inspiration from the regular lines and curves of London's Underground and bus maps, the steel structure comprises three undulating ribbons, clad in textured stainless steel. The middle of these ribbons folds downward at regular intervals to meet the ground and create the supporting structure. It also accommodates seating and glazed sheltered spaces within its loops. The outer elements oscillate between 5.5 and 6.5 metres (18 and 21 feet), providing enough clearance for buses to pass beneath.

The 12-metre (39 feet) wide canopy ends in a dramatic cantilever, as it divides and rises. This highly visible element creates an exciting new architectural addition to this somewhat neglected corner of London, with an aspiration that it will help regenerate the immediate urban precinct.

The entire scheme is designed to perform as a seamless sculptural artifact. Every effort has been made to integrate the paraphernalia of a public transport node into the architectural work. Elements like lighting, signage, seating, PA speakers, and CCTV cameras have been carefully integrated.

The canopy is accompanied by a cluster of small freestanding buildings, providing offices for staff, lifts to the underground station ticket hall, public toilets, and a unit for on-site bus controllers. The principal building is an asymmetrical two-storey structure wrapped in corrugated stainless steel. Its lines follow those of the canopy giving it a vehicular aesthetic.

Arup Associates has liaised closely with the Metropolitan Police to incorporate measures to reduce the risk of crime. In addition to CCTV cameras, excellent lighting, good sight lines, and material transparency, help deter criminals and drastically improve the urban environment.

Architectural drama at a bus station

BUSES
UNDERGROUND
Vauxhall Cross
30

Limited materials create maximum effect

Rendering of the sky-reaching ribbons

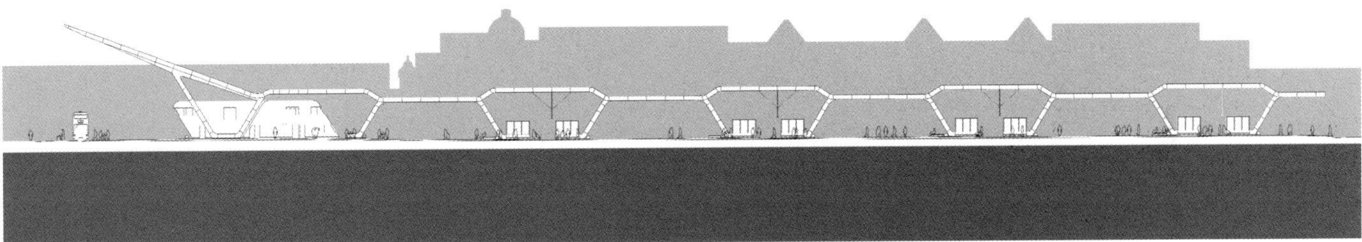

Section through the scheme

Aerial perspective of model

The undulating ribbons of Arup Associates' Vauxhall Cross Interchange have the dual advantage of creating a striking architectural intervention and being easily replicable for construction purposes. The form is uncluttered, even after the client has taken possession and decked it out with signage and other essential additions – a consequence of clear architectural planning from the outset.

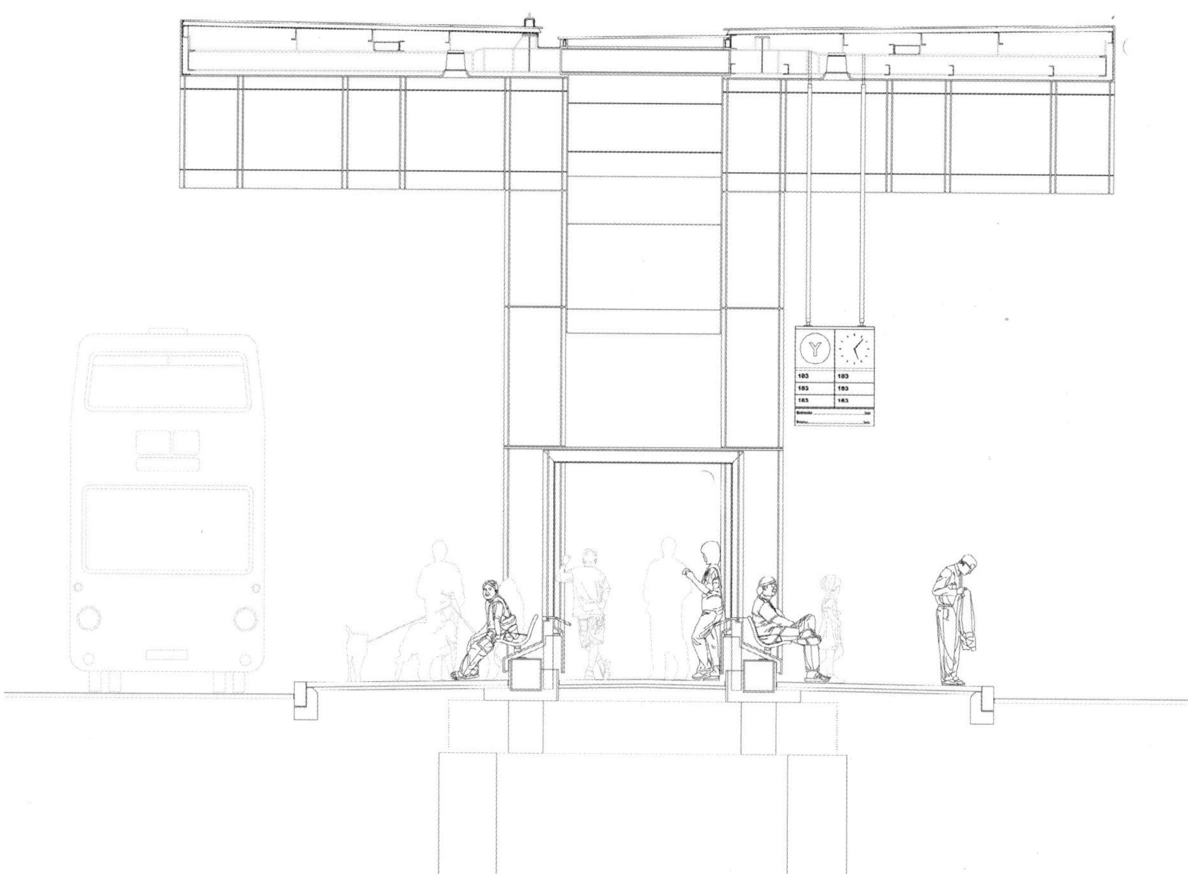

Section through element shown below

The central ribbon touches down

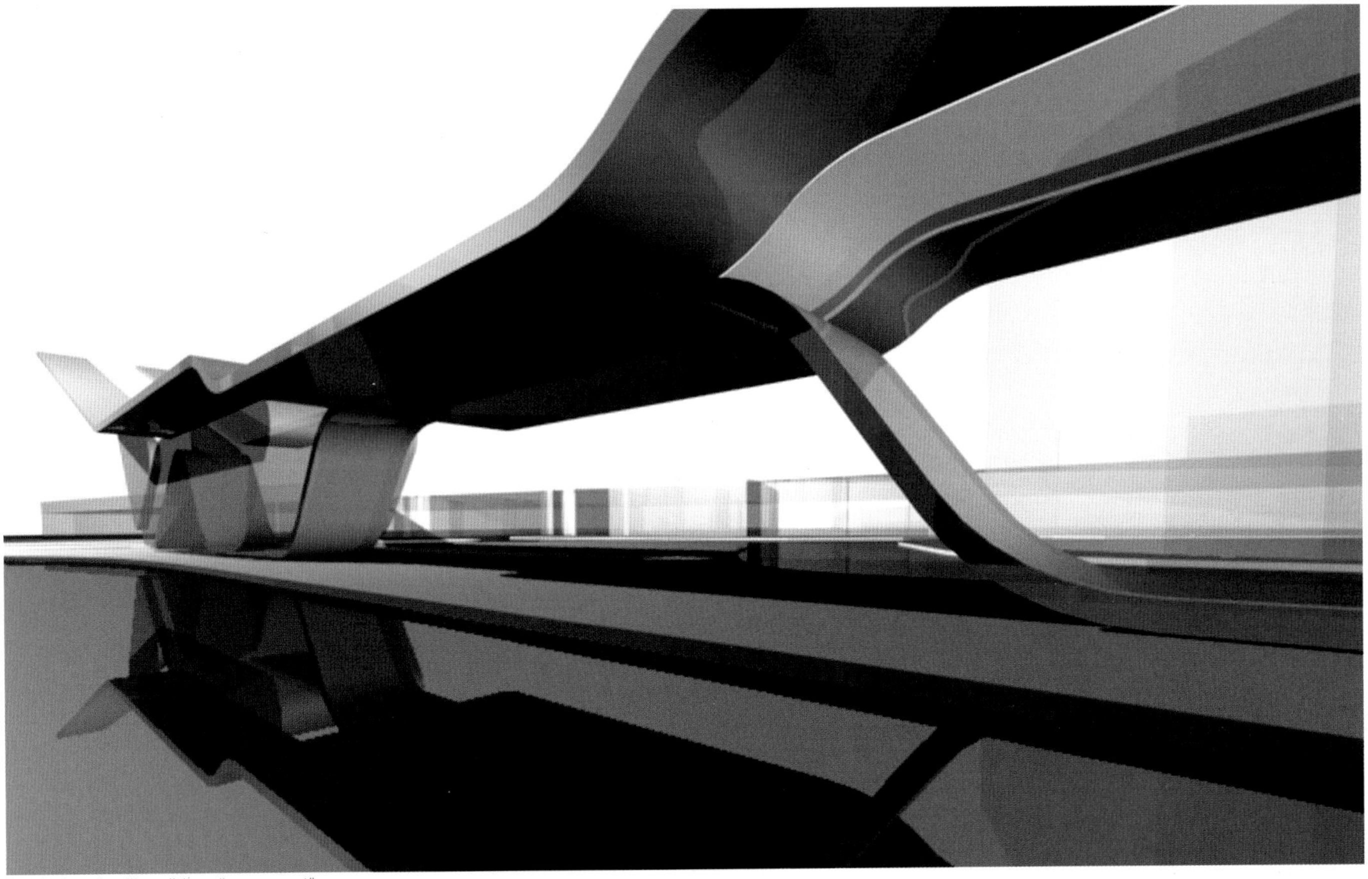

Rendering detailing ribbon "movement"

Size comparison of the ribbons to buses

The slender computer generated images don't reveal the scale and depth of the ribbons, for example that of the technical section (top left). Here, it is possible to see the space within the ribbon, which houses multiple services for lighting, signage and audio visual equipment. At night the interchange is open and well lit, discouraging would-be muggers or graffiti artists from operating in the area.

Bus crew control room

The only substantial building within the entire structure is the bus crews' quarters. This ribbed stainless steel-clad addition slopes with the lines of the upward-pointing arms to accentuate the "movement" of the architectural form. Indicative of the classic Air Stream caravan, its shimmering presence makes an interesting focal point within the lengthy interchange and gives bus crews a welcome secluded stop-off point in this extremely busy multi-modal travel interchange.

Night-time illumination

Car Park

DESIGN INGENHOVEN ARCHITEKTEN
LOCATION OFFENBURG, GERMANY

Following the completion of a new media park on the outskirts of Offenburg, a small town near Strasbourg in Germany, the demand for car parking outstripped the available ground level space. Ingenhoven Architekten were commissioned to design a multi-storey car park in a prominent position in a semi-rural area just off one of the main arteries into the town.

The architect's solution is like no other car park. Instead of the usual multi-levelled box structure, this car park is cylindrical in shape. It is five storeys high and 60 metres (197 feet) in diameter and can accommodate 474 vehicles. Two independent helical ramps offer ascending and descending routes for cars, giving the structure a flowing, almost filmic feel. The entire structure is cloaked in a translucent lattice of Oregon pine, suspended on stainless steel cables.

The load-bearing structure of the building is a mix of concrete and steel. The ramps and their surrounding walls are constructed of in situ concrete, forming a drum-like core that stiffens and stabilizes the whole structure. From this, the car park floors are projected outwards – prefabricated concrete elements carried on steel beams extend to the perimeter, where they are supported by steel columns.

It is the facade, however, that catches the eye. Round Oregon pine sections are suspended on stainless steel cables with specially designed clips. Horizontal wind movement is restricted at each floor level by steel brackets that anchor the cables. The roof is constructed in a similar way, with the cables adopting a catenary curve between the core and the outer steel compression ring. The poles and cables form a sort of enclosing pergola.

This beautifully light skin is wind permeable, allowing breezes to blow away the exhaust and fuel smells usually associated with multi-storey car parks. It also creates a delightful play of light and shade across the parking decks, making the mundane activity of parking your car a pleasure.

In time the pine will weather, turning from its current brown to a silver grey colour, blending with the slowly altering hue of the concrete. The people of Offenburg are privileged to have such a prominent architectural icon sign posting entry to their town. What is most remarkable though is that while many urban settlements now have a recognizable landmark building, no other can claim to have made such a statement from a building type that is universally regarded as purely ugly and functional.

Top-level parking beneath a tensioned cable screen

The Oregon pine facade

Ground entrance level

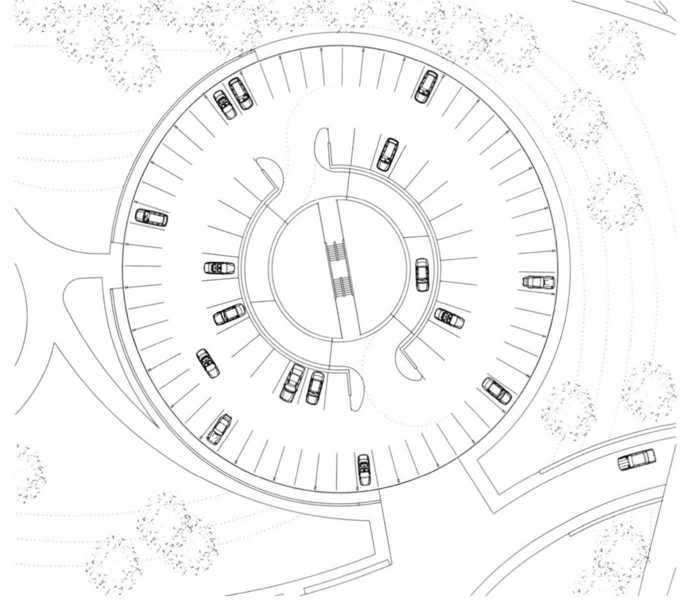

Intermediate level

Aerial view at night

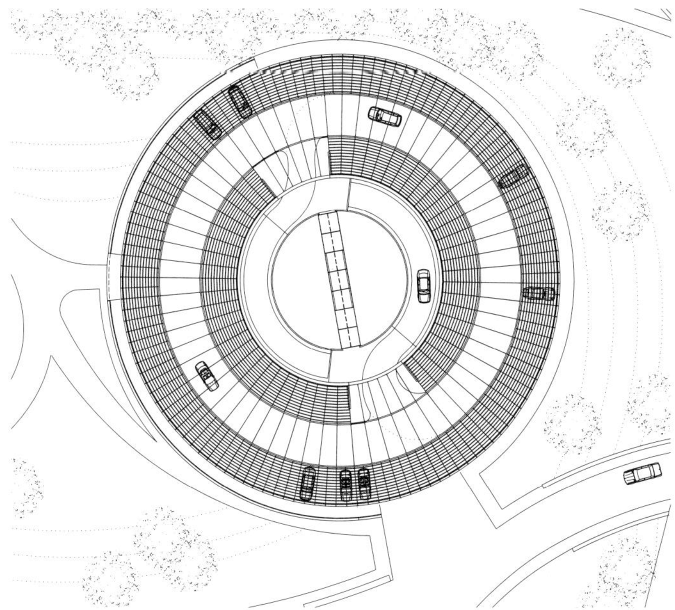

Top floor

Burda car park is unique. Its cylindrical form and Oregon pine slat cladding challenge our expectations of a multi-storey car park and so allow it to exist as a landmark and architectural statement in prime position, rather than being hidden away or an eyesore. In this way the architect has triumphed in its ambition to elevate the mundane to a level appreciated by passers-by. At night, lit from within and by the lights of ascending cars it makes a dramatic spectacle.

The spiralling ramp

Glazed bridge to the central pedestrian lift

Central ramp

Aerial view of the top floor

From within, the design is as considered and aesthetically pleasing as from afar. Clean, fair-faced concrete ramps with sheer walls spiral upwards, allowing no view of what is to come until drivers exit on to the parking floors. Once on the parking decks, the pine and steel cable screen allows views out over the landscape. For pedestrians, descent involves journeying across the abyss on glass-clad bridges, which lead to lifts at the car park's structural core.

The Whale Jaw

DESIGN NIO ARCHITECTEN
LOCATION HOOFDDORP, THE NETHERLANDS

There can be no stranger bus station in the world. The Whale Jaw, by NIO Architecten, is unlike anything else built: is it a relic from prehistoric times or an alien form cast down from outer space? Even the architect has difficulty describing it, stating that the building was conceived in the tradition of Oscar Niemeyer, "a cross between white modernism and black Baroque", before pondering the form again as "a large boulder worn down by footsteps and sight lines".

However, in purely functional terms, the Whale Jaw is a bus station sitting in front of the Spaarne Hospital in Hoofddorp. It serves the rather mundane purpose of a turning point for the local bus service and it is precisely because of this that NIO wanted to create something that was more than the usual bland shelter.

The structure creates shelter and seating for those waiting for a bus, as well as space where conductors and drivers can take breaks. A restrictive budget meant that the architect had to think creatively to create a Niemeyer-esque monument. So instead of using concrete, the building is completely built from polystyrene foam and polyester. The result is the world's largest structure in synthetic materials.

The design and construction process was experimental from start to finish. The form was factory-cut from huge blocks of expanded polyurethane foam. This created the form, but all rigidity and strength to resist both wind loading and the effects of downward forces caused by the frequent winter snow falls comes from the coating of polyester, sprayed onto it in gradually built up layers. The entire structure is anchored using plates of Contraclad, which are connected to steel plates bolted to the concrete pad on which it sits.

Due to the experimental nature of the project, NIO had to test the materials used against conventional loads and deliberate tampering and vandalism. Tests were carried out to ensure that the polyester coating could not be compromised by knives, cigarettes, or the solvents in spray paint. The coating passed all destructive tests, but it remains to be seen whether the structure will stand up to the test of time.

Every person that experiences the Whale Jaw will form a different opinion of it and its meaning but, as the architect concludes: "Like the white face of a geisha, every opinion and image can be projected on to the building and yet it has no answers of its own and no need for them."

The belly of the whale – the waiting area

2609

Side elevation facing the pedestrian set down point

End containing bus crew quarters and toilets

This grotesque and yet intriguing form is born out of the lack of imagination usually expressed on building types as simplistic as bus stops. The architect has deliberately set out to shock in an environment where people least expect it and the result is astounding. The surface texture is akin to a cross between concrete – an immediate assumption for built form – and the skin of a dinosaur – because we can't be sure of what we are looking at. Our beliefs are suspended until safely back on the bus.

Side elevation showing covered seating to rear

The waiting area illuminated at night

The structure is vandal proof, although not graffiti resistant. However, the architect hopes that the unusual nature of the bus stop will endear it to locals and so protect it against overt acts of vandalism. Alternatively, good graffiti art could actually work in harmony with this creation enhancing the structure even more.

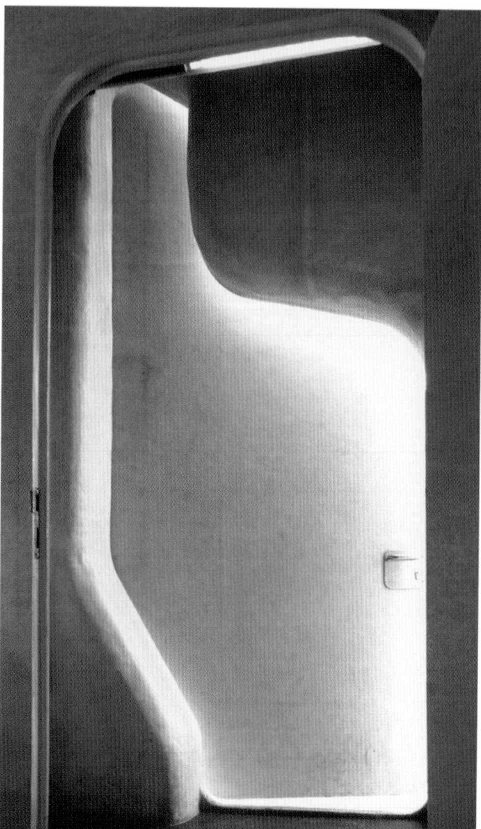

Entrance to the toilets

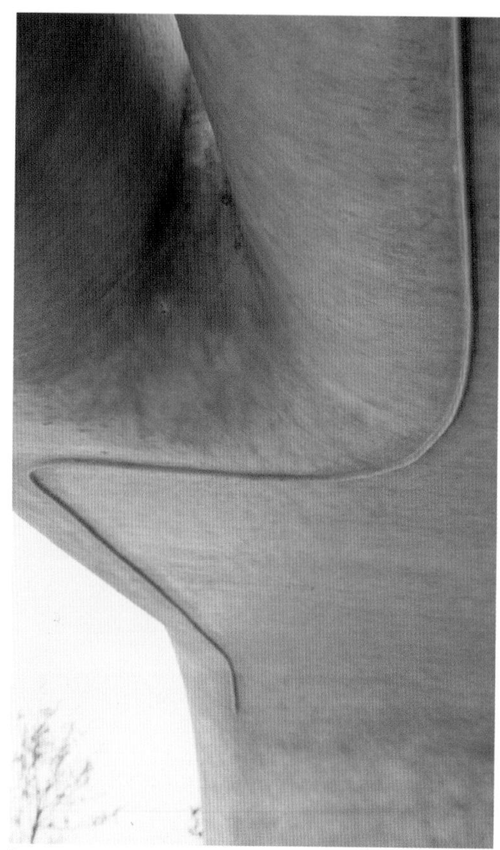

Detailing on the ceiling

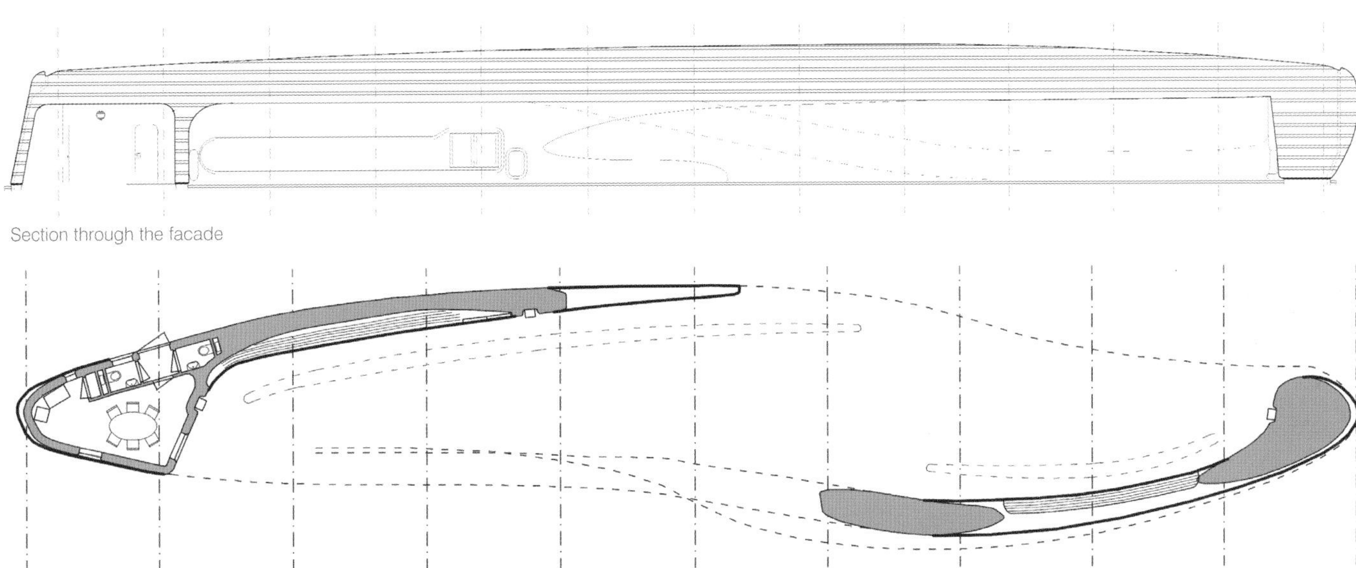

Section through the facade

Plan view at floor level

View from an elevated road nearby

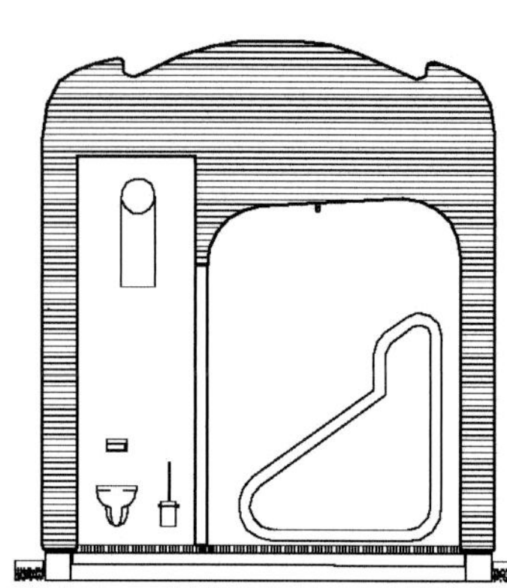
Section through toilet cubicle

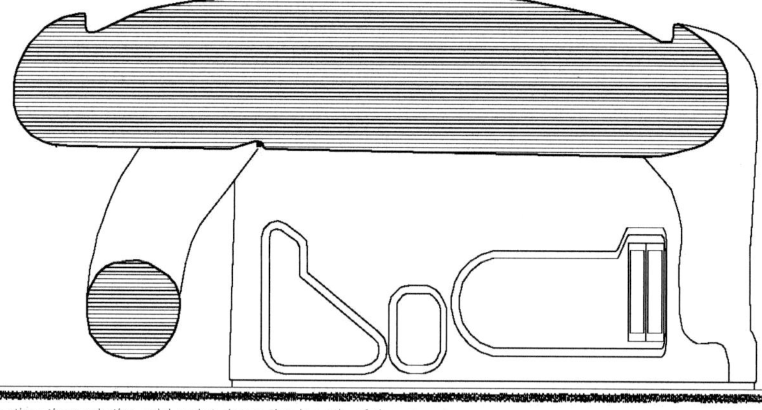
Section through the mid point down the length of the structure

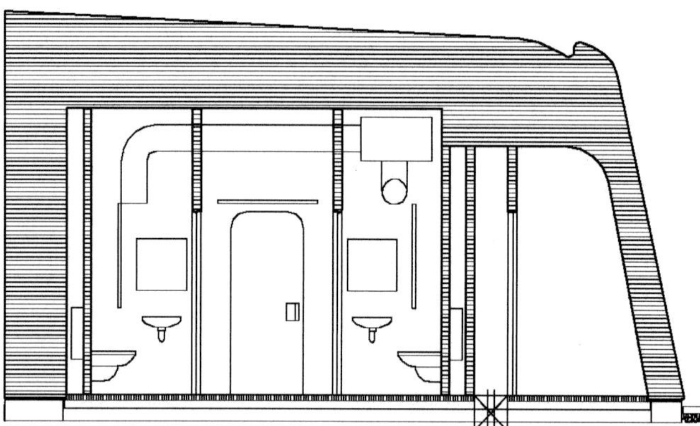
Section through toilets, showing door to crew quarters

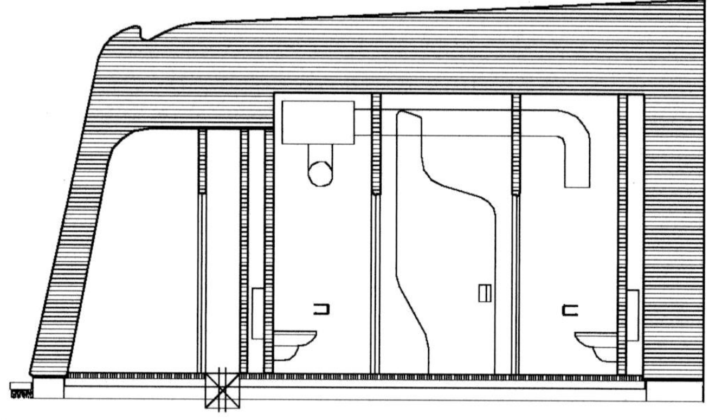
Section through toilets, showing door to exterior

The curvaceous rear elevation

Travellers accentuate the structure's size

Due to the use of expanded polyurethane foam, the structure can be massive without being heavy. This has allowed the architect to create a deep roof section, which is virtually unsupported, adding drama to an already bizarre spectacle. Internally, the crew share their bathroom amenities with the public via a door from their quarters. This reduces the requirement for separate WCs that would impact on the aesthetic of the design.

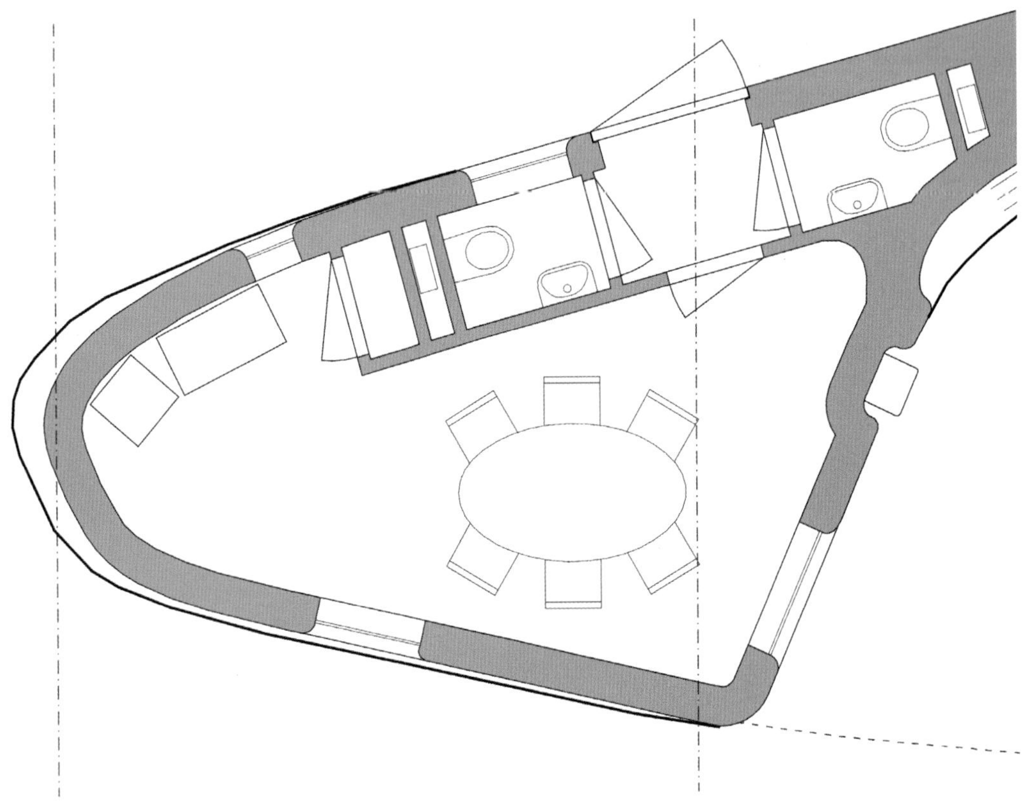

Plan of the crew's quarters and public/crew toilets

Cycle Parking Garage

DESIGN VMX ARCHITECTS
LOCATION AMSTERDAM, THE NETHERLANDS

The construction of a new metro line, bus station and underground pedestrian passage at Amsterdam Central Station necessitated the closure of indoor cycle parking facilities and the clearance of the main station forecourt, where further bicycle racks had been situated. The works created a problem of where to park the 2500 bicycles that are regularly left at the station by commuters and tourists. VMX Architects has provided an innovative and endearing solution, designing a temporary cycle parking garage that floats on and above the water in a quay near to the station.

The design is suitably quirky and yet wholly practical, mimicking the ethos of this very individual city. It is based upon the simple functionality of a basic multi-storey car park. The building is 110 metres (360 feet) long by 17.5 metres (57 feet) wide. It is self-supporting and independent of the quay, with minimal contact with the water. Six metre (20 foot) wide ramps, sloping at a constant three degrees take cyclists up from one of the three entrances on a red asphalt 'carpet', lined on either side by cycle parking racks. Just as in a car park, users ride up the inclined ramps until they find a space to park. The colour of the 'carpet' is taken from that of the cycle tracks that snake around the city and the country. Four staircases make for easy, safe descent by pedestrians. However, due to the structure's complete lack of walls, the architect says that after parking their bikes most cyclists like to stroll back down the ramps, surveying the city from this unusual elevated platform.

To avoid contact with the quay, the building is supported by 13 double columns that run through its centre. It is constructed from prefabricated metal parts and assembled to create a dramatic cantilevered structure that overhangs the water. The cantilever enables maximum space to be retained on the water to allow boats to turn around. The cycle garage's weight, loaded with bicycles, is counterbalanced by a concrete ground floor on the land-side of the structure.

The temporary, inexpensive nature of the project has not detracted from the architect's desire to create something that makes a real impact. From the red colouring to the industrial sloping forms of the ramps, the cycle park has become a tourist attraction in its own right. Instead of being a temporary eyesore at one of the entrances into Amsterdam, the cycle garage is an energizing addition that echoes the avant garde nature of the city.

View of the multi-storey cycle parking structure from the water

hotel ibis
ibis
LOVERS
André van Duin

This dramatic addition to the Amsterdam cityscape has become a tourist attraction in its own right. This multi-storey cycle park is a world first and not something that many cities currently require. However, as fuel prices escalate and eco-taxing is boosted to reduce greenhouse gases, the bicycle will once again become a major transport option in the western world. VMX's concept could soon catch on.

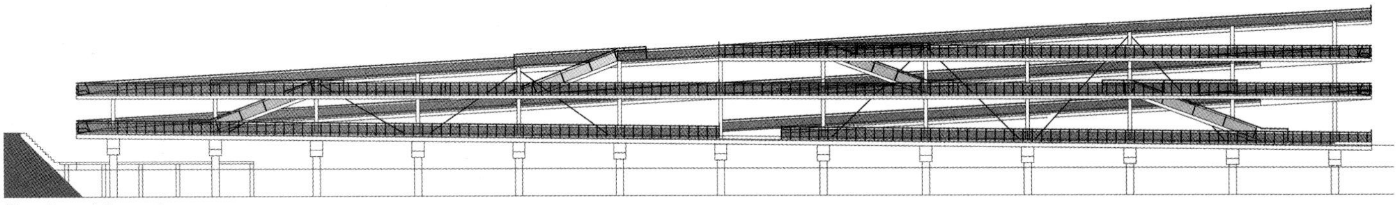
Elevation of the cycle garage

Night-time illumination creates a spectacle on the waterfront

Red carpet treatment

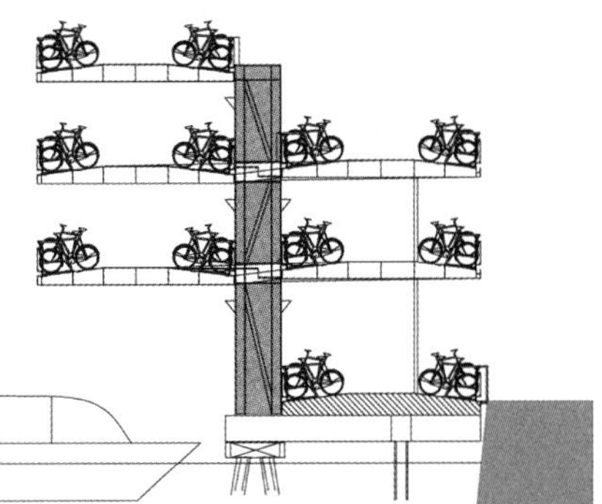

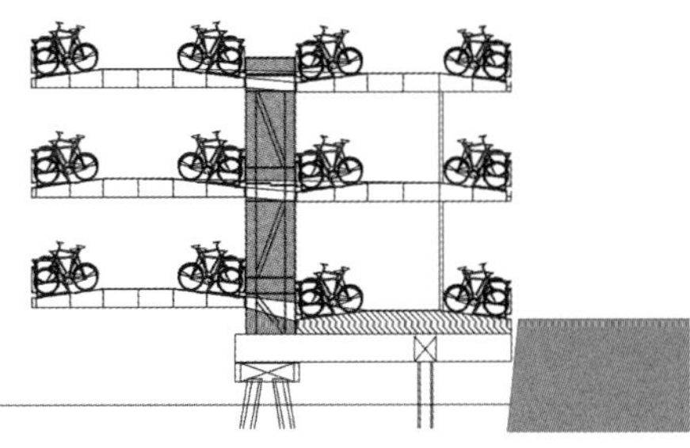

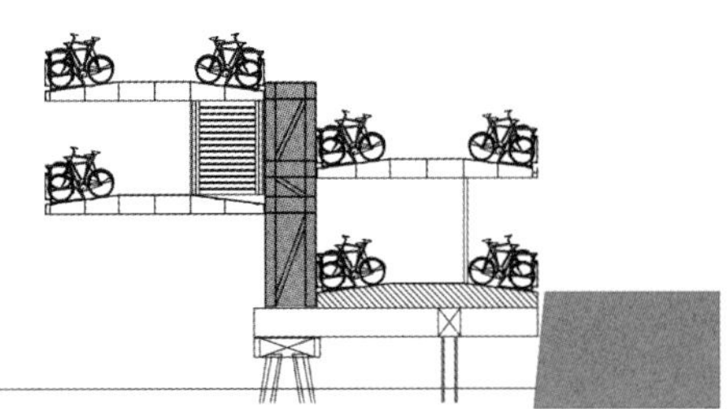

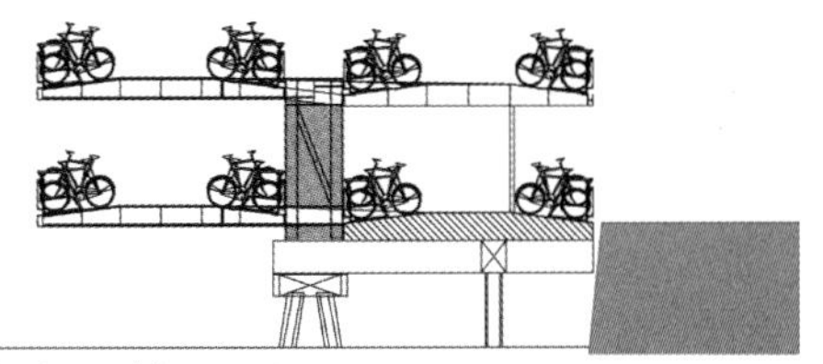

Sections of the structure

The continuous ramp features cycle racks on either side

The striking contemporary structure of the cycle park ascends as one continuous ramp to the highest point overlooking the historic Amsterdam Central Station. The ramp is cambered to allow rain run-off. Its red colour could signify the importance of the bicycle to the Dutch city both historically and today: more mundanely, it is the same colour as all the cycle paths around Amsterdam.

View of the interior with exit stair in the background

Border Station

DESIGN ROSS BARNEY + JANKOWSKI
LOCATION SAULT ST. MARIE, MICHIGAN, USA

Border stations and ports of entry have been undergoing a major makeover all around the USA for the last decade. And with the North American Free Trade Agreement resulting in increased border traffic from Canada, the latest to be rebuilt and increased in size by a staggering nine times is the crossing at Sault St Marie on the Michigan/Ontario border.

Designed by Chicago practice, Ross Barney + Jankowski (RBJ), the building and surrounding roadways, carparks and facilities are informed by two factors: a steeply contoured site and the efficient processing of vehicles through the station. A lower level of inspection lanes are determined by the turning circle of an articulated truck, while the proportionally smaller navigational requirements of cars shape the high level plaza.

Depending upon where the building is viewed from it can be seen as a dramatic architectural statement or a sensitive addition to the landscape. Set into the hillside, the office element is located away from the noise and fumes of passing vehicles and a green, vegetated roof helps to blend the large structure with the natural environment.

The driver's view of the border station is punctuated by translucent inspection canopies which glow gently to provide a luminescent gateway. The main three-storey building towers over the scene, its extensively glazed facade providing inspectors with views out over the vehicle inspection stations. This wall of glass also reassures, according to the architect, breaking down the barriers between official and driver.

Sustainable design considerations are mainly of the passive variety, including the vegetated roof and large expanses of high performance glazing to facilitate the ingress of natural light. The building's shape and positioning, nestled into the side of the hill, also lessens its exposure to the harsh local climate. The building's reception centre was designed by artist Terry Karpowicz as an "Art in Architecture" project using hardwoods salvaged from shipwrecks in Lake Superior. In addition to glass, copper and stone are the cladding materials, each heralding the natural resources of Michigan's Upper Peninsula.

The project is one of a number of showpiece border stations currently being completed across the states. It has been described by General Services Administration project manager, Donald Melcher, as, "a unique design and innovative response to a difficult site that is a signature addition to the inventory of federal architecture".

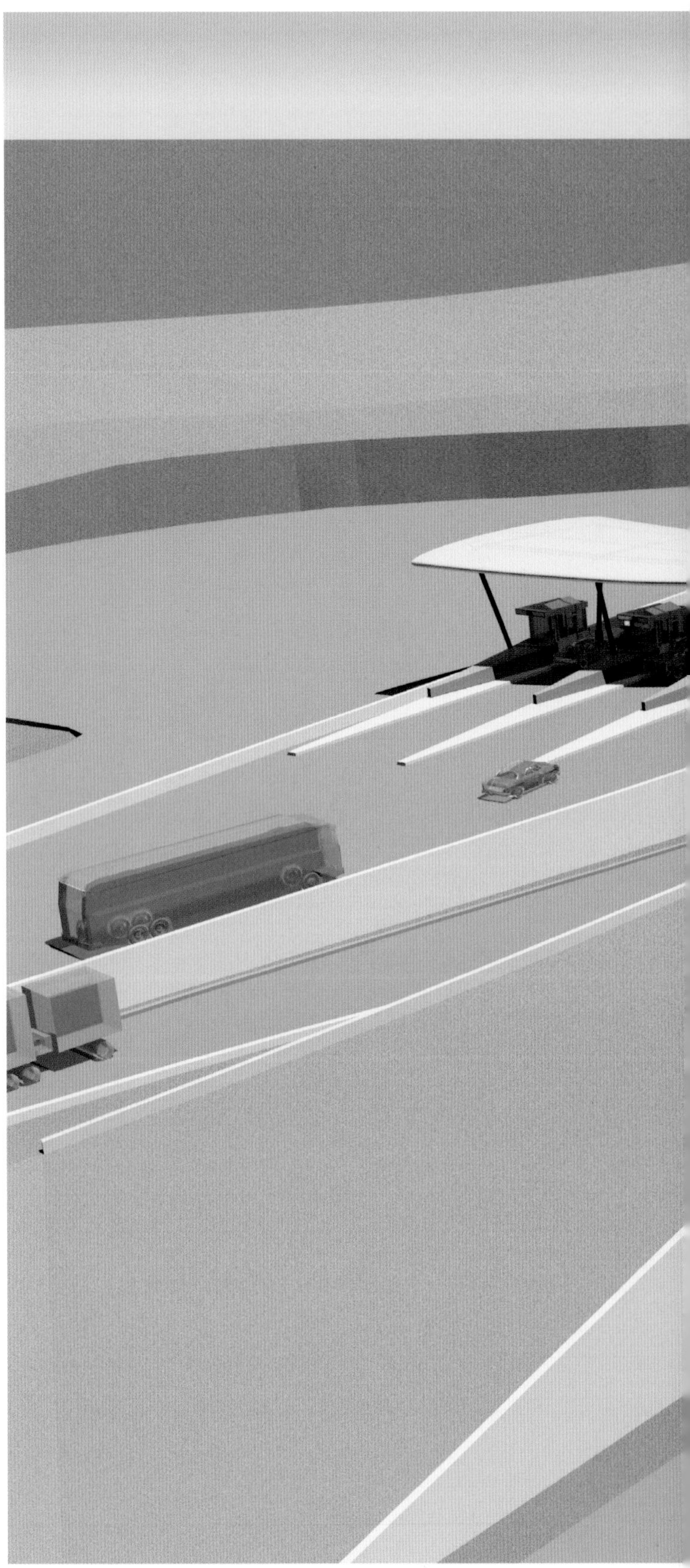

View of main building and toll booths

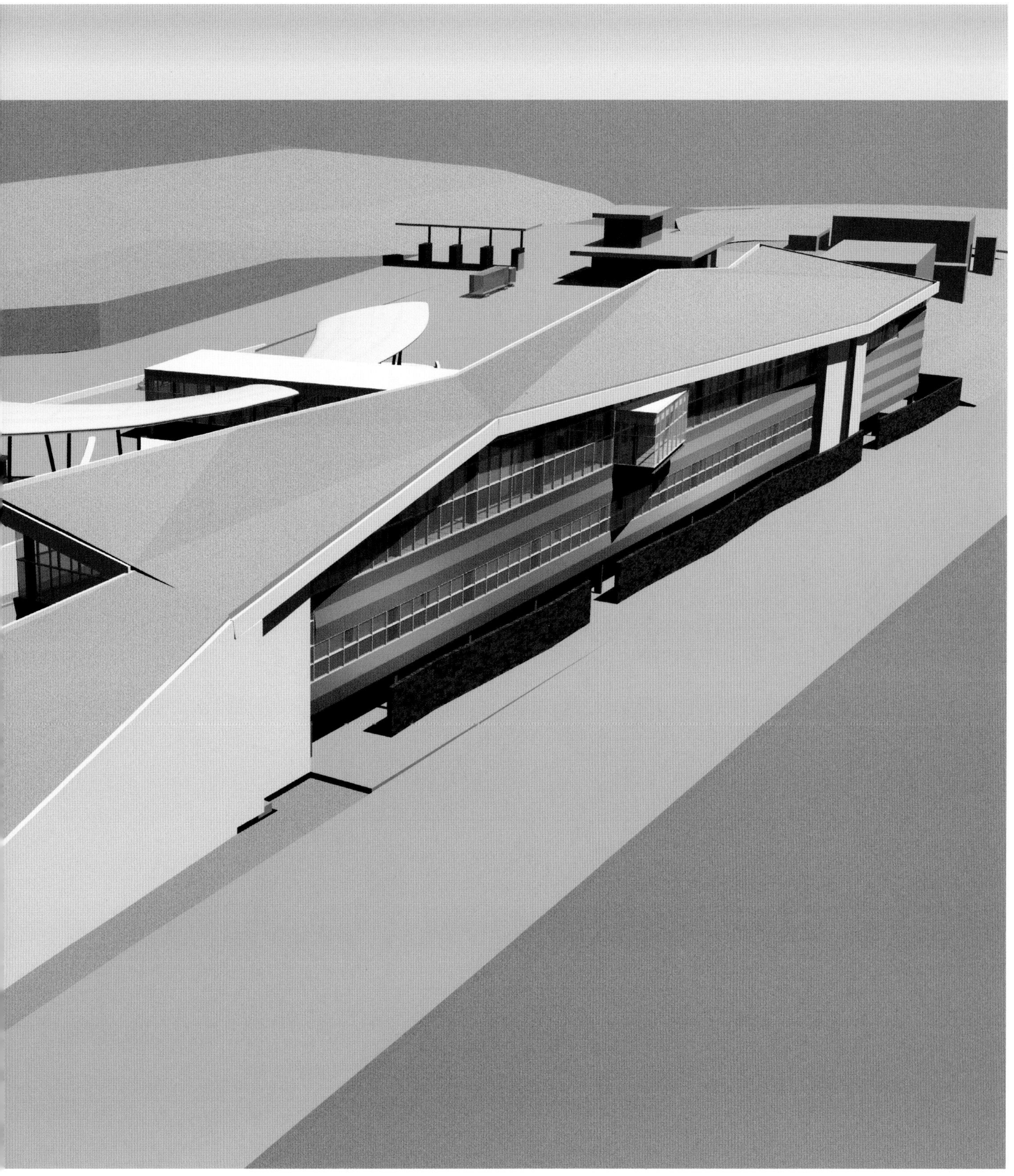

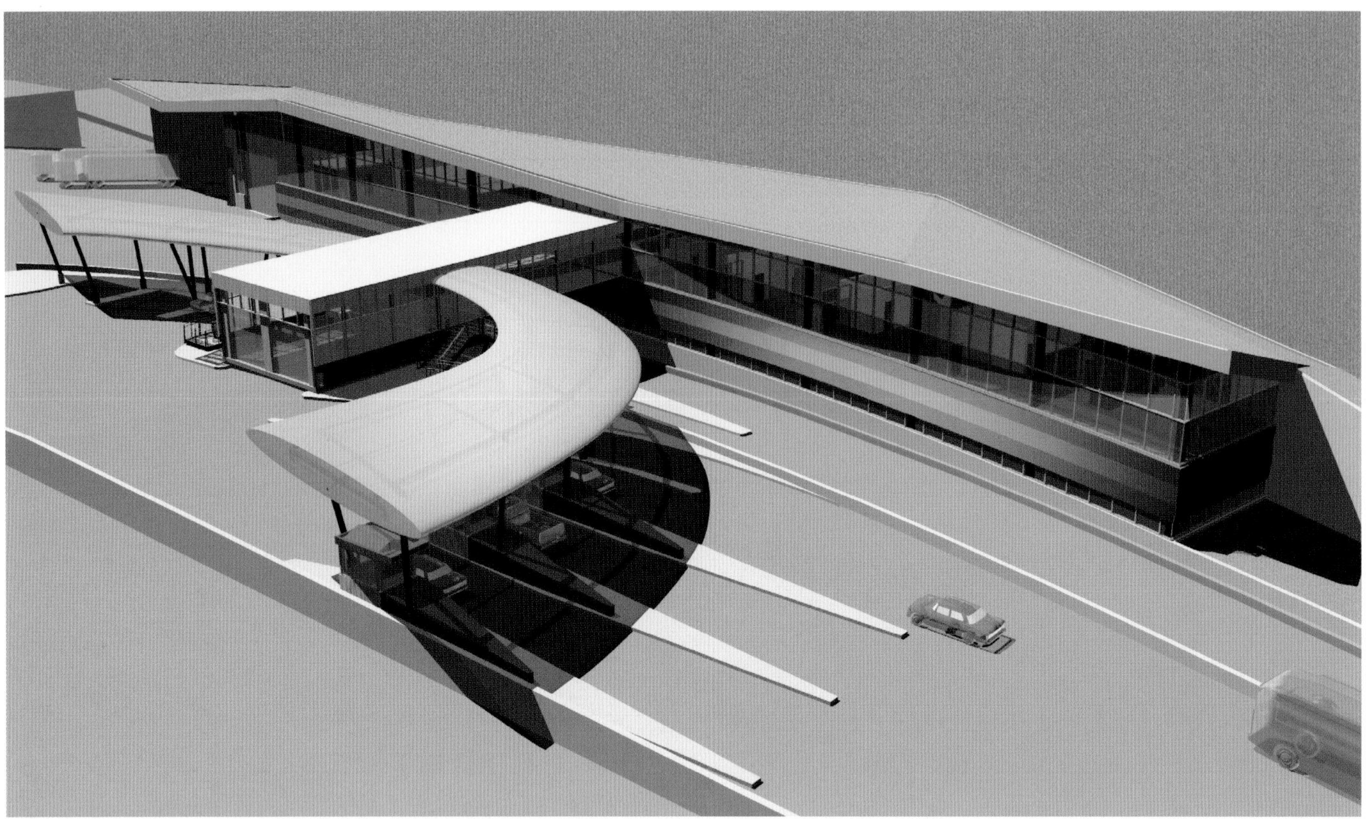

View of the curved inspection booth roof

View from the rear of the building

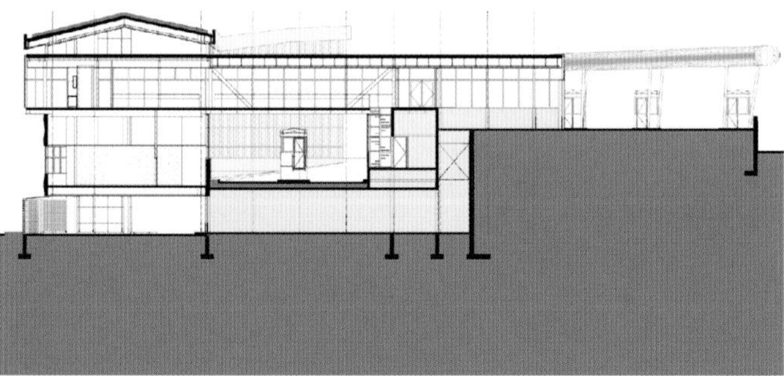

Section showing the building built into the hill

The dual height inspection lanes

View from the gantry leading from main building to the booths

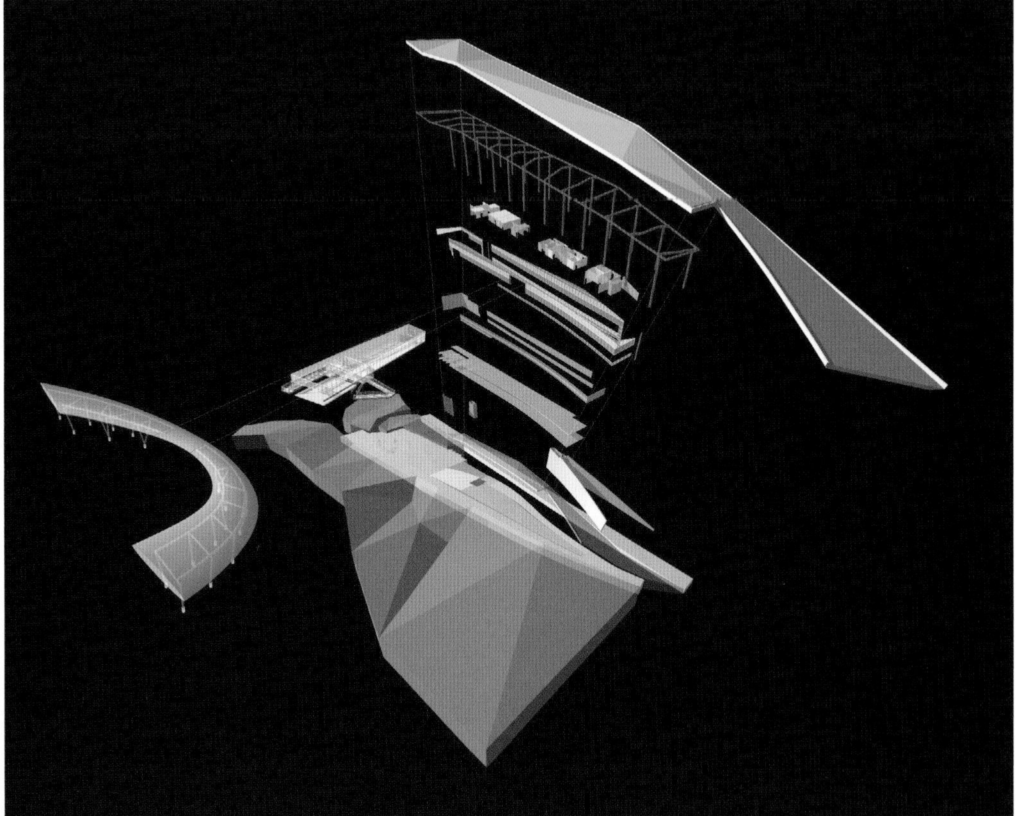

Exploded elements diagram

The design of the border crossing is a triumph of design over necessity. Not only does the complex include inception areas for both cars and freight vehicles and offices, it also houses detention cells, search dog kennels, a veterinary station and even a shooting range.The functional requirements of this building type often means that aesthetics are overlooked in a bid to save time and cost: strange ideals for a building which is quite literally the gateway to and from a country. This project is an exception, as can be seen by the interesting form of the inspection booth roof and the use of high grade materials throughout.

View from the lower roadway

Exciting architecture does not have to be a city hall or an art gallery. While a relative few will experience these civic buildings, everyone interacts with transport architecture on a daily basis. This is why considered, dramatic designs such as this border station are important. With glazed bridges, sharp lines and the curving roof, it makes a statement that is seen by all.

Sound Barrier and Cockpit

DESIGN ONL
LOCATION A2 HIGHWAY, UTRECHT, NETHERLANDS

Throughout Europe acoustic barriers stretching for miles along the side of major autoroutes are a common occurrence. However, the aesthetic qualities of such noise-reflecting devices have not, until now, been fully considered. Dutch practice ONL, headed by Kas Oosterhuis, has taken on this challenge and produced a combined noise barrier and car showroom that defies exclusive description as either architecture or pure engineering, noise barrier or building.

ONL's exciting approach to the project saw the team attempting to design "at a speed of 120km per hour". While the building does not move, it will be viewed mainly from the road from speeding vehicles. In order that the building interacts with this moving audience, the architect has stretched the Cockpit car showroom ten-fold in the longitudinal direction. This effectively speeds it up to the velocity of the passing cars and allows time for motorists to properly take in its presence.

The continuous flowing lines of the acoustic barrier add to the perceived speed of the structure while providing the horizontal members of a complex grid that changes along its length from angular to smoothly curved, convex to concave. On the road side the grid is clad in a system of glass elements, producing a sleek automotive feel. The other side is clad with an open mesh that allows light to percolate through.

Produced according to a strict file-to-factory process, the design has been formulated using computer scripts that plot a cloud of points, each depicting a position that corresponds to a critical joint. From the cloud point diagram, individual elements are defined and their size, shape and strength is calculated and tested via computer and scale model to produce the structural framework. All information is then fed into a computer-aided manufacturing plant where each element is created. Assembly is simply a matter of bolting together the individually numbered pieces to form the massive 1.6 kilometre (1750 yard) long barrier and car showroom.

The defining element of the scheme is the car showroom. Designed as the hub or Cockpit, it is an integral part of the barrier and as such is constructed from the same materials. Four floors are defined by the curving contours of the facade. Natural light dominates, pouring in through the fully glazed, all-enveloping facade, while at night a subtle lighting scheme provides a distinct point of reference to the head of the acoustic barrier

High speed architecture meets sound barrier

Car showroom within the barrier framework

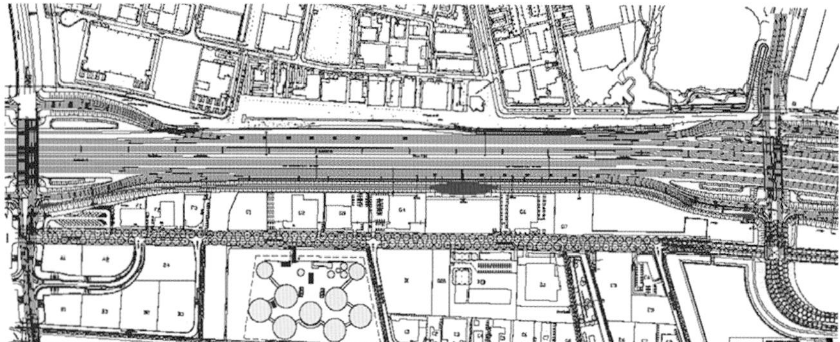

Plan of the barrier

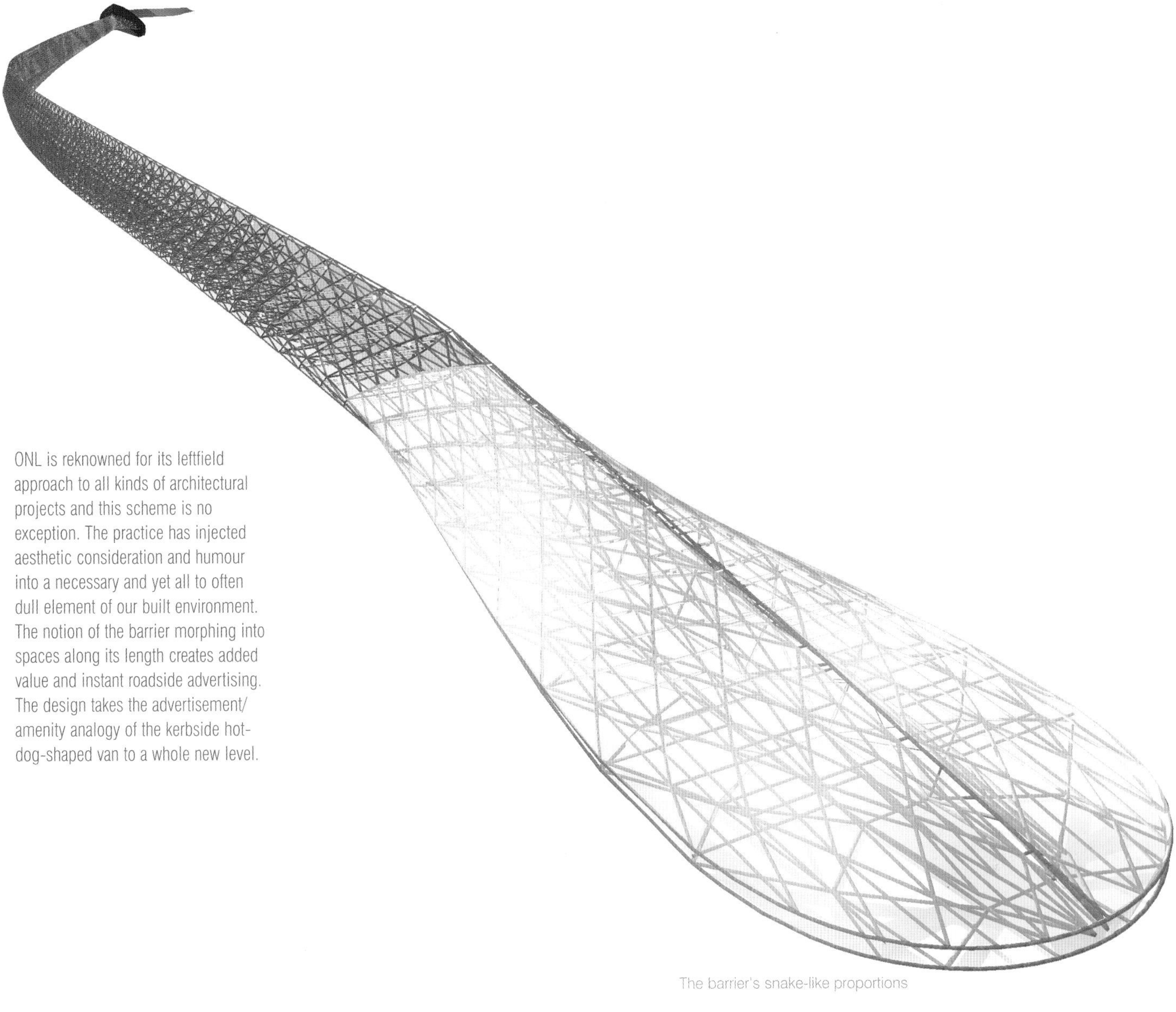

ONL is reknowned for its leftfield approach to all kinds of architectural projects and this scheme is no exception. The practice has injected aesthetic consideration and humour into a necessary and yet all to often dull element of our built environment. The notion of the barrier morphing into spaces along its length creates added value and instant roadside advertising. The design takes the advertisement/ amenity analogy of the kerbside hot-dog-shaped van to a whole new level.

The barrier's snake-like proportions

A section of the barrier's glass-and-steel facade

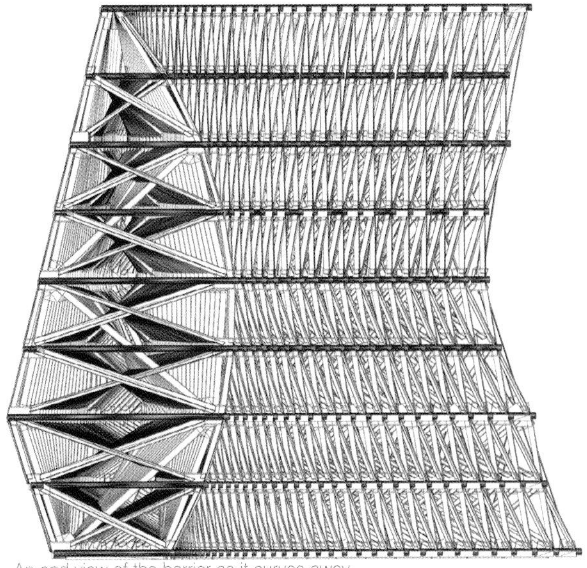
An end view of the barrier as it curves away

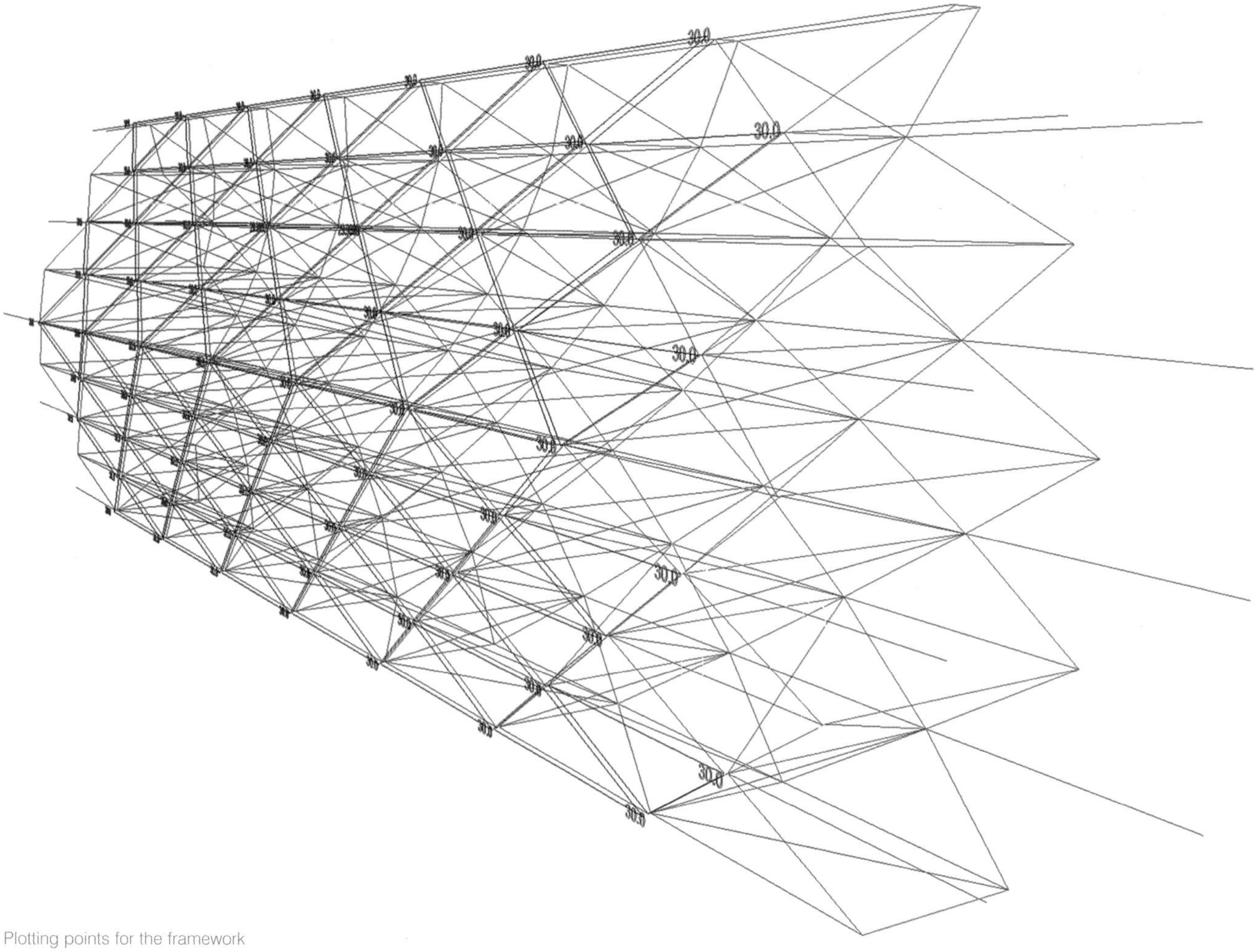

Plotting points for the framework

The barrier during construction

The continuous form of the barrier morphs through a variety of shapes along its length. While they may look random, these sections (right) are each calculated to provide best sound deflection and also accommodation within the barrier. The design genius of this project is the fact that the entire barrier is constructed from simple triangulated forms that easily replicable using CADCAM techniques.

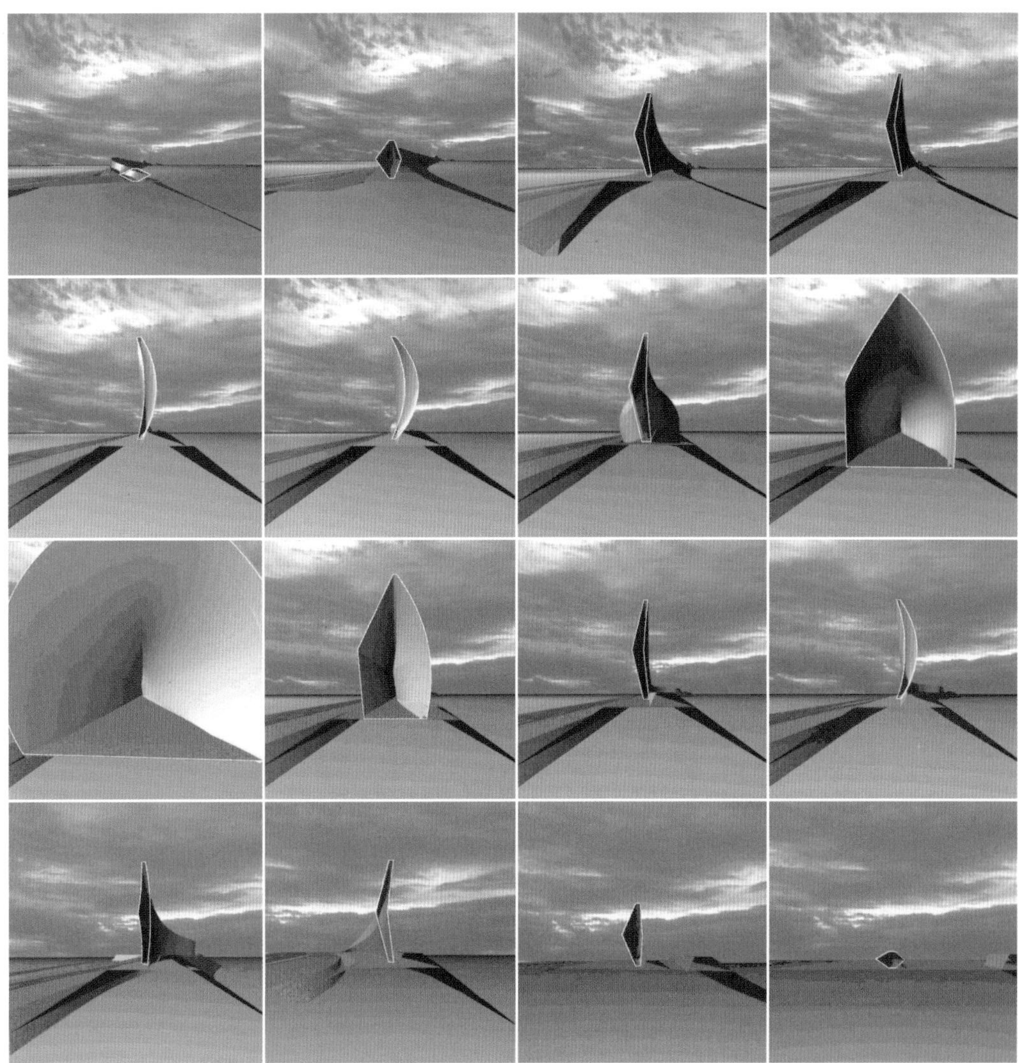

Sections taken along the barrier

Detail of barrier cladding

Rendering of cockpit at night

The showpiece element of the barrier project is the cockpit, a multilevel car showroom situated at the barrier's end, like the head of a gigantic serpent. Built from the same steel-and-glass components as the barrier, this bulbous form is enlongated to ensure that it has maximum impact when viewed from vehicles travelling along the adjacent highway, rather than a static position as wisdom would dictate.

Cockpit by day

Central Bus Station

DESIGN AUER + WEBER ARCHITEKTEN
LOCATION MUNICH, GERMANY

The new Central Bus Station in Munich takes its form directly from the vehicles that circulate within and around it. The sleek, low-slung design has a distinct resemblance to various makes of German luxury saloon cars, or the city's impressively well kempt public coach fleet. An external shell, or sheath, as the architect calls it, surrounds the station's various departments in much the same way as a vehicle's body encases and disguises the ugliness of its working innards.

The building's shape alludes to movement and speed, too. Streamlined and curvaceous, it is a deliberate break from the static, bulky impression that the city's other buildings present. The station does not try to compete with the skyward bound office towers, instead it hunches primed, ready to speed off along the rail tracks that border the site.

These tracks define the site that is bounded on one side by a raft of new development, of which the station is part, and to the other by the gentle curve of the railway lines. The building itself is five storeys in height, with another level below ground. It contains a main bus terminal, offices, a hotel and service providers. All are extensively naturally illuminated via four large atria that ascend up through the building at regular intervals to huge skylights cut into the roof of the outer shell. Both ends of the building are also open, allowing in more natural light, and, to the lower-slung extremity a large café and terrace features elevated views out onto a public square. On the first floor, the promenade deck is connected to the bus stops of the central bus station, the suburban railway station and Hackerbrucke by walkways and escalators, providing barrier-free access to all facilities.

The terminal's main lounge opens out onto the aforementioned external square that faces the city and main railway station. This gesture is designed to give gravitas to the new building and harks back to traditional design of the interface between travel hubs and the public realm, reiterating the importance of the building to the city and its people. From the square, people can see views of the bus stops below, the rail platforms and main station, all set against the backdrop of downtown Munich.

Superimposed design in the cityscape

Internal view of atrium

The bus station is intelligently designed to fit into the existing urban landscape. Positioned on a tapering site at the end of a city block, it makes good use of the land available. Internally, the building is naturally lit by four vast atria that allow light into the ground floor bus terminal and across intermediate floor spaces populated by offices, as well as the hotel and restaurant.

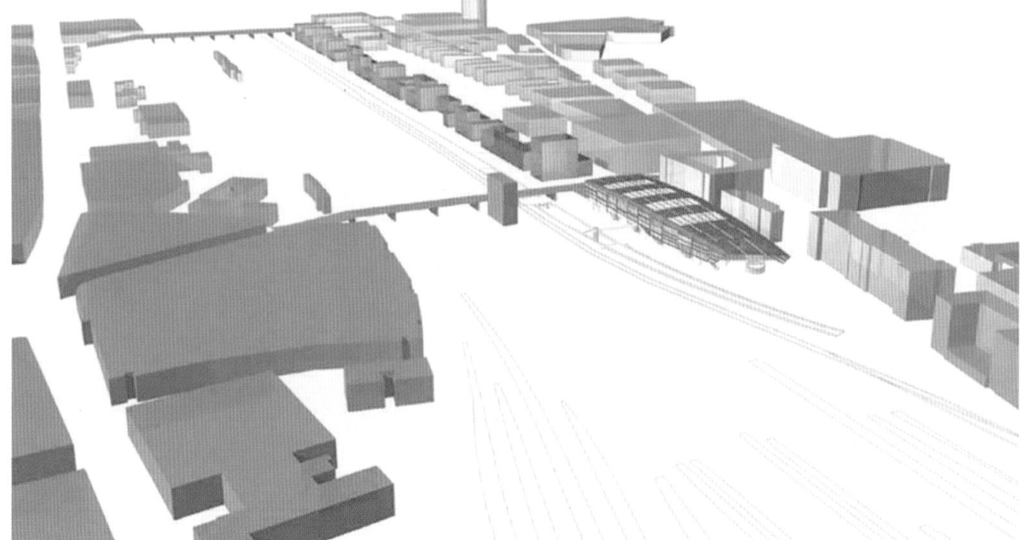

Illustration of alignment with other buildings

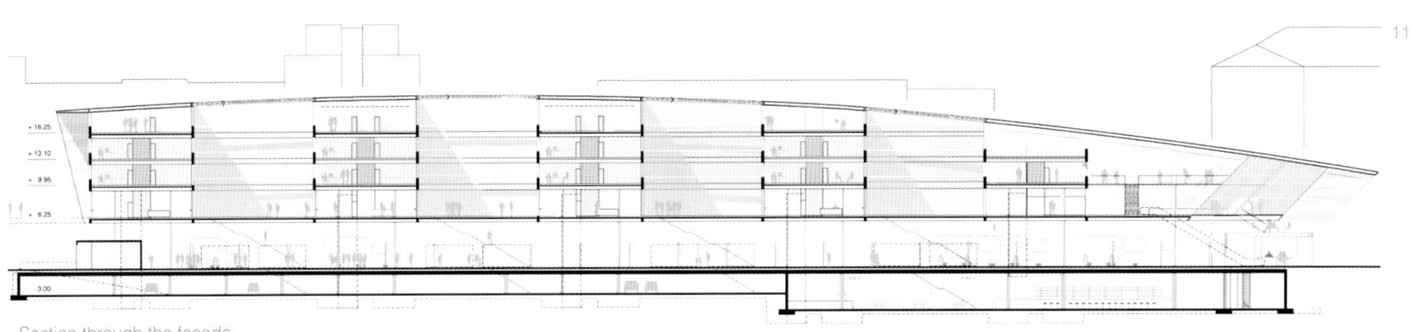

Section through the facade

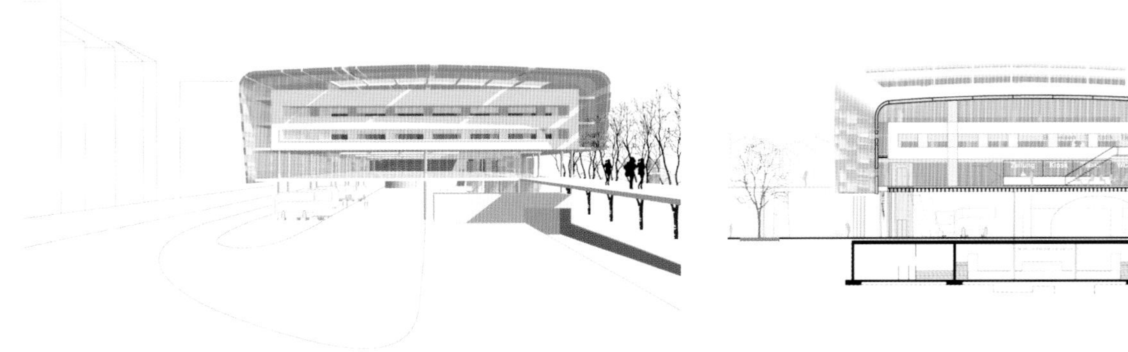

End elevation (office space)

End elevation (café and terrace)

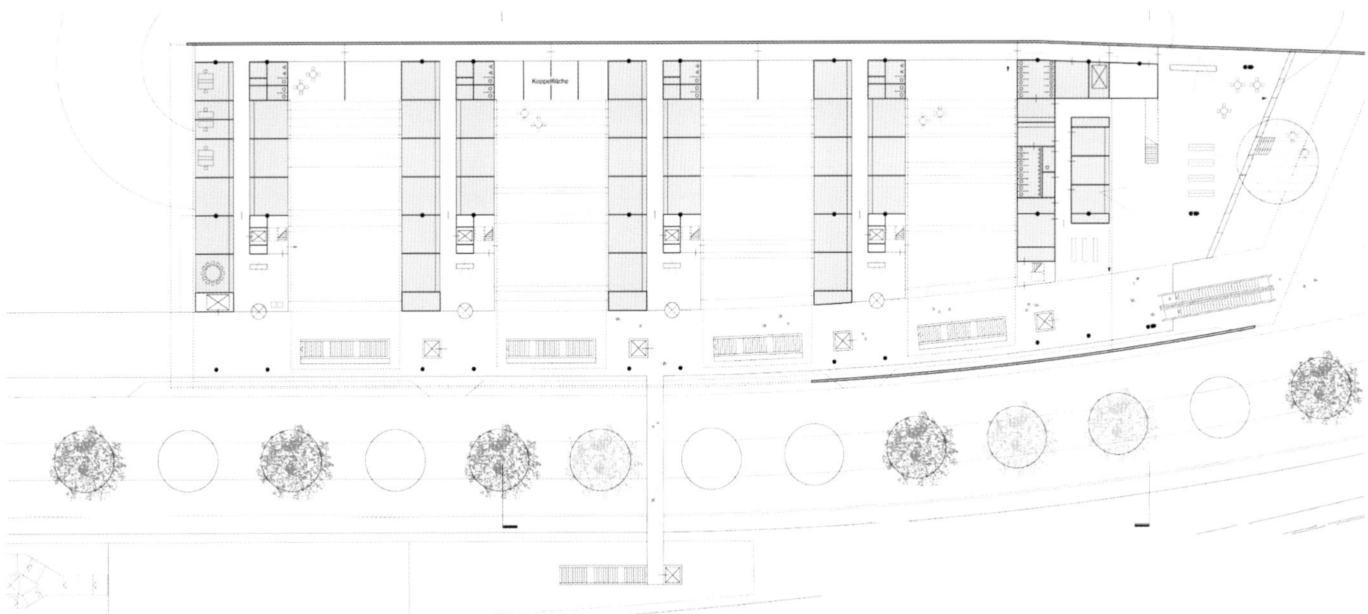

Plan, showing the positions of the atria

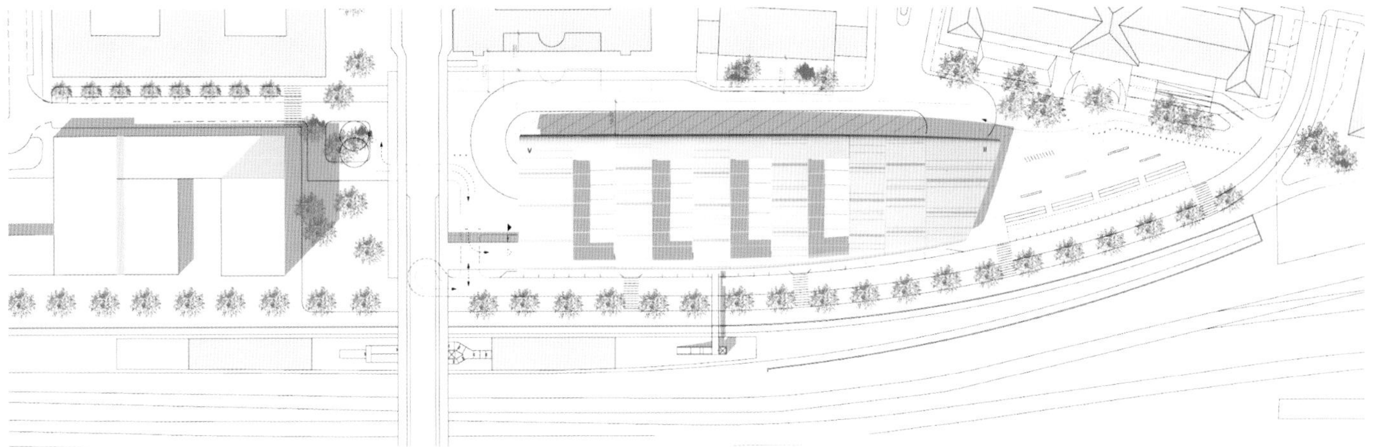

Plan indicating atria size

Underground Parking Garage

DESIGN SZYSZKOWITZ + KOWALSKI
LOCATION KASTNER & OEHLER DEPARTMENT STOREGRAZ, AUSTRIA

This demanding project is an unusual undertaking for an architect, as the underground car park is a necessary element of our urban environment almost entirely neglected in a design-conscious world. Apart from the formation of a new city square above part of the car park, there is no overground element to indicate the vast amount of work that has gone on beneath.

Szyszkowitz + Kowalski's task involved creating a five-storey car park directly under the historical city of Graz. Surrounding buildings included the 100-year-old Kastner & Oehler department store as well as a former monastery, city villas and urban dwellings of much earlier dates. In addition, the site is in the immediate vicinity of the River Mur, making ground conditions unstable.

The resulting underground car park is conceived in the form of ten ramps, expressed as a continuous spiral. Floor levels are gently sloping over the garage's entire length – motorists simply continue downwards until they reach a vacant parking place. On leaving, drivers use a steeper, spiralling exit ramp that can be accessed from all floors.

Within the parking floors, columns take on a "swung lens" form, maximizing space and viewing angles for drivers. These also conceal built-in units that wash the space with soft lighting. Wall and floor colours contrast with the white ceilings in a range of tones including apricot and yellows. The effect is altogether less harsh than most conventional parking garages.

From the exterior, standing in the new square, one can look down through a glass floor into the abyss at the centre of the exit spiral. Intriguing views are also available as users ascend from the parking levels up into the store via glass elevators and stairwells. This innovation also provides good visibility in areas that might otherwise be seen as opportune points for vandalism or crime.

The beauty of this project is not so much in its clean, considered styling, as in the ingenuity of its construction. To construct the car park, an entire city block had to be supported on temporary caisson piles. The colossal load-bearing walls of the buildings were then underpinned with concrete beams and the beams tied to the caisson piles, before over 64,000 cubic metres (2,260,140 cubic feet) of earth was excavated. The garage was built upwards floor by floor, and on completion of the last floor the buildings above were transferred from the temporary caissons to the new permanent columns.

View of the spiralling ascent ramp

Piles support existing buildings while construction takes place

The incredible task of designing and building this car park is graphically illustrated in the image above. An entire block of three storey residential buildings is temporarily supported while construction of the car park takes place beneath. While all evidence of this work is lost on completion, the architectural and engineering expertise employed on the project cannot be overstated.

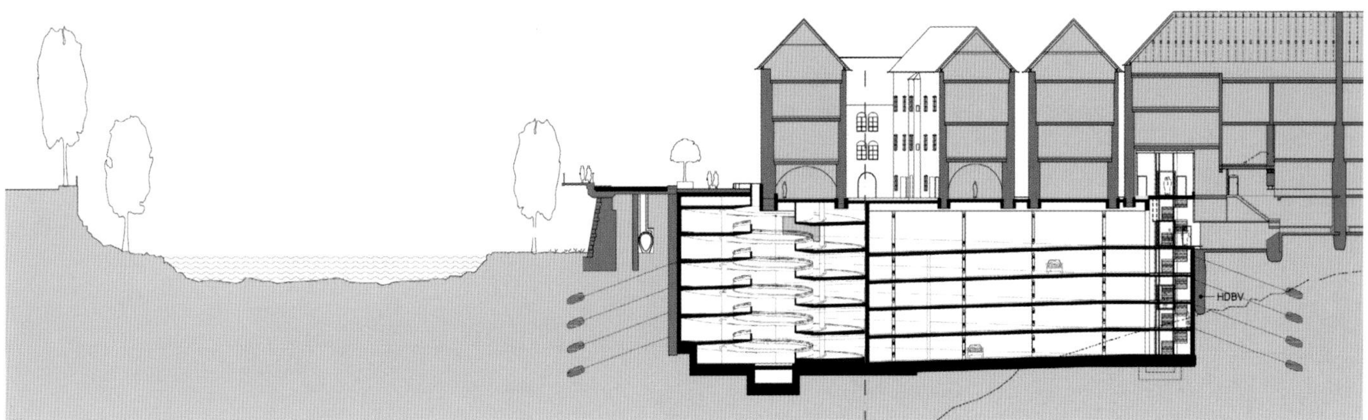

End section, showing the River Mur nearby

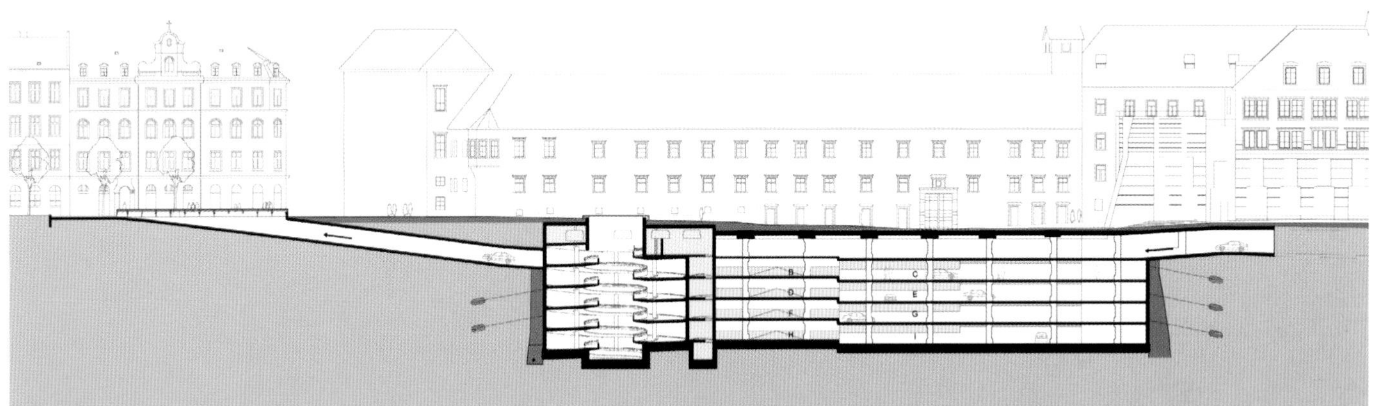
Side section, showing access and exit points

Three-dimensional view showing the supporting raft and piles

The well lit parking levels are painted in various colours

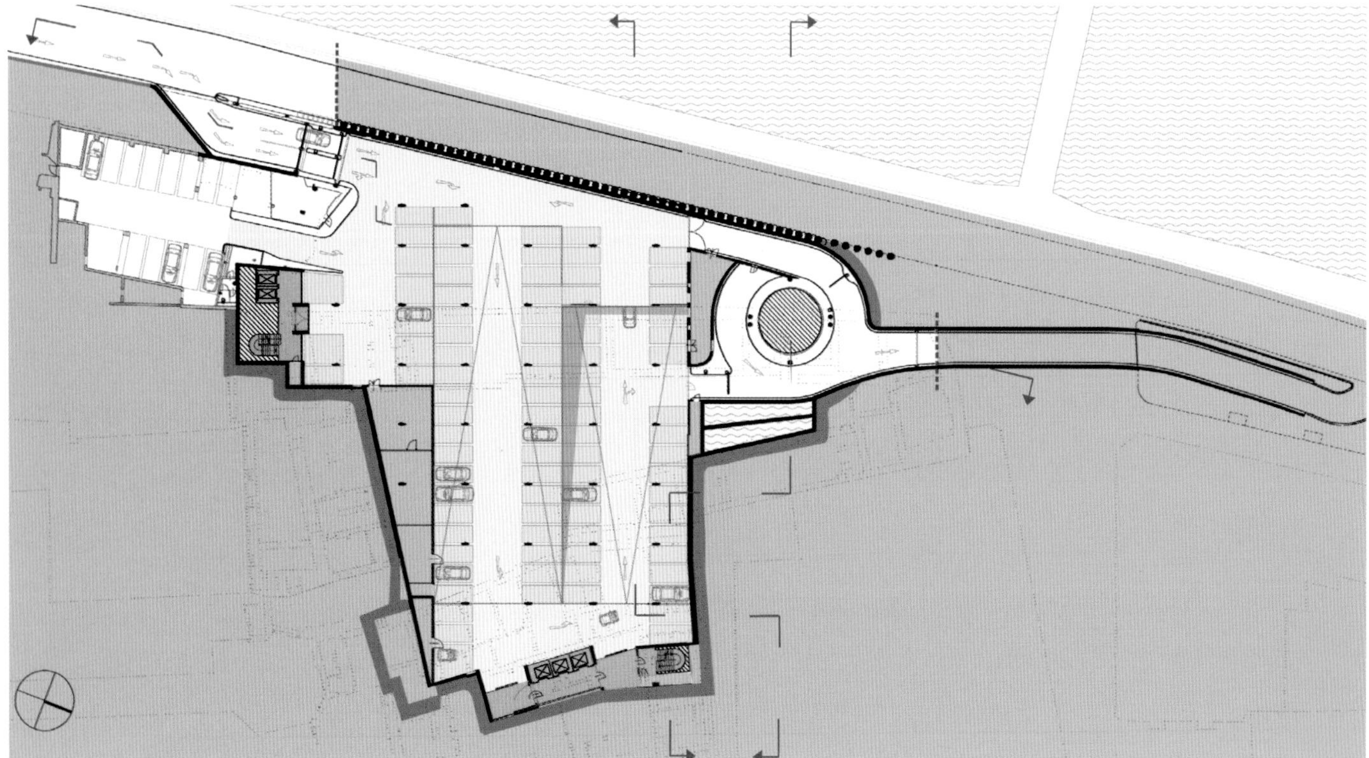

Plan, showing gradient of levels

Stair cores exemplify quality material use

The internal spaces of the car park are unusual in the fact that they are so well finished. It seems that the effort put into designing and building the structure, most of which is hidden, has spurred the architect to impress users with the quality of elements on view. Artificial lighting is excellent and materials are well chosen to provide a quality feel in an environment normally bereft of aesthetic consideration.

Mölndal Commuter Station

DESIGN WINGÅRDH ARKITEKTKONTOR
LOCATION MOLNDAL, SWEDEN

The municipality of Mölndal, outside Gothenburg, has invested heavily in architecture in an attempt to create order out of the chaos brought about by an ill-thought-out city centre plan. The latest addition is this dramatic new bus station which spans a major multi-lane highway.

Created as a functional landmark, the building's upper level is a multi-stop bus station, crowned by an angular roof canopy. The large expanse of roof is lessened but also made more dramatic by cutting away the elements under which the buses pass, "allowing the sky into the building", while leaving adequate shelter for travellers awaiting their ride. The underside of the roof is clad in strips of untreated larch, producing a warm glow in conjunction with the artificial lighting or when sunlight bounces up off the road beneath. The canopy edge is formed in the shape of a "W", in order to detract from its bulk and produce a slimmer profile.

The upper level of the station also serves to link the communities that live either side of the heavily trafficked road. And, as if the architect envisaged them meeting on the bridge, he has included a café within the complex geometry of the building. Situated at one end of the building, the café is a natural continuation of the station's angular form. Created by wrapping the roof canopy under and back on itself at a sharp angle, this overhanging space is supported on central columns, as is the rest of the upper level. The design limits the café to a small rectangular area for the service counter and several chairs and tables. The architect creates further space to sit and eat by incorporating a sharply angled feature wall and adapting it to produce a cantilevered terraced seating area.

While the extensive covered canopies protect travellers from the weather, Wingårdh has employed glazed screens to deflect the wind. The majority of these glass barriers are clear, affording views through and from the elevated station. However, at irregular intervals tinted glazed panels inject colour and humour into the design. It is this playful attitude to the design of a purely functional building that endears it to users.

The architecture enlivens an otherwise drab urban transport intersection and creates a sense of transition and movement. Travellers crossing over the main road are taken on a mini journey as they enter the pedestrian escalators, with their tinted panels and slate floors, or out under the canopy. Travel, even bus travel, doesn't have to conform to the norm.

Bus station as architectural drama

4-11

Material choices accentuate the unusual design

Site plan showing the location over a major highway

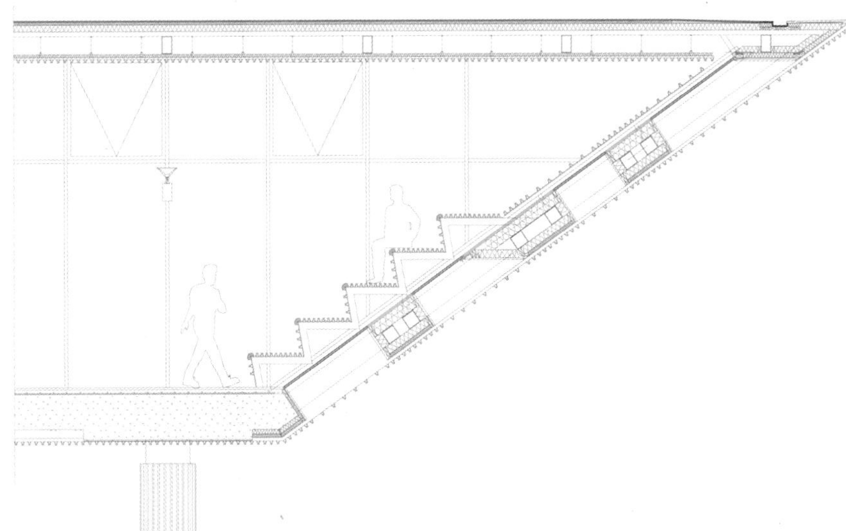
Section through the café

View of the café with its sloping terrace

The project is awash with eye-catching elements that distract from the building's rather mundane function as a bus station. Interesting material use, including coloured glass, produces unexpected reflections and plays of light, while the sloping wall of the elevated café makes a statement from afar and provides interest internally. Mölndal is enriched by this new architectural addition that will be experienced by all sectors of society.

The angular platform shelter roof

Sharp lines and acute angles play a prominent part in the design of the entire project, both in material form and architectural design. They culminate in the fiercely angled extremity of the café and the thrusting point of the shelter roof. Both could be harsh and uninviting, but the slatted timber cladding tempers the design, making it intriguing rather than foreboding.

Detail view showing coloured glass panels and timber seating

Night-time illumination of the café and lift shaft

Box Hill Transport Interchange

DESIGN MCGAURAN SOON ARCHITECTS
LOCATION MELBOURNE, AUSTRALIA

Box Hill Transport Interchange is already a bustling centre of activity within the Box Hill Central retail complex in Melbourne. It operates as the city's largest interchange between buses, trains and trams and as such was earmarked by the Department of Infrastructure for major refurbishment in 2002.

Architect McGauran Soon (MGS) and engineer Arup headed up a project team that developed new designs to create a world class transport interchange within the urban design framework study. Initially a study was carried out in order to create a full concept plan for Box Hill shopping centre and the transport interchange. This included re-siting the bus station to bring it closer to the train station and tram depot as possible to minimize road transport conflicts, provide facilities for bicycles, and add new bus shelters and covered walkways.

In studying not just the micro anomaly, such as train passenger numbers using the station, but also the macro effect on the wider transport network, the team produced a detailed study of all forms of travel in the area. These included studying congestion points and conflict between transport types, as well as the potential for new retail and commercial elements.

Conclusions gleaned from the year-long study resulted in a three-storey interchange to fully integrate all traffic movements, both vehicular and pedestrian, into the scheme. The result is a building that re-engineers the routing of passengers between the retail complex and the numerous transport options to ensure the most efficient flow of pedestrians. Key to this strategy has been the relocation of existing rail and bus station entrances to create a clear architectural "spine".

This clarification of space has also improved the footfall past retail outlets in the centre, which is situated below the new transport interchange. MGS's design creates a bus station that hovers above the main shopping area and the train station. Lightweight glazed canopies with a striking saw-tooth profile provide shelter for those waiting for buses while allowing light to filter down into the lower tiers of the interchange.

The new interchange will have a major beneficial impact on the neighbourhood, both in terms of easy access to and linking between transport facilities, enlarged retail operations and the overall safety of pedestrians and vehicle occupants in and around the Box Hill area.

Internal view from ground level to the platforms

TRAIN
LILYDALE
RINGWOOD
BUS
4:27
4:34
4:45
4:31
4:42
284 DONCASTER
SHOPPINGTOWN
202 EAST KEW
302 CITY
231 HEIDELBERG
233 GREENSBOROUGH
235 THE PINES
270 RINGWOOD
271 SPRINGVALE RD

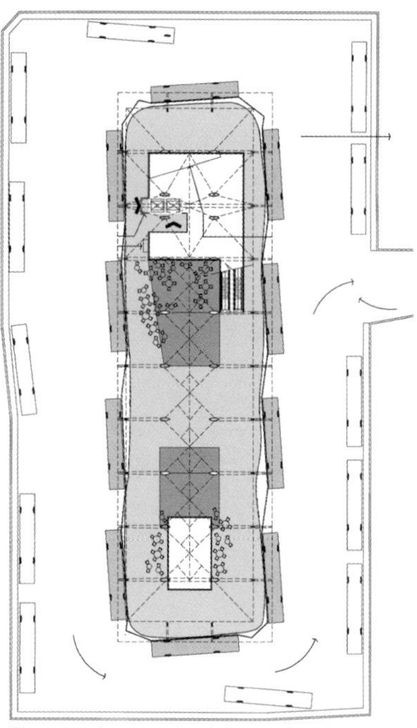

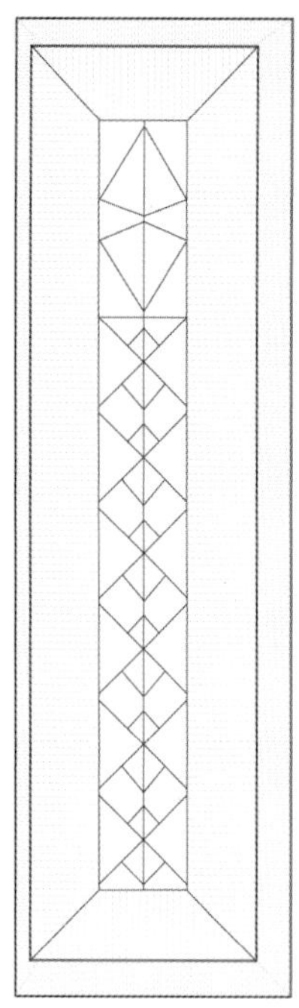

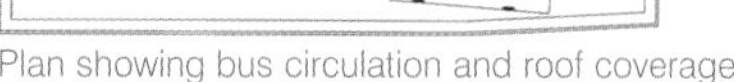

Plan showing bus circulation and roof coverage

From street level, Box Hill Transport Interchange is a relatively diminutive development of steel and glass, much like many retail malls in Australia. It is only when seen in section, including all of the elements situated below the ground, that the scheme can be fully appreciated. Then, the true extent of the project is realized, with sub-basement level platforms for trains, which are linked to street level and bus stops by a subterranean shopping complex.

Box Hill pedestrian plaza

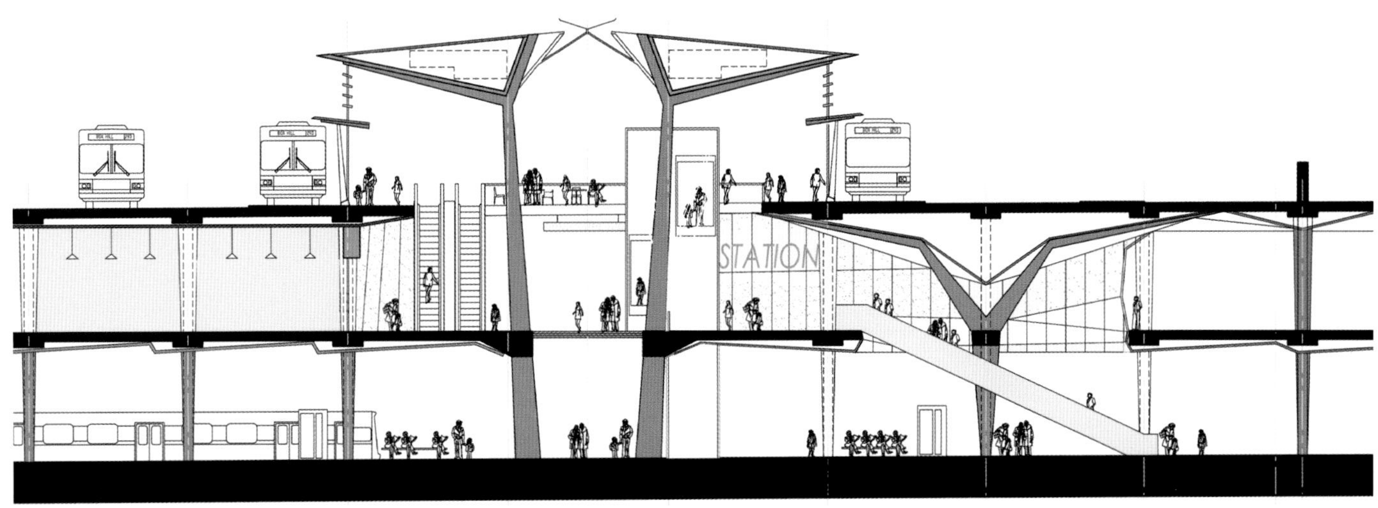

Section showing transport options

Cycle Station

DESIGN FOURTH DOOR RESEARCH AND THE ARCHITECTURE ENSEMBLE
LOCATION ANYWHERE IN THE UK

The Cycle Station project is a new environmentally conscious experiment that combines green design and architecture with new media networks and capitalizes on the opportunities provided by a UK initiative, the National Cycle Network.

Originated by Fourth Door Research's Oliver Lowenstein, with a prototype designed by Steve Johnson of the Architecture Ensemble, the Cycle Station is part eco-information centre and part rest-and-refreshment location. Housed in a structure of sustainably sourced materials, and powered by roof-mounted solar or photo-voltaic panels and wind turbines, the essential functions of this environmentally friendly vision include a bicycle hire and repair centre, a restaurant and cafeteria, toilets and washing facilities, a quiet room for rest, overnight sleeping facilities, and an information centre providing maps, route, and weather data using new media and high-tech satellite links.

The building is to be situated on the National Cycle Network, which is currently being completed. The aim of the initiative is to provide everyone with access to a safe cycle path within two miles of their home, in an attempt to improve health and awareness of local surroundings and beauty spots.

The architectural design of the Cycle Station is adaptable to suit site-specific conditions, and Lowenstein sees the concept as just one segment of a broader sustainable design approach. This currently hypothetical vision would contribute to education about sustainable travel and the realisation of a more sustainable transport infrastructure across the country.

Key objectives of the design include tackling environmental problems that affect western society, including the transport crisis – congestion, pollution, climate change and fossil fuel use, the despoilment of the environment, eco- and energy-literacy and education, and health. The Cycle Station encourages a shift in the way we travel, decreasing the dependence on cars, the promotion of a "slow" culture, and increasing the use of low energy transport.

Sited at various strategic points along the National Cycle Network, all Cycle Stations will be designed for zero energy use. The stations will not be restricted to use by cyclists, but also walkers and even drivers – what better way to introduce them to a greener modes of transport. And, while their primary function is to both assist and educate travellers, the aesthetic nature of the designs will make them tourist attractions in their own right.

The innovative timber frame complements countryside settings

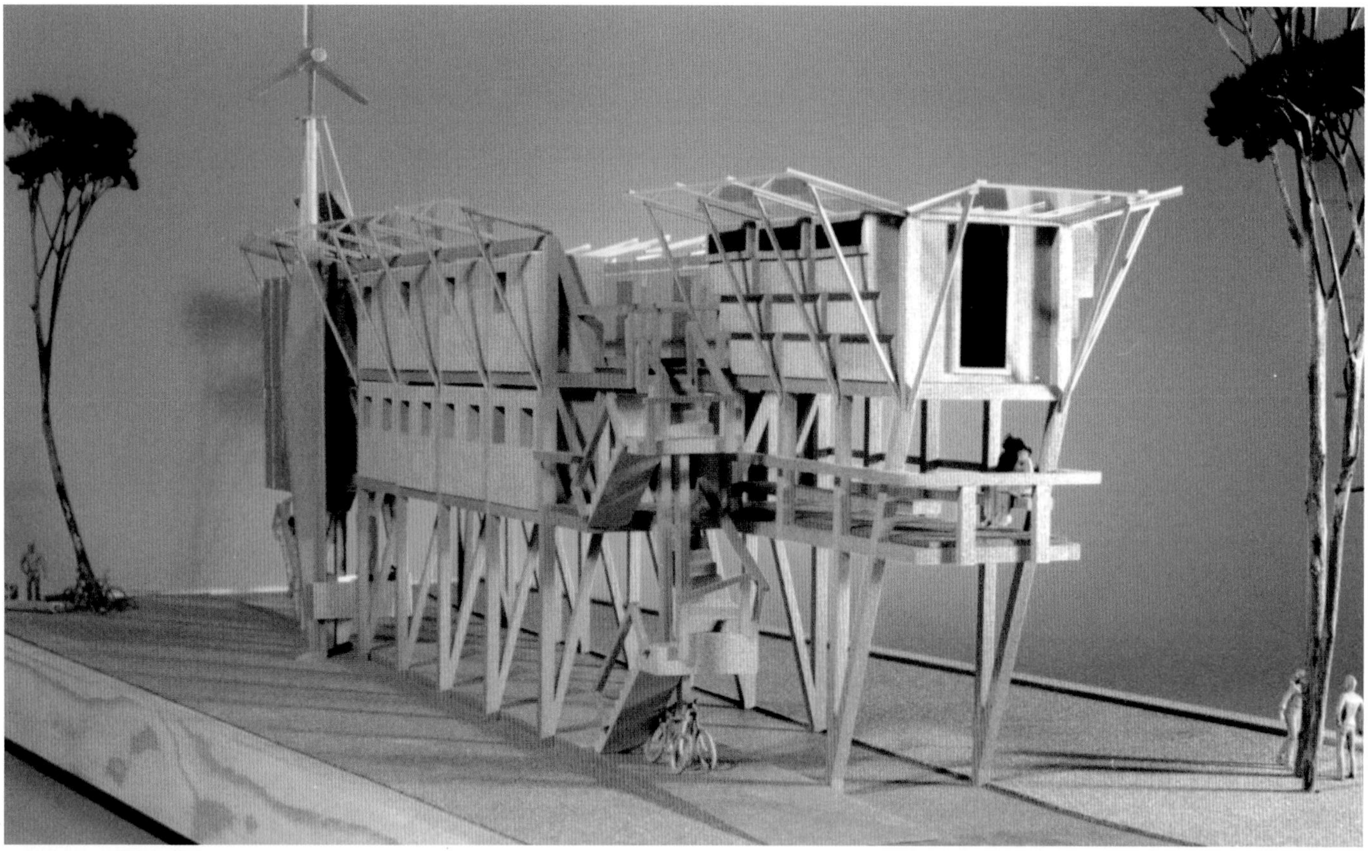

Model view showing the viewing platform

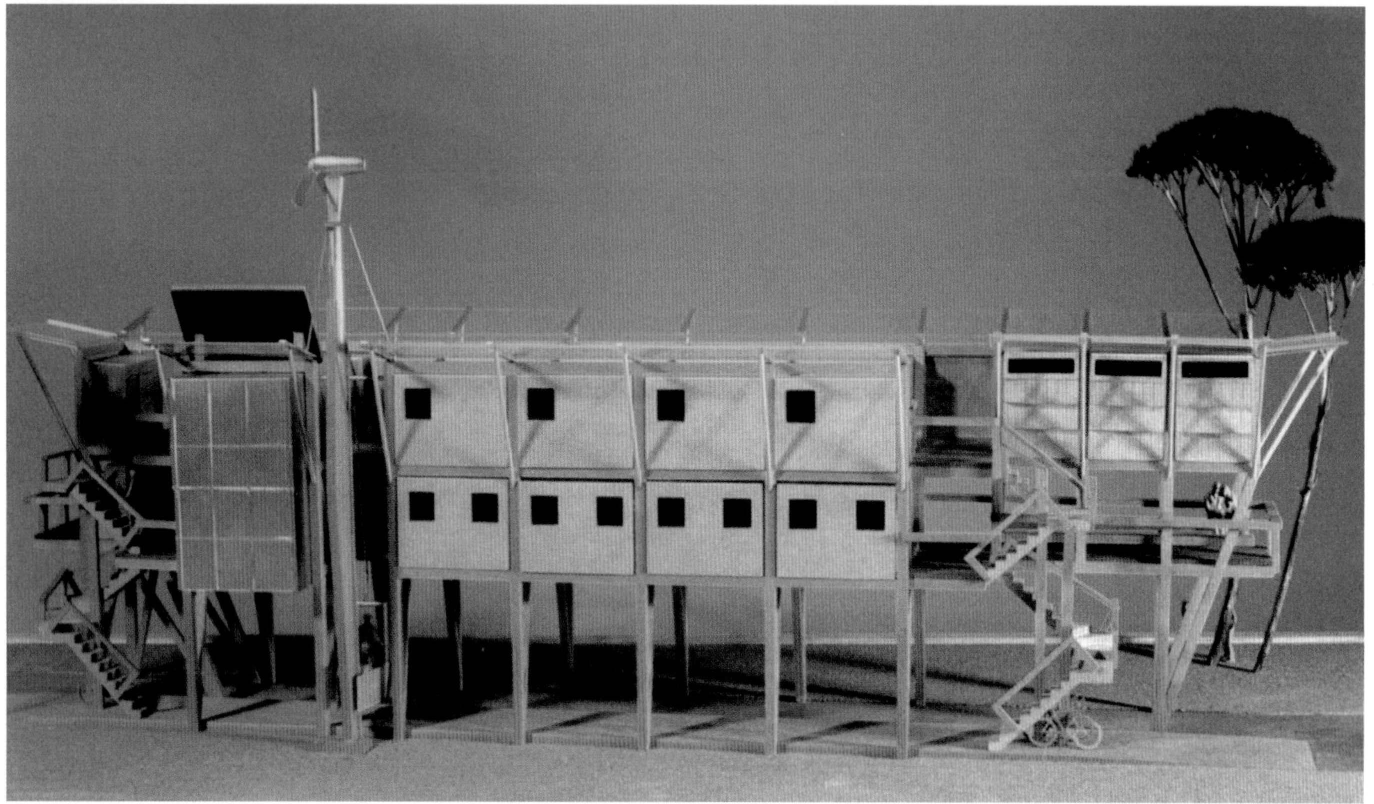

Model of the Cycle Station showing the services and power plant to the left

The design of the Cycle Station combines craft and computer to create an outstanding addition to any space. Home-grown timber and other resources are utilized by local tradespeople to construct the easily replicable building. This in itself, is a tourist destination, with the added bonus of providing information and accommodation for tourists and commercial travellers alike. The Cycle Station is gaining support from many designers and environ-mentalists in the UK. The project is in its fledgling stages but support from Sustrans, the organization behind the National Cycle Network, will hopefully see the first Cycle Station built in the near future.

View of a Cycle Station in an urban setting

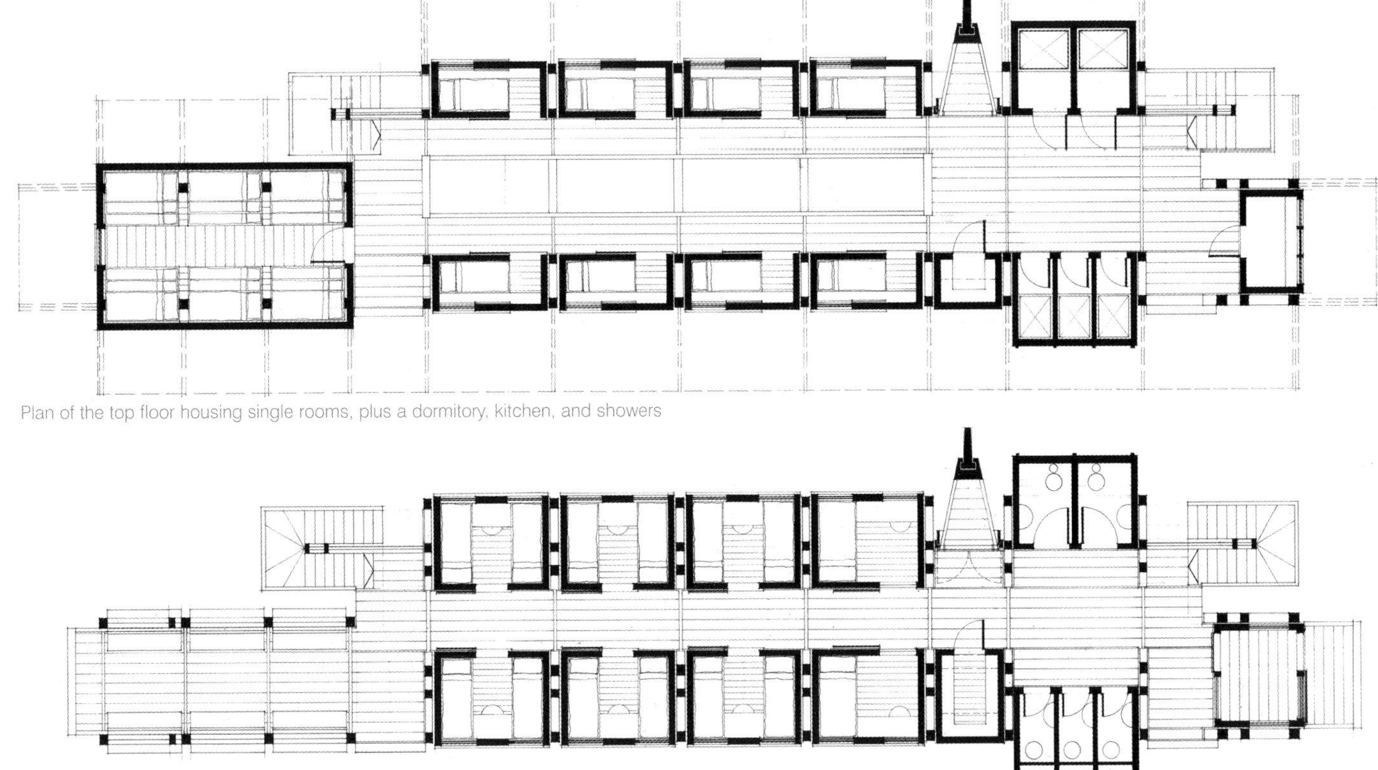

Plan of the top floor housing single rooms, plus a dormitory, kitchen, and showers

Plan showing double rooms, WCs, kitchen, and viewing platform

Engineering in Transport Architecture

Richard Prust
Richard Prust is a civil and geo-technical engineer. As associate principal at Arup, he leads the firm's infrastructure business in the US Pacific Northwest. He has 20 years' experience, ranging from the design management of major subway projects to major infrastructure schemes.

Transportation projects embrace a wide variety of modes of transport and include airports, subways, light rail, heavy rail, highways, ports, trams, and bus systems. The roles of architects and engineers in these projects vary significantly with the type of project tackled.

On many of these transportation projects the role of the architect, defined by the Merriam-Webster Dictionary as "a person who designs buildings and advises in their construction" and the civil engineer as "an engineer whose training or occupation is in the design and construction especially of public works" appear to overlap. Airport and subway stations for instance, are clearly both public works projects as well as buildings.

This essay looks at the intertwining of the roles of architects and engineers in subway station design focusing specifically on how these roles were addressed on the preliminary engineering design of the underground stations for the Second Avenue Subway in New York City.

From the earliest days of the New York Subway engineering has played a leading role in the planning and implementation of subway projects. The design and construction of the first subway in the city was lead by engineers. More recent projects have recognized that a successful design requires a multidisciplinary approach which combines architecture with all the engineering disciplines.

A matrix organization was adopted for the Second Avenue design team which placed engineers as team leaders for geographical areas along the route. These teams were truly multidisciplinary and included architects along with geotechnical and tunnelling engineers, structural engineers, mechanical, electrical, and plumbing engineers. Other disciplines such as systems, trackwork, and tunnel ventilation were also integral parts of the design team.

The architects' primary role within the concept and preliminary engineering stages recognized their strengths in developing designs, schemes, and layouts which best accommodated the many and often competing programme elements of the station, which were largely driven by the engineering disciplines. Other issues such as urban integration, finishes, facades, lighting, and signage, which in the early design stages required a less geographic and more system-wide approach, were dealt with by specific task groups often lead by architects.

Here, we consider the background to the project and then look at some of the key engineering decisions and requirements and how they impacted on the layout and architecture of the stations.

History

The Second Avenue Subway has been on the drawing board since the early 1920s, when the line was proposed as part of a major expansion of the subway network. The need for it became ever more pressing when the elevated rail viaduct along Second Avenue was demolished. The cast iron viaduct had carried steam trains along Second Avenue to South Ferry in downtown Manhattan since 1880. Its demolition, along with that of the Third Avenue El train left the East Side of Manhattan served only by the already overcrowded Lexington Avenue subway.

Detailed plans for the new line were developed in the late 1920s and construction was due to start in 1931. However, the problems associated with the Great Depression stopped the project before construction started. The plans were resurrected in 1944; however, progress slowed on the outbreak of the Korean war in 1950. A bond issue aimed partly to fund the plans was passed in 1951, however the funds were eventually used to upgrade existing lines and the project slowed again through the late 1950s and 1960s. In 1968 approval was given for a revised Second Avenue subway which would provide two tracks for the full length of Manhattan with connections into the Bronx. Ground breaking for this scheme was carried out on 27 October 1972 and three sections were completed amounting to about 1.6 kilometres (1 mile) of cut and cover tunnel. However, fiscal issues again got the better of the project and work was again stopped in the mid 1970s.

Project Background

The current programme for the Second Avenue Subway began to take shape in 1995, when the Manhattan East Side Alternatives (MESA) study looked at 20 transportation alternatives to reduce the overcrowding on the Lexington Avenue Subway Line. In 1999 a full subway line from the existing Metro-North Station at 125th Street and Park Avenue, east along 125th Street to Second Avenue, and then south along Second Avenue to downtown Manhattan was approved. On November 8, 2005 a bond issue was approved that will contribute US$450 million to the construction of the first phase of the project. The project will ultimately include 13.6 kilometres (8.5 miles) of twin-bored tunnel and 16 new underground stations. The line will also connect to an existing stub tunnel at the east end of Lexington and 63rd Street station to provide a service on to the Broadway line. The existing Lexington and 63rd Street station will be refitted to accommodate the new line. Connections are proposed between new and existing stations at a number of locations.

The client's vision for the new subway is that it will be a 21st century system that will stand the test of time as well as the subway of the previous century had. This theme ran through the planning and design of the project.

The Stations

The designs of the stations were approached in an integrated manner from the outset to ensure that all competing objectives and demands were satisfactorily achieved. The high level project objectives were to:

- Provide a subway that is safe for customers.
- Provide a 21st century subway service.
- Provide a temperature controlled environment in all new stations.
- Reduce overcrowding on existing subway lines, particularly the Lexington Avenue Line.
- Improve accessibility to the east side of Manhattan, provide connection to the Broadway line, evaluate transfers to existing stations, and not preclude future extensions to The Bronx and Brooklyn.
- Provide facilities to handle the predicted passenger forecasts.
- Incorporate the existing 1970s tunnels.
- Provide train storage facilities.
- Develop a fiscally responsible procurement plan that would include construction phasing.
- Allow for convenient intermodal transfer.
- Minimize property takings and other displacements.
- Maintain the character and compatibility with existing neighbourhoods and land uses.
- Minimize community disruption during construction.
- Provide a subway system that meets environment goals and opportunities established for the project.

Station Form

Engineering plays a major role in the basic form and function of subway stations. The station form is defined by the method of construction used to build it, and this method resulted from the design of the track alignment for the project. The station function is defined by the prime subway station function, which is to serve as a transportation hub between the subway and above ground means of transport and to house the many services and facilities required to operate and maintain the system.

The 1970s scheme placed the track and stations close beneath the road surface. This followed the design principles used on the majority of the rest of the system and was expected to reduce cost and excavation quantities as well as allow passengers a quick descent to the trains. A closer inspection of this premise showed that the cut and cover construction required to achieve this would lead to major surface disruption impacting on both traffic and pedestrians, and reducing accessibility to stores and residences along the route. Major utility diversions would be required and the risk of impacts to properties along the route would be greatly increased.

An examination of the ground conditions showed that a major portion of the Midtown and Upper East Side sections of the route were built on the very competent Manhattan Schist rock strata. A deeper alignment was therefore proposed that would allow Tunnel Boring Machines (TBM) to be used for the majority of the length of the route. This enables caverns to be excavated in the rock to provide the station spaces, while minimizing the travel distance for passengers from street to platform and accommodating the many existing tunnels that cross the route. This subsurface excavation would significantly reduce disruption and the use of TBMs and mining would not increase the excavation quantities or cost of the project.

The deeper alignment arose out of these engineering decisions and effectively defined the two basic forms of stations used for the project: rectilinear cut and cover stations, and arched mined cavern stations.

A planning goal of the station structure was to provide a mezzanine above platform level to allow passenger circulation and to provide ticketing and control functions. These were incorporated in all stations and were typically of the order of six metres (20 feet) above the platform to allow the platforms to be accessed or egressed quickly.

Entrances

The typical New York City Subway entrance is a small structure in the sidewalk with stairs leading down to a high level mezzanine or high level platform. However, a combination of pedestrian modelling and urban planning, combined with two of the project goals led to a departure from this approach. The first was to provide mechanical vertical circulation (escalators and lifts) from street to platform wherever possible for passenger convenience. This approach, however, would require a structure too wide to fit on to the sidewalk. The second, reducing the obstruction caused by building structures in the sidewalk and allowing the entrance to provide its own identity and fit within the urban fabric of the site, also led to entrances being located off the sidewalk either in existing plazas or within existing buildings. Entrance locations were selected primarily based on the results of passenger modelling so that entrances were located where the predominant ridership originated. Specific buildings or plazas in the appropriate locations were selected to satisfy the planning needs of the station layout and to reduce impacts to existing structures. In this respect, architectural and engineering disciplines worked as one team to develop the optimal solution.

The entrances to the cavern stations, which are to be constructed within adits mined in the rock, will descend to and then punch into the side of the cavern spaces, sometimes with other mined entrances or utility duct adits nearby. These required detailed co-ordination between pedestrian planners, mechanical engineers, architects and tunneling engineers to ensure that the rock pillars between adjacent excavations were sufficiently robust and that the rock structure could accommodate all the required openings while maintaining good pedestrian flow and allowing direct utility routes.

Public Space

The public spaces within the stations include the entranceways leading to the main station cavern, the unpaid ticketing area, the paid circulation area of the mezzanine, and the platform area. The key to designing these heavily trafficked stations was to define the number and location of the vertical circulation elements. For the majority of stations, escalators were the only way to provide adequate capacity for passengers both under normal operations and in the emergency case. Real time computer simulated passenger modelling was carried out for each station for both cases. This enabled the numbers of escalators to be defined along with the location and direction of rise, allow exit times from the platform to be kept within reasonable limits, define queue lengths and times, and allow circulation paths to be defined to avoid conflicts. This modelling, along with code compliance for fire and life safety, and disabled access, also defined the width of platforms and hence the width of the station boxes and caverns themselves. Pedestrian modeling also defined the number and location of fare gates and Metrocard vending machines, which impacted on the layout of the unpaid area. Escalator locations were defined both by the needs of pedestrian modelling and the mechanical space requirements for escalator pits and machine rooms.

The architectural finishes and layouts within the public space had to accommodate many engineering issues. The New York City subway runs 24 hours a day, 7 days a week. The fixtures and fittings were selected to ensure that maintenance and cleaning could be carried out at any time.

Wall finishes allowed access to utility corridors running behind them. Acceptable materials had to be selected for exposed duct work. Constructability of the finishes, particularly to the cavern lining, was designed by structural engineers, cavern designers, fire specialists, and construction engineers who worked with architects to develop a structure that was stable and constructible and would provide adequate fire protection and the architectural statement desired for the space.

Back of House Space

The back of house space comprises the areas at either end of the station beyond the public area. They house the majority of the station facilities including power rooms, ventilation equipment, signal rooms, plumbing rooms, and emergency access corridors, as well as the offices, work rooms, and locker rooms required for staff. This area constituted up to 50 per cent of the station length. The layout of these spaces provided one of the major challenges in the station design, as there were many conflicting demands. These included providing adequate space for the equipment, maintenance and replacement of equipment rooms of like function placed in close proximity, security, logical service duct routing, fire and life safety requirements, headroom requirements within rooms, structural requirements – height of structure, rock cover to caverns, and electrical interference between communications and fan rooms.

The majority of these requirements were defined by the various engineering disciplines; however, this kit of parts was put together by architects in the most efficient way possible to keep the station size to a minimum to reduce cost.

Ancillary Buildings

The majority of the station functions were located underground within the station box or cavern to improve accessibility from the station. However, in locations where properties were required for other functions, such as entrances and ventilation shafts, some of these functions were consolidated above ground to minimize station costs at a small increase in above ground construction cost.

The station and tunnel ventilation concept was to locate ventilation fans and shafts at each end of each station. In the event of an emergency within the tunnel this allowed air to be pushed or pulled in one direction away from the passengers to allow them to escape to the other station. This method required the construction of above-ground vent shafts and large fan rooms which in some cases were above ground and in other cases below ground at the ends of the stations.

The typical New York City subway station provides gratings within the sidewalk. New codes require that all new ventilation stacks intake or exhaust at least 3m (10 feet) above ground level. To achieve this in the constrained New York environment it was often necessary to acquire property on which to locate the shafts. To maximize the usage of these properties, the station ventilation intake and exhaust shafts were also located in these buildings, as were emergency stairs.

Conflicting requirements also governed the design of these above ground structures, for example shaft sizes, structural impacts on adjacent buildings to accommodate minimum distances between intake and exhausts, circulation requirements for emergency stairs, space requirements for facilities rooms, zoning requirements, and urban context. Again these requirements resulted from a multitude of disciplines and were brought together in the most efficient manner by the architects.

Conclusion

The Second Avenue subway project is one of the most significant transport infrastructure projects in the USA and will be built in the heart of its most densely populated city. The objective of building a 21st century subway system that will stand the test of time was foremost in the list of project goals. The objective, to emulate the success of the existing New York City subway system, which has transported billions of passengers reliably and safely for more than 100 years, is a major challenge for any team.

The aspirations of New York are high. It is a global city that deserves an infrastructure worthy of its international stature. The system must satisfy the needs of the community, provide social justice (in the form of affordable and efficient public transportation) and meet a demand for transport that has existed for more than 60 years. It must be accessible to users, and its construction must be achieved with a minimum of disruption.

Successfully bringing all these requirements together into a coordinated design was achieved by integration of a multidisciplinary team of engineers and architects working collaboratively to define the optimum scheme. This was achieved with the tremendous support and drive of a client who fully understood the demands of the project, the historical and institutional context of the existing subway, and the aspirations of the city and subway staff. In this sense, the architects and engineers of the designer and client left their discipline tags behind and became members of one team.

Water

140 Yokohama Internation Port Terminal

148 Naviduct Lock Complex

152 DFDS Terminal

158 Maritime Terminal

162 Leith Ferry Terminal

170 Ferry Landing Stage

174 Falkirk Wheel

182 St George Ferry Terminal

190 Whitehall Ferry Terminal

Water

Boats are not the oldest form of transport, but from ancient times up until the invention of steam they were the mode most easily advanced. Global exploration and navigation was pioneered via the sea, while inland the movement of mass loads for trading and construction purposes was predominantly facilitated by boat on rivers or man-made canals.

Architectural additions connected with water travel were similarly limited until very recently. Those credited with advancing the canal systems are almost invariably engineers. However, some of the water structures achieved are quite breathtaking. Undertakings such as those of Persian emperor Darius I, who built canals throughout Mesopotamia and one in Egypt that linked the Nile and the Red Sea, or the Sui Dynasty's Grand Canal in China, linking the Yangtze and Yellow Rivers, would be mammoth tasks even today.

Later engineers controlled the water running in their canals, inventing locks that would allow them to navigate boats up and down steep gradients safely. Chinese engineer Chiao Wei-yo invented what is considered the forerunner of locks in the 10th century AD which is still used today. Leonardo da Vinci refined the design by combining it with mitred gates, on a project in Milan in 1500.

This new invention allowed canals such as the Briare, which joins the Seine and Loire in France, to be built in 1642. The Briare includes a staircase of six locks that cope with a descent of 20 metres (65 feet) over a minimal horizontal distance. Even more remarkable is the Canal du Midi, completed in 1681, joining the Mediterranean to the Atlantic with 240 kilometres (150 miles) of man-made waterway linking the Aude and Garonne rivers. At one point the canal descends 63 metres (206 feet) in 50 kilometres (32 miles). Three aqueducts carry it over rivers, and a 165 metre (180 yard) long tunnel allows it to flow through a patch of high ground.

Engineering is still an essential part of our inland waterways. However, architecture is now being integrated with it to create some wholly functional and yet visually stunning interventions such as the Falkirk Wheel by RMJM in Scotland (page 174) or Zwarts & Jansma Architects' Naviduct lock complex in The Netherlands (page 148).

From land to sea

Large coastal ports have developed in tune with seagoing vessels. Naturally accommodating coastal waters were soon colonized as ports, often initially by the navy, before merchant trading took over. This is exemplified by James Cook's discovery and naming of Port Jackson in Australia. This most sheltered bay, perfect for harbouring ships, is now better known as Sydney Harbour.

Before this the sea-port at the lower end of Manhattan Island, New York, was established in the 1600s, while Peter the

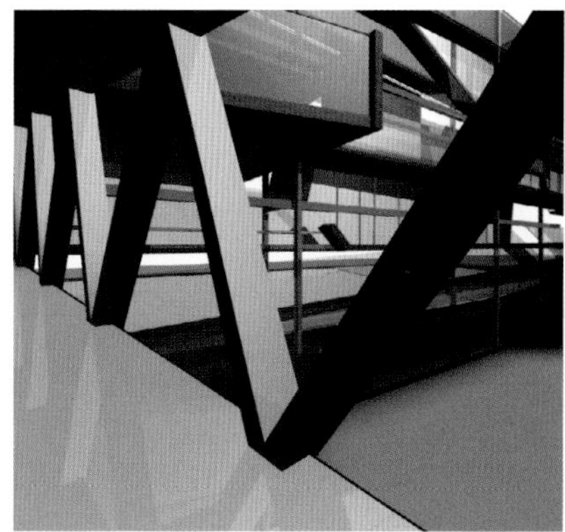

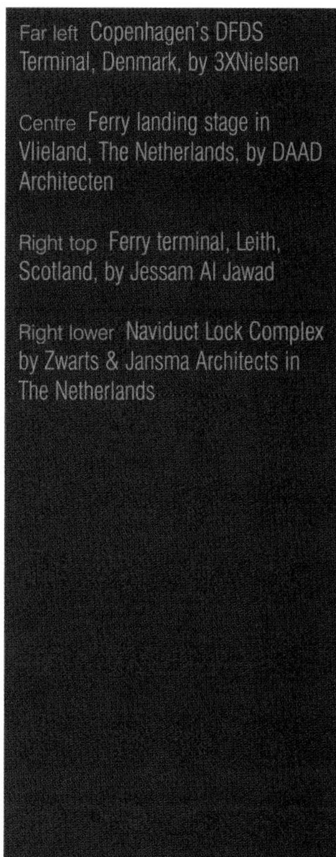

Far left Copenhagen's DFDS Terminal, Denmark, by 3XNielsen

Centre Ferry landing stage in Vlieland, The Netherlands, by DAAD Architecten

Right top Ferry terminal, Leith, Scotland, by Jessam Al Jawad

Right lower Naviduct Lock Complex by Zwarts & Jansma Architects in The Netherlands

Great built St Petersburg including its port and shipyard from scratch on desolate marshes in 1703 "to stand firm on the sea as Russia's window to the west".

Such ports and the associated buildings that surrounded them were almost invariably of a functional nature, as many still are today. It wasn't until much later that ports changed to accommodate mass passenger transit – the move from the gangplank to the passenger terminal has been swift in terms of architectural progression and yet slow due to the near death of the passenger cruise industry.

The advent of the train and plane put paid to much sea travel. Where as at the start of the 20th century the ultimate in luxury was an ocean cruise – up until the 1912 Titanic disaster – those lucky enough to be able to travel were soon setting out on plane journeys instead. Only in the 1970s and 80s did the cruise ship make a comeback. New reliable vessels that were virtually floating towns came into operation and with them a new era in water architecture was born.

The international traveller was now used to airport terminals and so ports had to adapt. Similar style cruise terminals came into being both as a fast and efficient way of processing passengers and as an updated method of actually boarding these huge ships. The more standard form of terminal building is a long, medium-height block, that to some extent mimics the vessel that draws up alongside it. This is exemplified by Alsop & Stormer's Hamburg Ferry Terminal, built 1988–92. New terminals are also designed along these successful lines – DFDS Terminal by 3XNielsen in Copenhagen (page 152) or Jessam al Jawad's Leith Ferry Terminal (page 162).

However, the port terminal has, in recent times, been a building type that could do more for a location than simply load and off-load passengers. Japan pioneered the dramatic waterside architectural statement with the Nagasaki and Shichiruiko terminals built in 1994–95 by architect Shin Takamatsu. These wondrous apparitions look nothing like a ferry terminal and as such have become tourist destinations in their own right. Continuing the trend, UK practice Foreign Office Architects designed a "landform" style terminal for Yokohama (page 140). This radical approach produced a building disguised as an extension of the land and created an open park-like space on the edge of the city.

Once again water transport is in vogue but we should exploit its potential as fully as possible. Many countries have vast inland waterway networks that link their major cities. Is it not time to re-utilize them in a move to lessen pollution and congestion on our roads? And, while flight is fast and convenient, it is our most polluting transport mode, so why not take to the seas instead?

Yokohama International Port Terminal

DESIGN FOREIGN OFFICE ARCHITECTS
LOCATION YOKOHAMA, JAPAN

The concept of *ni-wa-minato* was the starting point for the design of the award-winning Yokohama International Port Terminal. Roughly translated it means a mediation between garden and harbour, or between the citizens of the city and those outside. The resulting building is like no other – a 70 by 430 metre (230 by 1410 foot) extension to the city that, while operating as a ferry terminal, also creates precious open space in one of Tokyo's busiest satellite cities.

The terminal has a maximum height of only 15 metres (49 feet) above water level. This alone makes it considerably different to more common medium-rise terminal buildings. This is a new architectural form in a sector so governed by standards – standard sizes, tried and tested layouts, and preconceptions of what a terminal should look like.

The building is split into three levels. The lowest, entered through a wide gaping mouth festooned with white directional markings, is set aside for car parking, machinery, and plant area. Above this is the main terminal floor, housing arrival and departure facilities, customs, meeting and waiting areas, restaurants and shops. However, this isn't like any other terminal. While travellers are usually treated to cathedral-like spaces, the Yokohama Terminal has an almost foreboding ambiance. The huge structural steel beams that arc across the space feel so close that you could almost touch them.

Vertical movement is via escalators and a series of ten "sloping floors", creating a feeling of continuity between facilities. Travellers enter the passenger terminal deck via customs, immigration and quarantine facilities. They are then guided through the wide low hall via the timber decked "gangway", just as those promenading above flow round the external park space on a similar walkway. Above, the ceiling, an origami pattern of projecting triangles, cuts across space and against the grain, or length of the hall. It is at odds with the perceived flow, making travellers slow and take a breath, before entering the chaos of the streets of Yokohama.

FOA has transformed the ground plane into an active surface that changes the symbolic gate-like quality of the building. While mystifying, the terminal attempts to throw off the historic shackles of this building type, demystifying the exclusivity of foreign travel and welcoming both travellers and locals on to common ground, ground that both aesthetically and realistically obeys no rules of occupation.

The gaping mouth of the terminal transport entrance

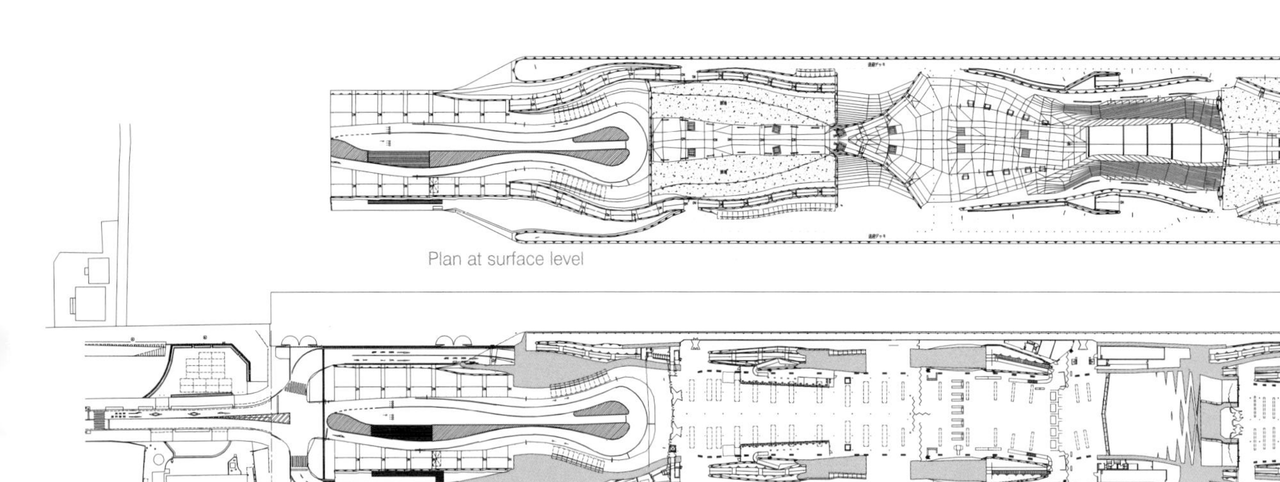

Plan at surface level

Plan of interior spaces

This outstanding example of architecture as landscape drew worldwide acclaim for Foreign Office Architects. The true scale of the project is best appreciated from the air (see opposite page). The terminal, seemingly floating in the harbour, is an extension of the city and an important piece of new open space that cannot be developed further. Only when a cruise liner is docked alongside can the terminal's size be effectively gauged, and then the real benefit to this crowded city becomes clear.

End elevation from the water

An aerial view with docked ship.

Ceiling detail to the main waiting area

Emerging via a timber-clad walkway

While citydwellers and tourists alike promenade above, the interior of the terminal is striking and unusual in its own ways. The timber boarding of the external walkways is continued to the interior, giving a sense of connection and flow. The main passenger terminal waiting area features a dramatic triangular vaulted ceiling, which overpowers everything beneath it.

Graduated timber walkways and large sun shades

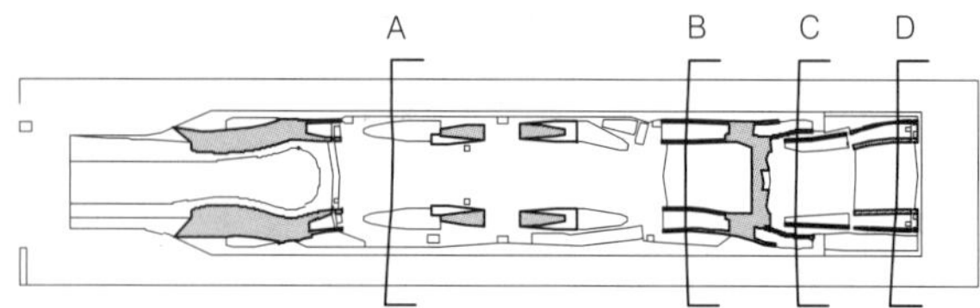

Plan with sections marked

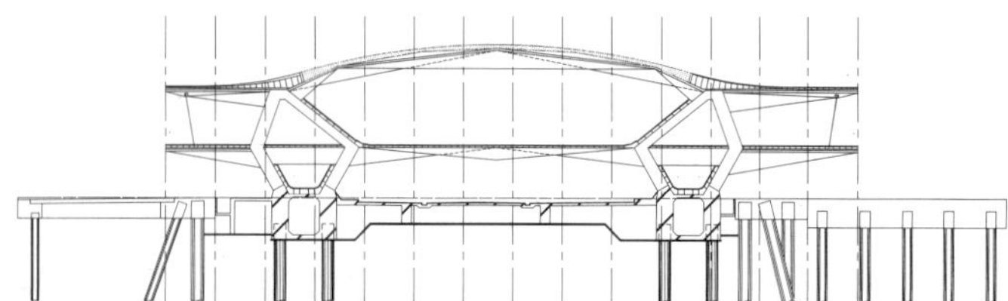

Section showing supporting structure

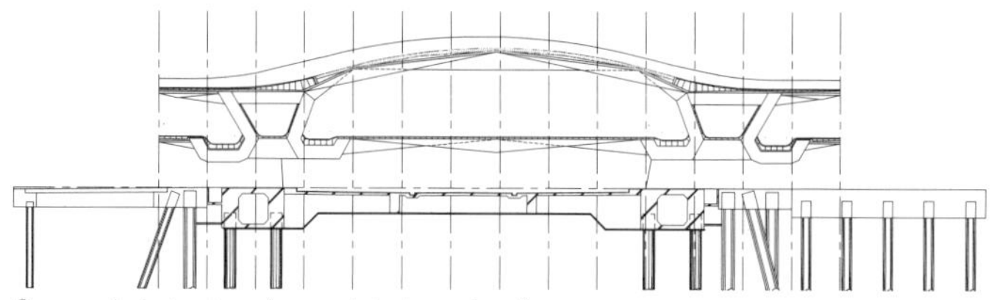

Suspended structure (car park to lower level)

The terminal has become a tourist destination in its own right, attracting foreign and Japanese visitors to its alien surface. Giant leaning sunshades hover overhead, while the walkways and lawned areas undulate, creating an ever-changing landscape of grass and timber; a departure from the city's steel and concrete. Foreign Office Architects has excelled with this unusual architectural statement. Time will tell whether the practice and the city can ever better Yokohama's International Port Terminal.

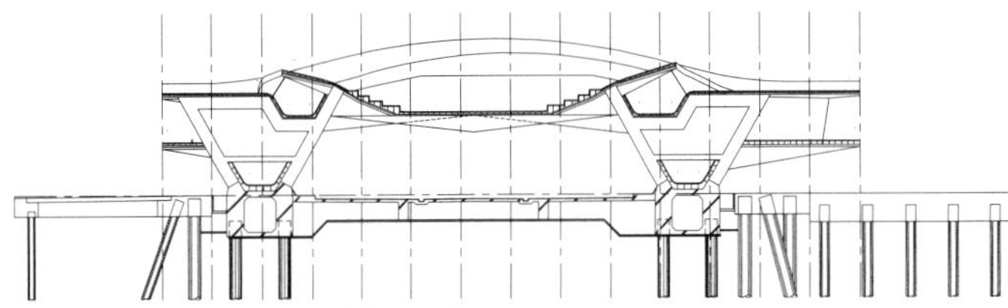

Stepped decking above main internal space

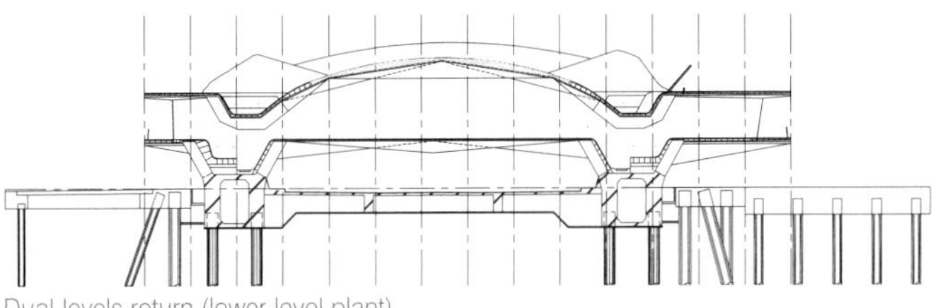

Dual levels return (lower level plant)

Naviduct Lock Complex

DESIGN ZWARTS & JANSMA ARCHITECTS
LOCATION ENKHUIZEN, THE NETHERLANDS

This part-architectural, part-civil-engineering project came about because the drawbridge at the Krabbegat Lock in the Houtrib Dike, some 72 kilometres (45 miles) north-east of Amsterdam, could no longer cope with the volume of road traffic. In the summer, road and river traffic had to endure long waiting times and queues while the bridge was raised and lowered. In response, Rijkswaterstaat, the directorate-general for public works and water management, commissioned a new lock complex to the east of the original bridge.

Zwarts & Jansma Architects became involved in the architectural aspects of this largely civil work. The complex consists of two lock-chambers, each 120 metres (394 feet) long and 12 metres (39 metres) wide. These function independently and are suitable for both merchant and pleasure craft. A roadway now travels under the lock, creating a structure that is simultaneously a lock and an aqueduct. The design team dubbed this new civil engineering type "Naviduct".

The most striking element of the project is the control building. Clad in polished stainless steel, its ellipsoidal form adds a point of reference in the flat surrounding landscape. The stainless steel finish stands in sharp contrast with the heavy, stony substructure on which it sits. A transparent glass stairwell connecting the sub- and superstructures exaggerates the floating effect of the lockkeeper's control building even more emphatically.

The building's position above the lock complex is dictated by sight lines. The position of the actual control room is elevated to afford the best possible overview of the complex and is kept separate from the two-storey substructure. This orthogonal volume is partially embedded into the embankment on which the building sits to accentuate its solid character and provide a degree of thermal mass. All lock operations that have no need for a view are incorporated in the substructure.

The reinstatement of the natural environment around the Naviduct was also of great importance. A landscaping and ecological design was implemented in collaboration with the landscape architect Lodewijk Baljon. This included integrating two million cubic metres of surplus silt from the digging of the locks, which was used to raise an embankment, creating a habitat for wildlife, while also providing a protective windbreak for vessels sailing into and from the dike from the Ijsselmeer.

The control building overlooks the lock and road tunnel

The control building

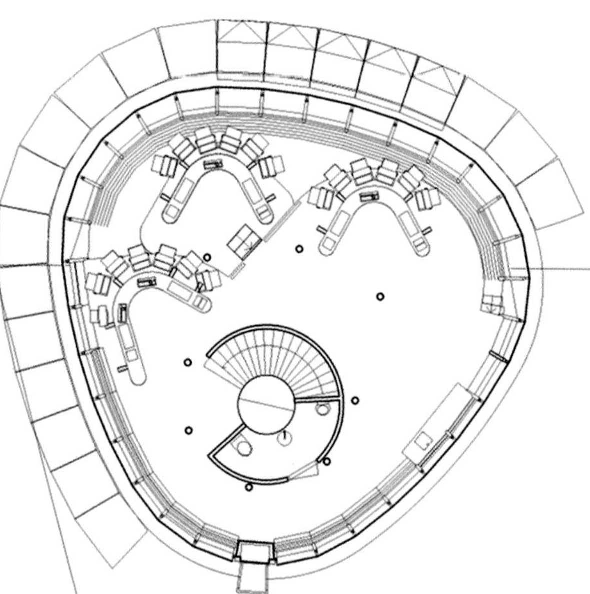
Floor plan

View of the landscape

A barge entering the lock

The vast flat landscape of the Netherlands lends itself to the inclusion of iconic structures on differing levels. However, while it could be tempting to overindulge, the Naviduct lock complex control tower presents a distinctive addition to the vista without being overly intrusive. Its polished steel surface, curved glazed facade and sculpted "peak cap" add a futuristic, alien-like form to the water-going tradition, so long an indelible part of the Dutch way of life.

DFDS Terminal

DESIGN 3XNIELSEN
LOCATION COPENHAGEN, DENMARK

The classic, precariously steep gangplank, used by passengers to disembark cruise liners in so many vintage films, is no longer a feature of the ferry port. Instead architects are designing facilities more in tune with airport buildings to assist in the movement of people to and from the fleets of ever-larger cruise ships that sail our seas.

The new terminal for DFDS routes from Copenhagen to Oslo, Norway and Gdansk in Poland is no exception. This huge rectilinear volume has the capacity to process the cargo of three ferries – some 2000 passengers and 400 cars or 130 lorries. Sitting on heavy black concrete pillars, the terminal is the epitome of functionality. There is no room for spatial extravagance and the Scandinavian sensibility of its designer doesn't allow for aesthetic frivolity. The building is planned to operate as a machine, processing its cargo with maximum speed and efficiency.

On the lower floor is a combined arrivals and departure gate, featuring ticket desks, café, customs, and a waiting area, with DFDS administration areas, offices, meeting rooms, and passport control for Polish visitors above.

The building's exterior is punctuated by protruding boxes which accommodate lanes for foreigners to queue for customs and extra waiting areas. The only other adornments are the horizontal stripes of the facade, comprised of glazed elements, within a steel framework. Built of glass of varied transparency, the facade informs and exaggerates the building's strong form, metaphorically pushing it out into the dock and back towards the harbour control station, also designed by 3XNielsen.

Its form is inspired by the transition from ship to shore. In one long movement, harking back to that romantic movie gangplank, the traveller is guided from the approach area up into the terminal's glass volume and out on to the pier to board the vessel some 150 metres (492 feet) from the quayside.

However, those occupying the terminal will not appreciate its true visual impact. It is at night that the architect's imagination and skillful artistry comes into its own. Illuminated via internal ambient lighting, the glazed building glows from within. Its heavy black legs disappear into the darkness and the terminal floats serenely, mirrored in the calm water of the harbour. The DFDS Terminal is a symbol of all that is good in constrained Danish design and a beacon of style and efficiency for travellers coming to and venturing from Denmark.

The terminal is dwarfed by a cruise liner

LYS-LINE
LYS-LINE

The elongated box of the DFDS Terminal pushes out into Copenhagen harbour and also backwards, connecting with the architecture of the city. It is a striking addition that visibly links land and sea both aesthetically and functionally. 3XNielsen's unashamedly Modernist design is horizontally striped to add length to its already overtly linear form. Only when ships draw in adjacent to it is the building's relatively conservative size revealed: until then, it dominates its immediate surroundings.

End elevation with cruise liner

The terminal from the city side

View towards the city

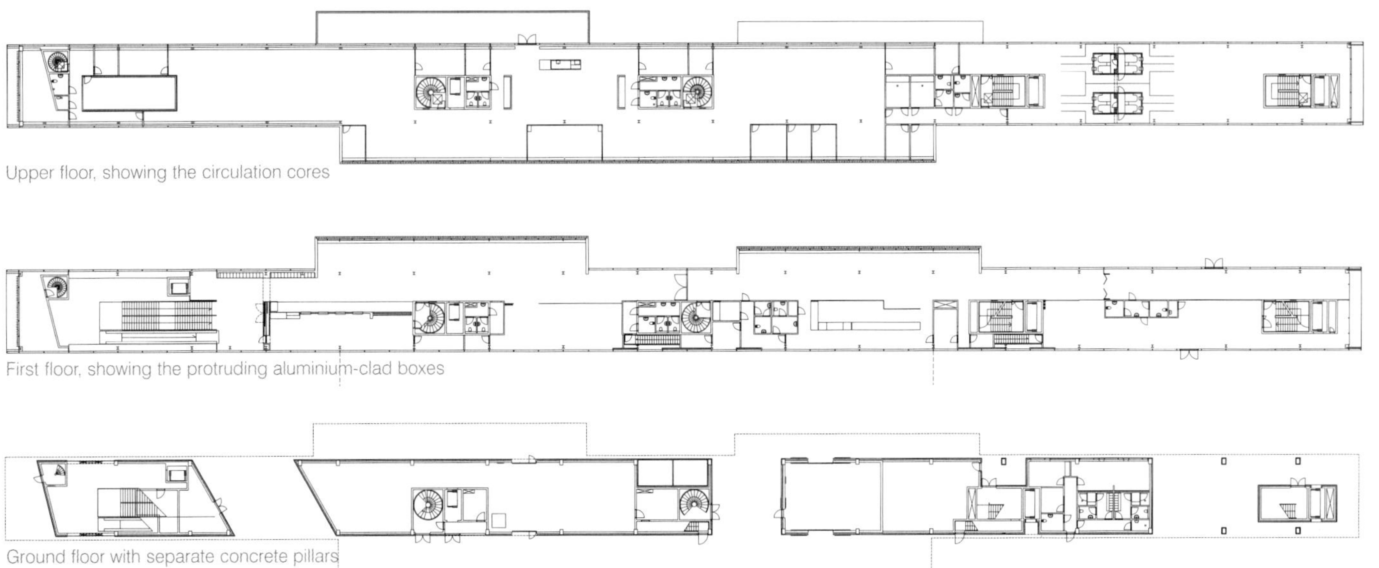

Upper floor, showing the circulation cores

First floor, showing the protruding aluminium-clad boxes

Ground floor with separate concrete pillars

The "land end" elevation

Functionality is at the core of the building's design. However, functionality and machine-like efficiency do not detract from the terminal's great visual impact. 3Xnielsen describes its design as a statement that punctuates a visitors view of the architect's homeland. "It is the traveler's first and last impression of Denmark." Viewed from afar across the harbour, it looks to float out into the dock: the black frames of glazed boarding tunnels detracting little from the overall architectural form.

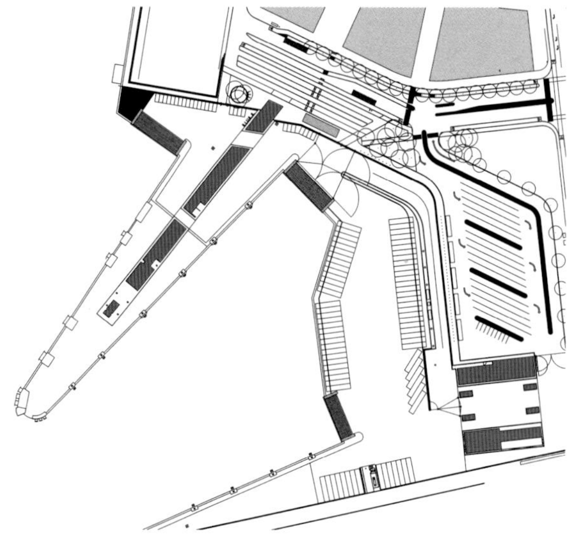

Site plan (including associated service buildings)

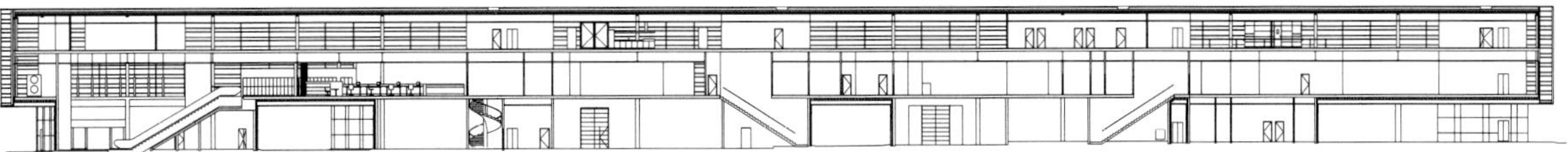

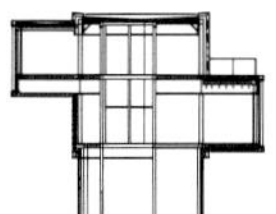

Section through side and end facades

East elevation

West elevation

Maritime Terminal

DESIGN ZAHA HADID
LOCATION SALERNO, ITALY

Described by the architect as "like an oyster, with a hard outer shell that houses soft fluid elements within", Zaha Hadid's design for a new ferry terminal in Salerno is one of the most eagerly awaited transport projects since the Yokohama Ferry Terminal in Japan, by Foreign Office Architects.

Situated in of the smaller Italian ports capable of accommodating two small cruise liners of approximately 600 passengers each or one larger one (2500 passengers), the new terminal is scheduled for completion in April 2007. It features an outer skin of two reinforced concrete shells between which is a glazed facade. This "valved" roof provides protection against the Mediterranean sun, while allowing ample natural light to illuminate the cool, naturally ventilated interior.

The building will house all of the usual requirements of a ferry terminal – passport control, luggage handling, ticket and waiting area, toilets, cafeteria, car rental, tourist information, and office facilities for staff, police and port authorities. The building is split functionally into three interlocking areas: the office for the port authorities and other administrative requirements; the ferry terminal; and the cruise ship terminal. These differing journey types are recognised and catered for in the architecture. Daily ferry passenger movements are fast and business-like, and as such, the design aids a quick entrance and exit on one level. Cruise liner passengers, however, are on a more leisurely journey and so are transported up flowing ramps to the upper level and vessel entrance.

The architect describes the journey through the terminal as "an intensified, smooth transition between the land and the sea; an artificial landform that is solid melting into liquid". As passengers step off the boat they are transported through a "swathe of dynamic spaces". Each area flows into the next almost imperceptibly – apart, perhaps, for the odd metal detector and passport control check. The entire building sits on a smooth sculpted hill that draws passengers through the length of the building, as an oyster slips from its shell. This fluid movement continues outside to connect the terminal with the town, the land with the water.

Lighting also plays an important part in the terminal's design. It is a directional tool, aiding passengers on their journey. It also enhances the almost cryptic design, however, marking the terminal at Salerno out as a wondrous beacon or lighthouse, jewel-like to be marvelled at from the sea.

The fluid form of Hadid's Maritime terminal

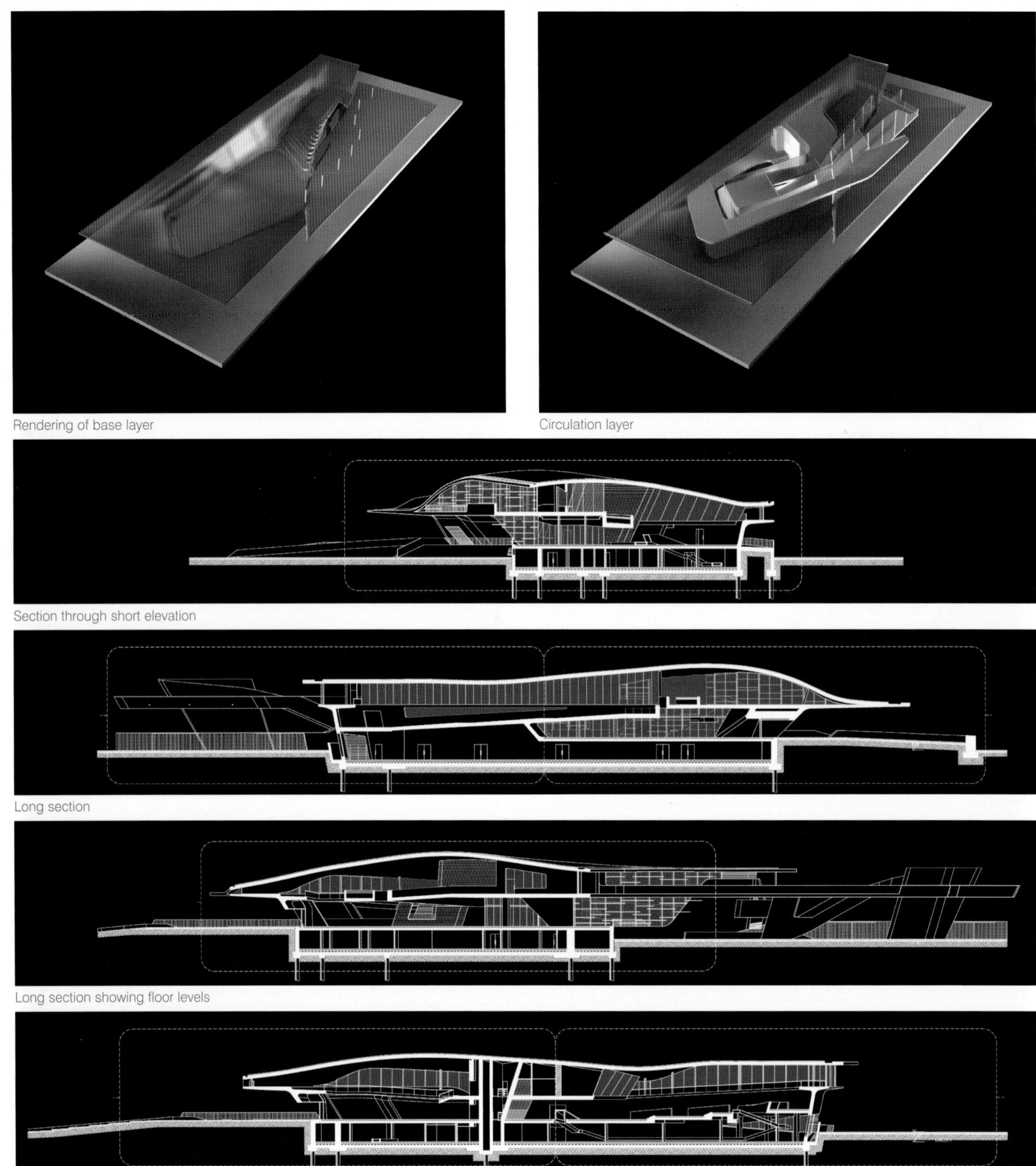

Rendering of base layer

Circulation layer

Section through short elevation

Long section

Long section showing floor levels

Long section through centre line of building

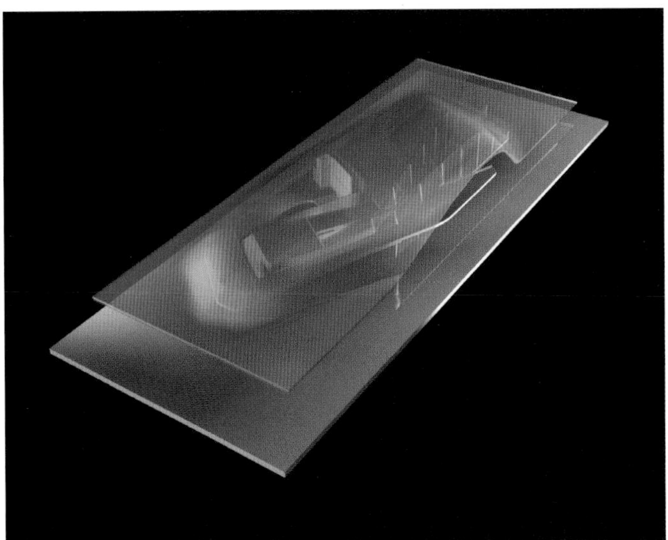
Roof shroud

Currently being constructed from Zaha Hadid's trademark material, concrete, the Maritime Terminal will be an unusual tourist-grabbing addition to the harbour side of the Italian town of Salerno. The shell-like form is totally different from the local architecture, as is Hadid's method of design. The concrete elements are almost impossibly thin for structures that span 30 by 96 metres (98 by 315 feet), but concrete is Hadid's speciality and the building's inherent strength comes from the valved shape. Built up in layers: base; middle, with functional elements; and shroud-like covering (see left), the terminal's contents are wrapped, as the architect describes, "like a pearl within an oyster".

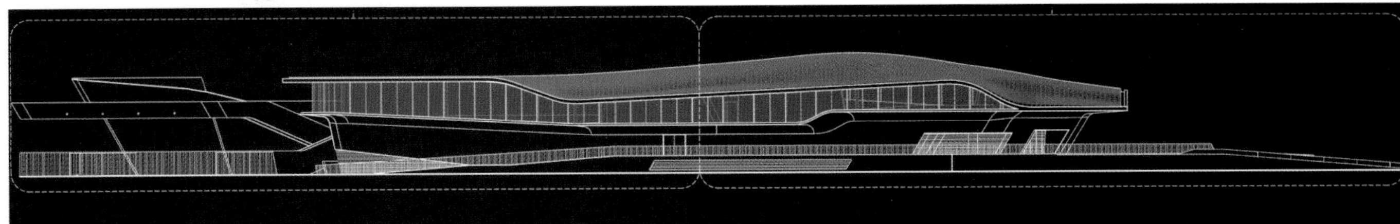
North east elevation

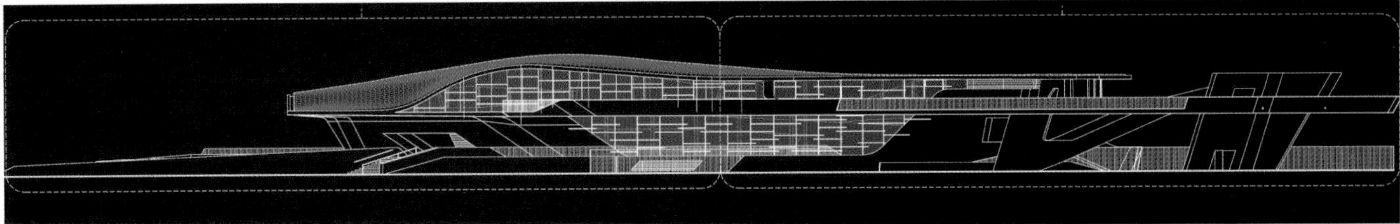
South west elevation

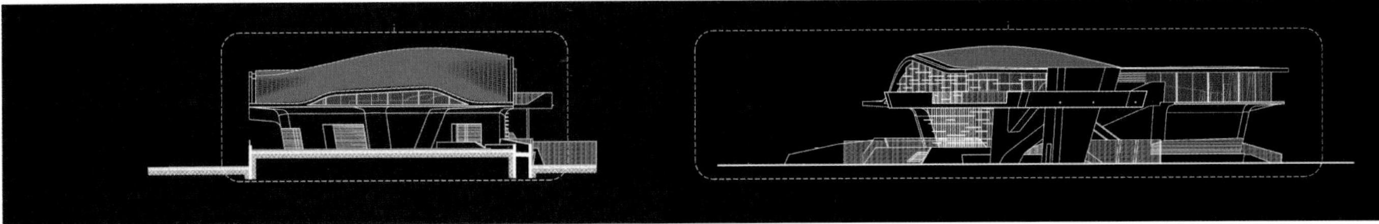
North-west (left) and south-east (right) elevations

Leith Ferry Terminal

DESIGN JESSAM AL JAWAD
LOCATION LEITH, SCOTLAND

This design for a ferry terminal in the ex-industrial port of Leith, Scotland is an elegant exercise in problem solving, coupled with a desire to revisit the golden age of travel. The requirement to include the essential elements of any transport hub is matched by the need to re-empower the site, returning its relevance within the city to that of half a century ago.

In many ways, while the architectural design is a statement in itself, the project focuses on the relationship between the port of Leith and the ferries' outward destinations. Historically port towns are thresholds that are doubly oriented – outwards to other trading centres, and inwards to the sources of goods to be traded. They are locations at which international and national space touch. As such, Al Jawad has reinterpreted this near/far experience within the very building that facilitates the travel that inspired it.

The site contains only the required functional elements: a gatehouse, dock controller's office and house and car parking. The slim volume of the terminal building facilitates access to and from the ships and houses a ticket office, waiting and observation areas and a café/restaurant.

The screen-like terminal building emphasises the relationship between the cars parked in the apron and the ferry by framing the boat when it is in dock. Its dimensions correspond to those of the ferry and the articulation of the structure and cladding make reference to the form of different parts of the boat. The building acts, in effect, as a register to the ferry and various elements of the terminal are positioned according to the corresponding location of parts of the boat. For instance, the control room of the terminal aligns with the ferry's control bridge when it is in dock.

The slim design of the building brings the passengers departing and those arriving into close proximity yet they remain separated. As passengers disembark and walk the drawn-out promenades or venture upwards to board the ferry, the architect seeks to make a connection between the two sets of people and allow them to do the same. In some way this reinforces the mystery of and similarity between each of them and enhances the travel experience. The long promenades and the "movie drive in" nature of the inclined car park also heighten the sense of theatre that has historically been associated with travel. What could have been a mundane journey is turned once again into an adventure.

A ferry approaches the multi-storey terminal

Section through the end of the building

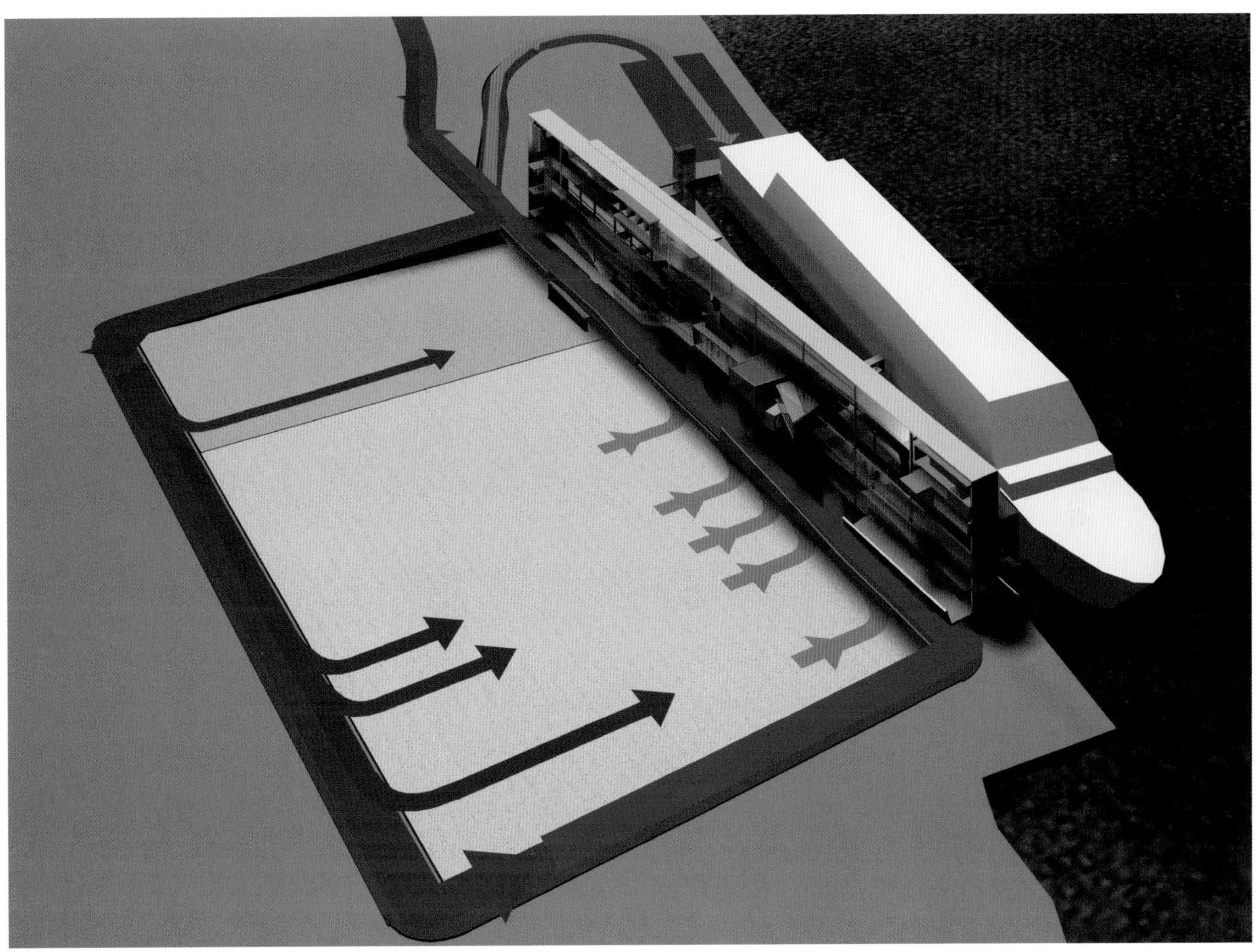

Transport and passenger circulation diagram

Like a stack of irregularly shaped steel beams, the design for the Leith Ferry Terminal is an unusual and innovative ramped format that presents a broadside to incoming ferries. Taller than other terminal designs, it echoes the huge industrial structures once common along the harbour and estuary of Leith in the heyday of this now impoverished Scottish town.

Road level aspect

Close-up view

View along the first floor

View along the floor including the ramp (right)

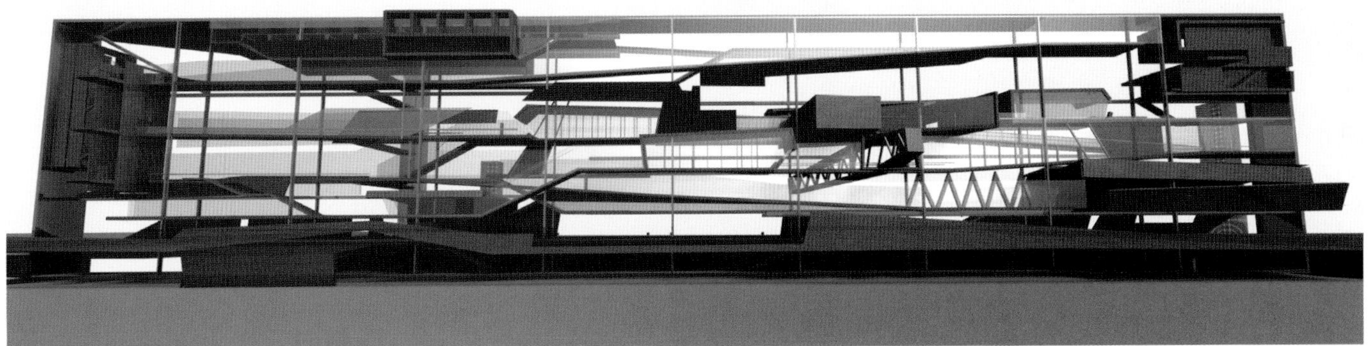

Side elevation showing the transparency of the structure

Although it has a large elevation, the mass is tempered by a large degree of open and transparent space. Architect Al Jawad proposes a series of ramps and stairways of differing gradients leading to box-like elements that house administration and other facilities. Visitors are protected from the weather by large glazed panels that offer views in all directions.

The terminal in Leith's industrial dockyard surroundings

Visiting ships enter into the large, fully protected harbour to dock alongside the terminal. Its high elevation adds further protection from wind off the sea as passengers depart onto the upper levels, while vehicles exit at ground level from the rear of the vessel. The terminal, although a hypothetical design, would regenerate Leith, which was for so long a vital connection between Scotland and its northern European and Scandinavian neighbours.

Landside lift and stair core

Sea side aspect and protected dock

Aerial view of the harbour

Ferry Landing Stage

DESIGN DAAD ARCHITECTEN
LOCATION VLIELAND, THE NETHERLANDS

Landing stages to enable both people and cars to load and disembark on trips between the islands and mainland of the Netherlands are a common part of Dutch coastal architecture. Most are situated within environments cluttered with huge-scaled harbour engineering and as such are seen as a small element, requiring no special architectural thought to blend with the overall industrial setting.

However, the ferry landing stage at Vlieland is situated in a small harbour with no visible industrial workings. This called for an architectural solution that would not create an eyesore. Having been involved in the design of other ferry landing stages, DAAD Architecten realized that the basic principles of the design had to be retained. A hinged bridge-like structure is suspended on steel cables underneath an engine room that sits atop heavy columns. This ungainly structure has historically been designed with no thought towards its aesthetic appeal. A typical example would take the form of a massive closed box with the bridge slung underneath.

With no possibility of redesigning the entire structure, DAAD had to consider how it could rework the structure to lessen its impact on its surroundings. The practice has sought to reduce the bulk of the engine room by cladding not in a solid material but with glass. The sides of the structure are fully glazed and the roof contains large skylights to allow natural light to penetrate the box and so relieve some of its bulk against the skyline.

This treatment necessitated the addition of a walkway around the exterior of the box for cleaning purposes. Again, the view through is of paramount importance, rather than the material in question – steel mesh walkways and box steel and cable balustrades provide a visually light solution. Finally a spiral stairway adds drama to the landing stage, looping up over eight metres (26 feet) from the dock to the engine room.

During the daytime, especially when the sun is shining, the glass box mirrors the sea and sky surrounding it, becoming as invisible as a large piece of industrial lifting gear can be. At night it is illuminated by the harbour lights, the glazed facade glinting in the soft yellow light and acting as a welcoming beacon to approaching ferry passengers.

Landing stage in action

45t

View from base towards engine room

This architectural solution is not inherently sculptural, but it does echo the surrounding aesthetic and exude a confident Modern aesthetic. The strong columns mimic nearby metal bollards in the dock, while the glass box reduces the mass of the landing stage engine room against the skyline. The architect has designed exactly what was required, rather than trying to overstate a relatively diminutive addition to the flat expanse of the waterfront vista.

View from the breakwater

Falkirk Wheel

DESIGN RMJM
LOCATION FALKIRK, SCOTLAND, UK

Architectural drama on the canal

This monumental piece of architectural engineering is the first ever rotating boat lift in the world, and the first new boat lift to be built in Britain since 1895. The Wheel connects the Forth and Clyde Canal with the Union Canal, some 35 metres (115 feet) below. The project also reconnects the waterways of east and west Scotland, providing a fully navigable canal system between Edinburgh and Glasgow for the first time in 70 years.

In the past, the two canals were connected by a staircase of 11 locks which descended the 35 metres (115 feet) over a 1.5 kilometre (1 mile) distance. RMJM's brief was to perfect the descent and lower two boats and raise two boats up the vertical drop in 15 minutes. They explored numerous methods of achieving this including a simple balanced lift, a counter-weighted circular basin, an oval wheel, and an imaginative rolling egg design. However, the final design is based on a rotating beam, not, in fact, a wheel.

The practice, along with engineers Arup, MG Bennet and Butterley Engineering, designed the aqueduct as a contemporary version of the simple yet beautiful forms of much older stone and brick aqueducts and viaducts. It developed as a series of reinforced concrete piers. Through these runs the flat bottomed aqueduct – the semi-circular gap left beneath each pier reinforcing the aqueduct as a continuous element.

From this came the first ideas for how the lift would look and work. The circular aesthetic is continued, but hooked leading edges are added to the lift elements to emphasize their movement. Between these dramatic hooked arms, two caissons, each capable of carrying two boats, are fixed to a system of gears that allow them to rotate in a stable fashion. The drive mechanism for the wheel consists of a series of eight hydraulic motors mounted in the last aqueduct support.

Perhaps the most challenging problem was that of providing a waterproof seal at the connection between the wheel and the aqueduct. Arup solved this using a special section of steel aqueduct located at the joint between the two structures. This accommodates all movement while taking into account the tolerances required to provide a waterproof seal.

Approaching from the Forth and Clyde Canal, boat users see the wheel through a veil of trees. It then disappears from site until boats slowly emerge from a preceding lock. On using the wheel, there is no obvious lifting mechanism and very little sound. The experience is quite literally uplifting.

British Waterways Scotland
welcome to
The Falkirk Wheel

The completed boat lift is the largest project ever undertaken by British Waterways in Scotland. It is an awe-inspiring site when viewed by visitors but really comes into its own when seen by users. Emerging from a 100 metre (328 foot) tunnel, boats on the higher Union Canal travel through the semicircular concrete hoops of the aqueduct 35 metres (115 feet) above ground level towards the hook of the wheel. The dramatic impact upon the landscape of this gigantic piece of architectural engineering can not be overstated. It is to the designers' credit, however, that the Falkirk Wheel is an exciting addition to the vista, which draws in visitors and users. It has achieved a sculptural quality that far exceeds its functional use and, as such, has become a valuable addition rather than an ugly necessity.

View looking along the aqueduct

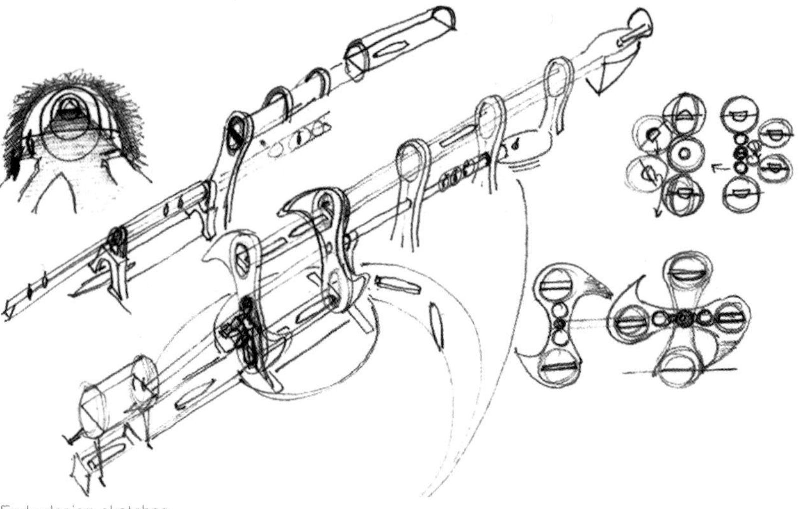

Early design sketches

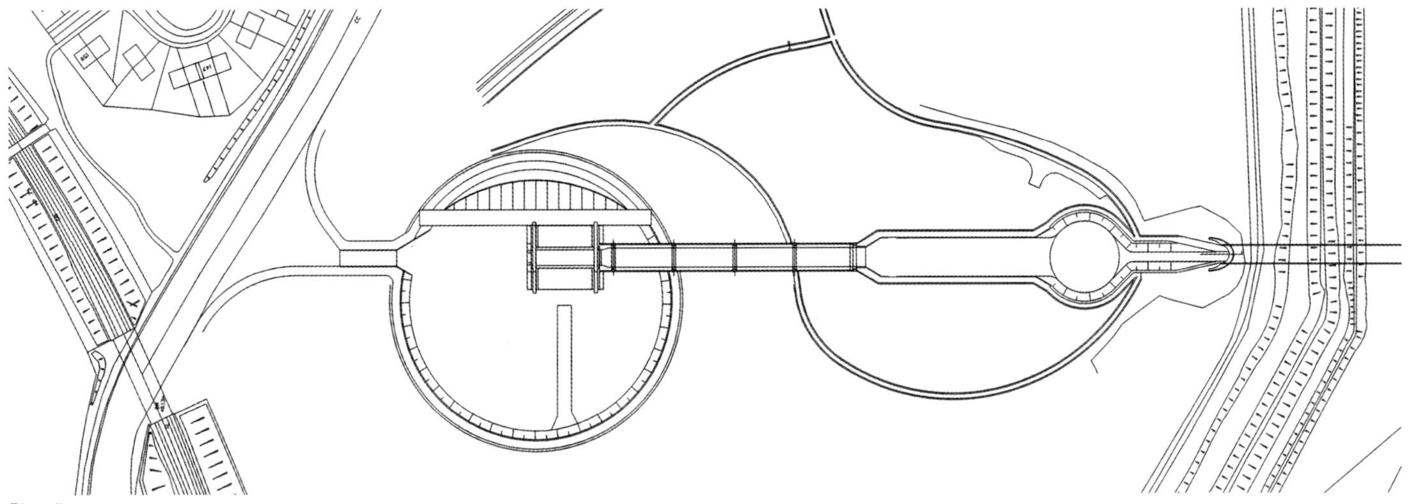

Plan diagram

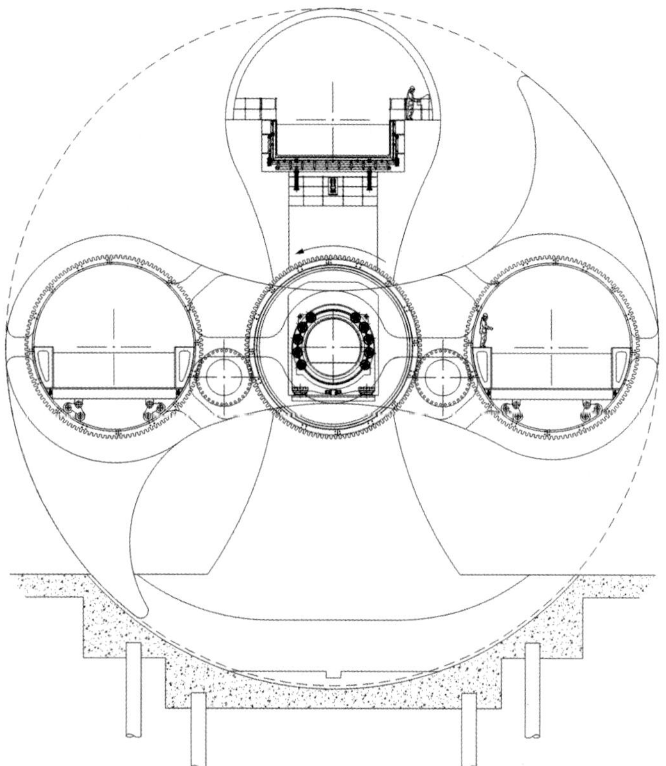

Section at the arm nearest to the aqueduct

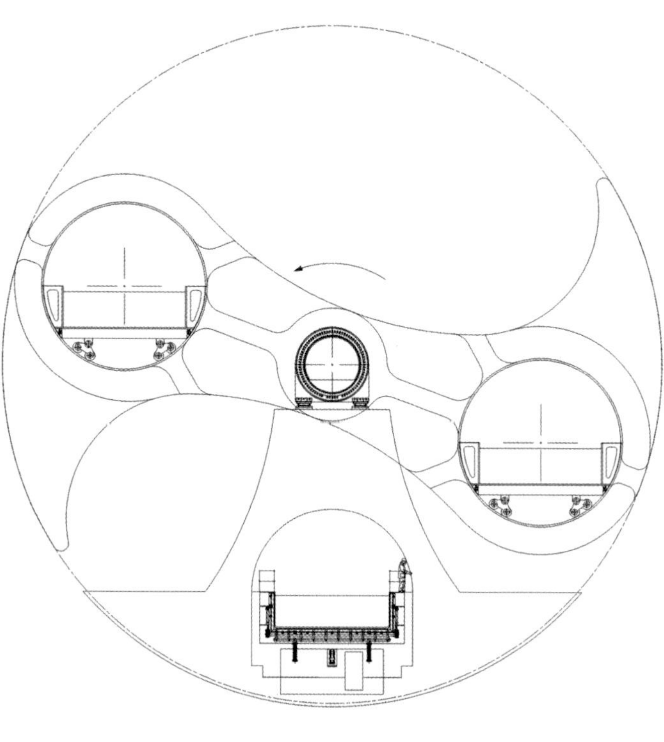

Section at the end of the arm

View of the wheel, at mid-rotation

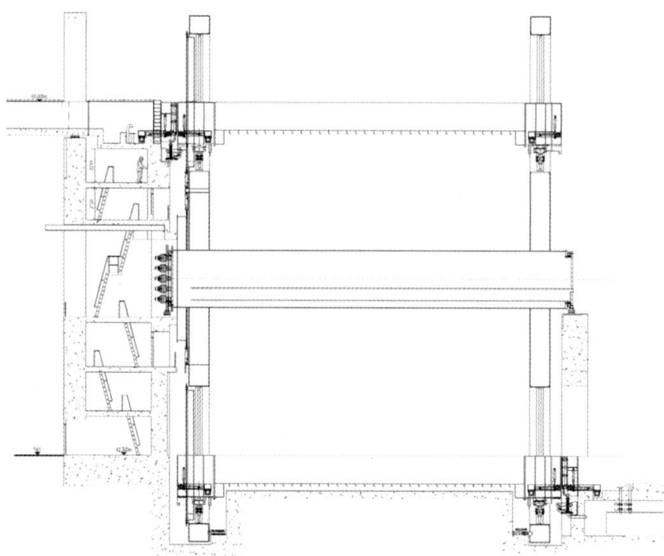

Side view, illustrating the emergency stairs

The shape of the vast arms is born of structural necessity and a keen eye for design. Circular forms are informed by the movement of the wheel but the dinosaur-like horn on the trailing edge of each arm is an element straight out of an architect's Art Deco wish-list. It creates movement and speed and adds drama and beauty to this lumbering beast.

View towards the aqueduct

View of spindle and caisson underside

The final built structure evolved from numerous alternative concept designs (see right): from counter-weighted cable lifts to a huge "rolling egg" design that would have involved sailors floating their vessels into a vast chamber, which would then topple over with them bobbing about inside. The finished article is the most rational and architecturally beautiful.

View looking along the aqueduct

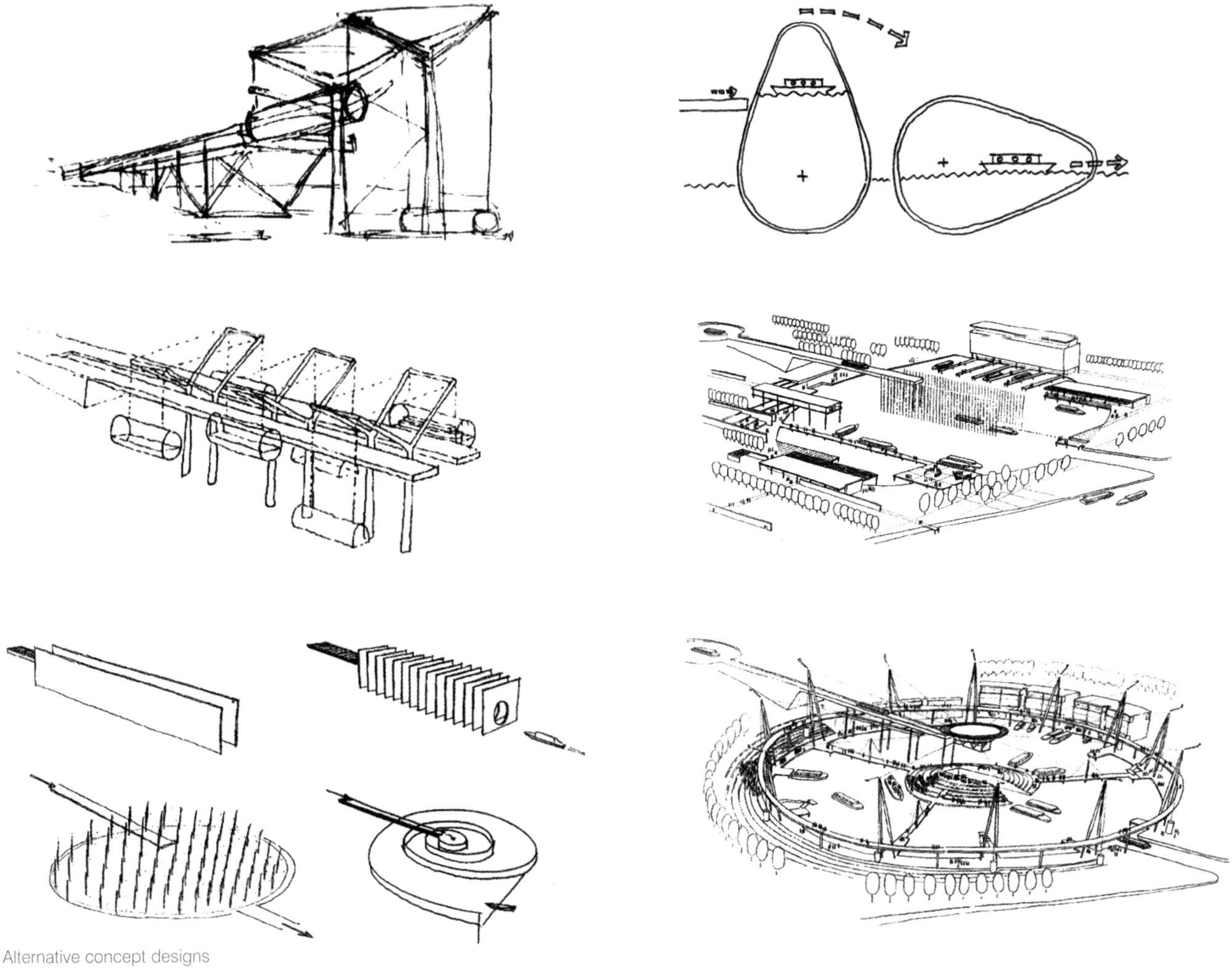

Alternative concept designs

St George Ferry Terminal

DESIGN HELLMUTH, OBATA + KASSABAUM (HOK)
LOCATION STATEN ISLAND, NEW YORK, USA

New York's drive to modernize its transport infrastructure sees new metro lines being bored under Manhattan Island, JFK Airport getting a face-lift and its ferry terminals being refurbished. A significant project in this programme is the restoration and upgrading of the St George Terminal on Staten Island. HOK's new building replaces what has for years been one of New York's most underwhelming tourist destinations.

The terminal is used by over one million tourists each year as a stop-off on trips to view the Statue of Liberty and other waterside landmarks. Until this renovation it was a cavernous, dimly lit shell of a building of no real interest to anyone. HOK's renovation has transformed the building into an airy space with clerestory windows on all sides. A 12 metre (40 foot) glass wall along the waterside provides views of New York Harbour, and two grand observation decks take advantage of spectacular vistas across to Manhattan Island. The building now has a new 106 metre (350 foot) arch which takes reference from the numerous bridges serving Staten Island.

HOK has embraced New York's drive to build more sustainably and the project is the first LEED Certified Sustainable intermodal transport building. Environmentally friendly strategies include measures such as maximizing the use of natural light to the inclusion of a living green roof and the reinstatement of oyster beds at the ferry slips.

The redevelopment of the passenger waiting area includes an extensive glass curtain wall, which replaces the old brick walls, and skylights, which allow natural light to flood into the main waiting area and new retail corridor. Old signage has been replaced with clearer and more internationally understandable visual assistance, while other enhanced passenger facilities include upgraded rest rooms, new information systems and public address systems and a map of the ferry route picked out of the terrazzo tile floor.

The building is a vital transport link to Manhattan Island for the 400,000 inhabitants of Staten Island and is an interchange with the Island's light railway and limited bus service. As such, the terminal remained operational throughout the reconstruction process, which was a public-private partnership overseen by the New York City Economic Corporation on behalf of the city's Department for Transport.

Detail of the feature arch

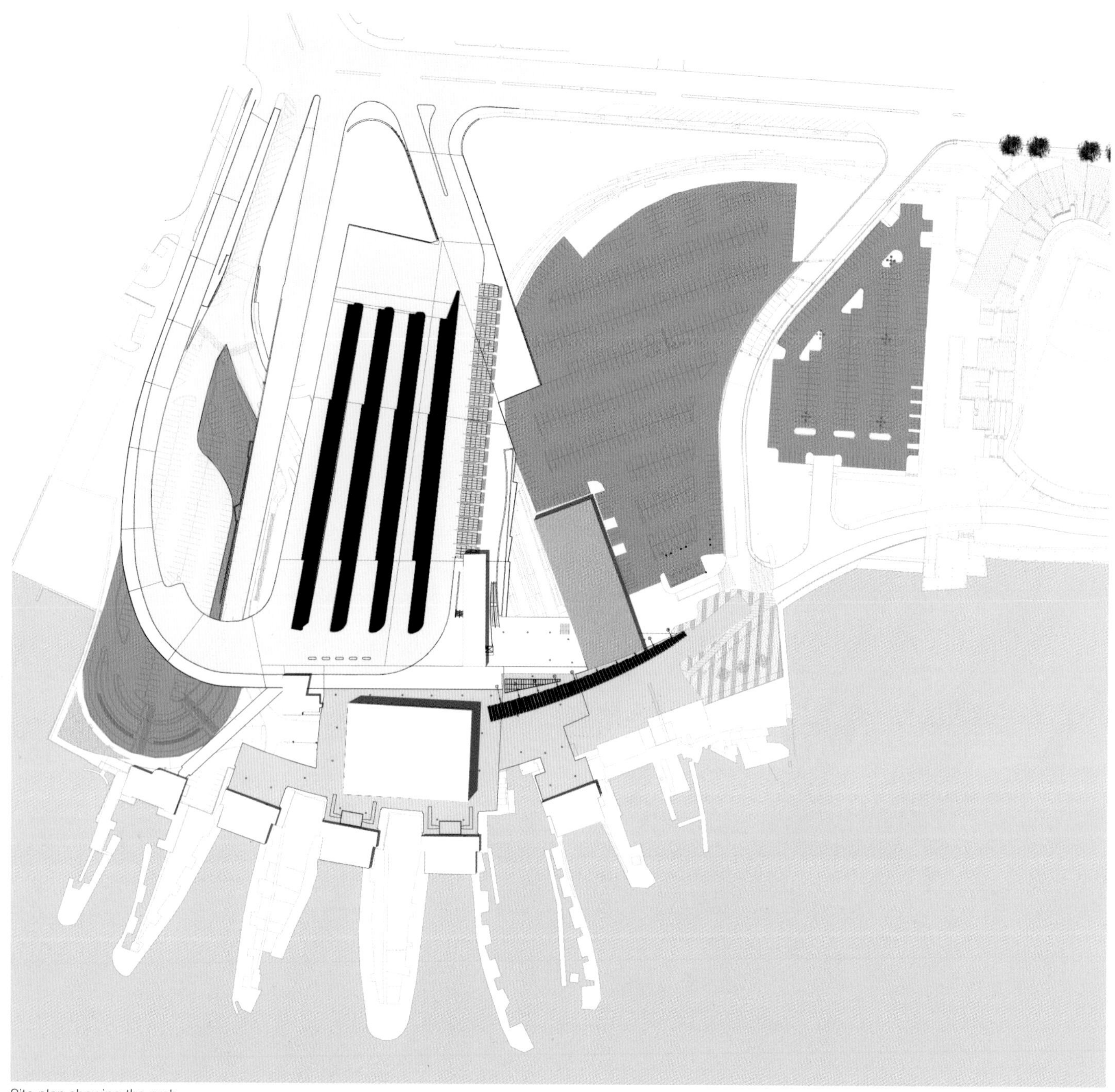

Site plan showing the arch

Externally, new landscaped areas create a waterfront plaza that offers views of the city skyline as well as open public areas and a new restaurant. The terminal is also the cornerstone of a much larger venture entitled the St George Station Project. This includes the new Staten Island Yankees minor league ball park and two new museums. The park and museums are expected to attract an additional 450,000 visitors to the island each year, many of whom will use the ferry and terminal, bringing much-needed work and revenue to the islanders who live so near to the monied elite of Manhattan Island.

Making a statement in the city of skyscrapers

The journey mapped out in the floor

Naturally lit waiting lounge

Column detail

Arch detail

The new addition to Staten Island's crowded waterfront will help cement the ferry's place in New York's history. More importantly, it provides an improved service to thousands of workers as well as the many tourists, and acts as a new core on which to re-energise local amenities such as restaurants and bars. Internally, the building now resembles a high grade transport interchange, with all modern facilities. Its defining feature, though, is the ferry route map set into the floor.

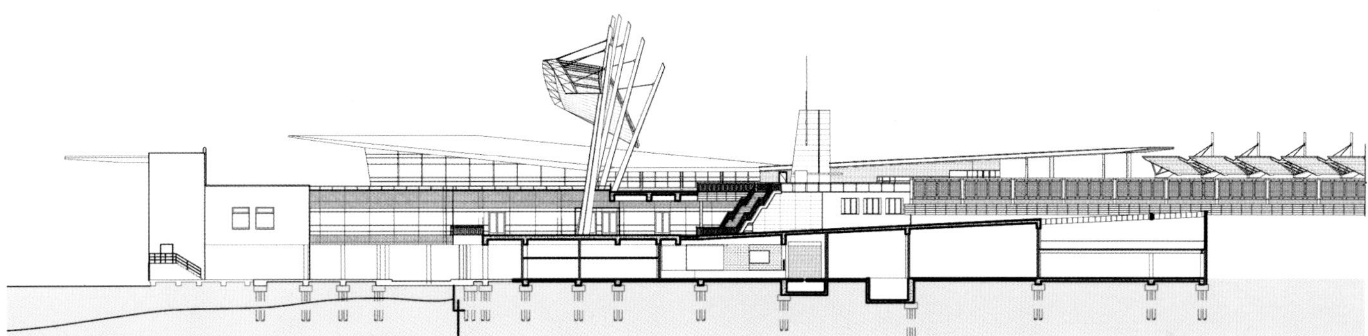

Elevation from the quayside

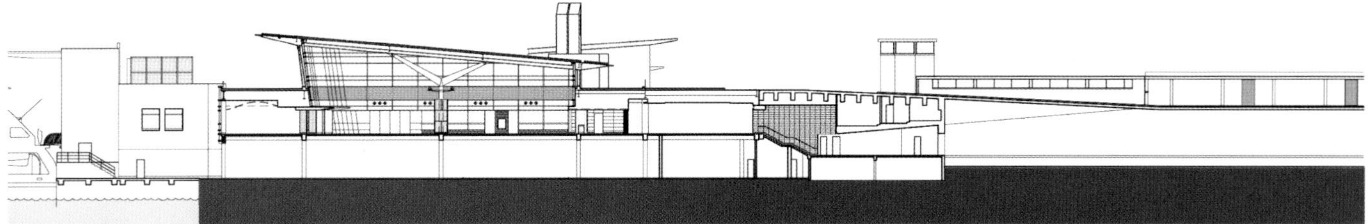

Section through main terminal building

Elevation showing main terminal centrally

Internal column detail with uplighters

Strong detailing and a clean almost industrial aesthetic presents St George ferry terminal as a place which is efficient and yet a pleasure to be in. Passengers are processed through the terminal quickly, a boon for locals wishing to get to or home from work, but there is chance for tourists take in the sights on the viewing deck high up on the front of the main building.

The viewing deck, atop the main building

Whitehall Ferry Terminal

DESIGN FREDERIC SCHWARTZ ARCHITECTS
LOCATION NEW YORK, USA

Winning an international competition in 1996, a team including Anderson/Schwartz Architects and Venturi Scott Brown & Associates, designed a new ferry terminal to replace the dilapidated Whitehall Ferry Terminal on New York Harbour at the tip of Manhattan. Following Venturi Scott Browns' resignation due to political interference, Frederic Schwartz Architects took on design responsibilities for the replacement of the building that is more widely known as the Staten Island Ferry Terminal.

This ferry terminal is the start of an unmissable boat ride for visitors to New York, but it is also a vital transport link for over 40,000 New Yorkers each day. As such, the design of a new starting point on the voyage to see the Statue of Liberty had to both embrace the everyday commuter and meandering tourist. The design does this by using a rational layout in response to circulation requirements while featuring destination-making elements like the rooftop viewing platform.

The building's earthquake-proof steel frame stands on drilled-in-place concrete and steel foundations, which include isolation sleeves near subsurface subway or highway tunnels. The facade is clad in a coated aluminium frame and glazing system to all sides apart from the waterfront elevation and slip openings, which are stainless steel. Photovoltaic panels on the building's south facade contribute to energy requirements and radiant under-floor heating provides the most economical method of heating the large waiting hall.

The waiting hall is situated centrally within the building. The vast glazed facade allows for good natural light and offers views out across the river towards Ellis Island and the Statue of Liberty. Around the waiting hall, perimeter concourses facilitate the swift transition of city-bound commuters to a variety of transport options including a covered taxi rank, subway lines and a dedicated bus loop. In addition to this main circulatory area the building includes concessions, office space and ancilliary support and ferry operations rooms.

Schwartz's masterstroke is the inclusion of a waterfront viewing deck on the roof of the terminal. This simple addition affords fabulous 360 degree views of the great New York Harbour, including a sweeping panorama that takes in the Brooklyn Bridge and skyline, the Governor's Island, the Statue of Liberty and Ellis Island, not to mention the towering skyscrapers of Manhattan. This feature alone makes the new Whitehall Ferry Terminal a tourist destination in its own right.

View of the terminal with its Manhattan Island backdrop

Section through the terminal

This iconic structure has been rebuilt in order to better serve the city in the 21st century. The new terminal takes on an airport-like feel with high ceilings and large expanses of glazing. Energy saving measures such as photovoltaic panels are used, but most important is the use of space and ease of circulation for this busy New York City transportation terminal.

Slip opening with a ferry docking

Landside passenger entrance

The glazed departure and arrivals hall

Inside the main building

Dwarfed in height by its high-rise neighbours, the terminal's bulk belies its true size. Once inside, travellers will appreciate the intelligently spacious design that is accentuated by the extensive use of glazed façades, which allow natural light to flood in. From the road, the building blends with the city, hinting at the Modernist "International style" – glass and steel – of illustrious New York City landmarks such as the Seagram Building and Lever House.

Initial concept sketch

Water-Based Transport Architecture

Eve Michel

Eve Michel is an architect and Senior Vice President of the New York City Economic Development Corporation Capital Program Division. Her responsibilities include the management of design and construction for a diverse portfolio of infrastructure, transport, and building projects.

Kenneth Drucker,

At HOK New York, Ken Drucker has directed many benchmark projects. His diverse, high-profile corporate and institutional clients include MasterCard and Amtrak. He has been the recipient of prestigious awards, including the GSA Design Award and the AIA Honor Award for Urban Design.

Historically, New York City has maintained a powerful link between its industrial edges and the waterfront. As industry gradually died out, however, the manufacturing facilities were replaced by a recreational edge. Today, the waterfront is again changing as the perimeters of all five city boroughs – the Bronx, Brooklyn, Manhattan, Queens, and Staten Island – are slowly and incrementally being reclaimed for public use.

New York Harbour is coming alive, mainly because of connections that are being reinvigorated by expanded ferry services. Two new terminals – the St George Intermodal Station on Staten Island and the Whitehall Terminal, its companion on the Manhattan side of the harbour, are supporting water-borne transportation links.

The New York City Department of Transportation maintains a fleet of 11 pumpkin-coloured vessels and five terminals, the largest of which are the St George Intermodal Station and the Whitehall Terminal. The nonprofit New York City Economic Development Corporation (EDC) has directed major renovations on each terminal that were completed in 2005. Appropriately, the Staten Island Ferry system also celebrated its 100-year anniversary in 2005.

About 70,000 passengers a day – more than 20 million every year – travel on the ferry between St George on Staten Island and Whitehall Street in lower Manhattan. The passengers are a combination of commuters and visitors who enjoy the majestic New York Harbour views on the five-mile, 25-minute ride, which, since 1997, has been free of charge. Ferry traffic has also significantly increased since 11 September 2001.

The authors of this essay have worked closely together for eight years on the planning, design, and construction of the US$130 million renovation of the St George Intermodal Station. This project added 1765 square metres (19,000 square feet) to an existing 17,650 square metre (190,000 square foot) complex. Lower Manhattan's Whitehall Terminal also opened recently, after a 13-year, US$201 million renovation designed by Schwartz Architects of New York.

Challenges

In describing the current state of this type of architecture, we focus on the St George project as a model. The challenges involved in giving new life to this busy intermodal centre were typical for a water-based intermodal transport renovation project in a dense urban location.

Water-based transport architecture gives designers opportunities to build connections – physical, historic, and cultural – and to create a sense of gateway and arrival. As with any building type, designs for water-based transport facilities must balance architectural form with pragmatic concerns. These buildings are primarily public and civic facilities that experience constant traffic and movement. Designers must understand the needs of commuters and tourists and then shape the architecture to satisfy those activities. Designs should respond to both the external requirements created by the site's context and to the complex internal technical demands of modern transportation and hospitality environments.

The low, horizontal, waterfront location made this a challenging project for the design team. In addition to enforcing a 27 metre (90 foot) height limit along the water's edge, city planning officials required the design to maintain all the existing view corridors to Manhattan. The EDC also could not build more than 2322 square metres (25,000 square feet) of new construction without triggering a review by the US Army Corps of Engineers.

The design team was asked to reuse the existing structure instead of building a new terminal and to leave intact much of the infrastructure and existing foundations and circulation paths. The challenge was to look for ways to design modern interventions – beginning with the waiting room at the heart of the facility and working out to the view terraces.

The existing building, which was built in the 1950s after a fire at an adjoining ferry terminal, lacked memorable spaces. There was, in fact, no "destination". The waiting room resembled a glazed-block high school gymnasium.

The Borough President wanted the new terminal architecture to create a "gateway". The terminal needed an identifiable image – a statement which announced to visitors that they were arriving in Staten Island. Local officials wanted to enhance the commuting experience while capturing tourists and convincing them to stay and use the terminal as a launching point for seeing the rest of Staten Island.

Another design goal was to create a central urban space that improved connections between various modes of transport, several Staten Island attractions, and the land, sky, and water. The team also wanted to capitalize on the scenic views of Manhattan and the New York Harbour and to bring as much natural light into the renovated terminal as possible.

The new St George Intermodal Terminal has transformed the ferry experience for riders and created a state-of-the-art gateway to Staten Island and its waterfront. The project is an important piece of the master plan to redevelop Staten Island's north shore.

Architectural Design: Integrating Sculpture, Art, Light, and Materiality With the Building Programme

Six key terms describe the terminal's architectural design: transparency, contextualism, tectonics, public spaces, connections, and poetry.

Transparency

The key to the design was to introduce transparency throughout the building and connectivity back to the water. The design replaces as much existing brick and terra cotta as possible with glass, corrugated silver metal, and painted white metal. The basic idea was to create a focus toward the waterside ferry arrival and departure activities.

The design is transparent in terms of revealing the programme and what the building looks like. The building's large amounts of glazing and day-lighting offers an honest reflection of what is happening within.

The dark and dingy main waiting area has been transformed into a light, airy space. The 12 metre (40 foot) high, 63 metre (208 foot) long, 30 metre (100 foot) deep aluminium and glass curtain wall along the waterside offers spectacular views of the Hudson River. Y-shaped metal beams on top of existing support columns lift the waiting room roof about 6 metres (20 feet) to create a clerestory element that draws in natural light. Two large observation decks take advantage of the expansive views.

The new waiting room can accommodate a total of 4000 people from two ferry boats. In the previous facility, passengers in the waiting room had no idea where the boat was, when it was arriving, how many people were disembarking, or how long it took them to do so. Adding a glazed curtain wall facing the slips allows passengers to participate in the arrival and departure sequence by watching the boats arrive and dock. People in the waiting room can now experience the water.

Contextual

One end of the new terminal responds to the rigid urban edge of St George's city grid. On the other side of the terminal, the design deals with how the island's softer edge meets the water. The composition results from how the two geometries – the orthogonal grid versus the lapping of the waves – come together.

The 1672 square metre (18,000 square foot) living roof draws inspiration from New York City's geology. Manhattan was formed by bedrock that has been covered over by a blanket of architecture. The design takes those bedrock forms, or what is called the "Manhattan schist", and extrudes them up to inform the roof shape.

Layers of meaning support the design concept. The idea of solid versus soft is carried out through features like the cantilevered forms and day-lighting. The team further developed that idea into the building details – the mullion shapes, for example – and into the material selections.

Tectonics

The design expresses the technology of how the building is constructed. Ideally, each building system should find an honest expression in the architecture.

The design goal was to turn everything – the lighting, ceiling, and structure – into its component. The steel columns and ceiling structure, for example, are part of the new waiting room, and the white-painted structure creates a nautical look.

Making Public Spaces

In making public spaces within water-based transport facilities, designers create a sequence of spaces that one experiences while moving through a building. This public space is integral to the project's memory.

The St George Terminal is not an "object" building on the waterfront – it is a destination. Because the building is so horizontal and spread out, the waiting room became the natural focus for the designers. Floor-to-ceiling glass allows panoramic views of the harbour and incoming ferries, which provide their own floating public spaces.

The original idea for the waiting room floor was to provide a map of New York Harbour with lights tied to the location of the ferries crossing the harbour. Those lights would be linked with a GPS sensor so waiting passengers could watch the ferries move across the floor. Inlaid bronze medallions would identify ferry terminals, the Statue of Liberty, and the locations of the old forts that protected New York Harbour. The value-engineered final design became a green, blue, and aquamarine terrazzo tile floor with a colourful oval map of the ferry's harbour route.

Connections

In addition to receiving the Staten Island Ferry boats, the St George and Whitehall terminals are each intermodal transportation hubs. The St George Terminal is the key intermodal centre for the roughly 400,000 inhabitants of Staten Island and is the home of the northernmost station of the MTA Staten Island Railway, which begins on the borough's south shore and terminates at the lower level of the terminal. This facility also houses the island's local bus service, with 23 bus lines ending here. These links to other modes of transport make the facility, which is a critical part of Staten Island's redevelopment, a complex organism.

The team created new pedestrian walkways linking the terminal to cultural attractions such as the new World Trade Center Memorial, the Lighthouse Museum south of the terminal, and the Staten Island Yankees' minor-league baseball stadium to the north-west. A new north–south esplanade improves circulation along the water's edge and provides spectacular New York City skyline views.

The design creates seamless connections by improving circulation between levels and through the site and adding a new signage and way-finding programme. Life safety was improved by adding a new lower-level lobby that separates the buses and taxis from the "kiss-n-ride" car drop-offs. Murals by local artists add life to the corridors.

The entry sequence for a passenger stepping off a boat at a slip begins with circulating from the boat around the waiting room to any of the four tubes that lead to the bus canopies. A stair next to those tubes leads down to the trains. A narrow stair goes up to Richmond Terrace. Passengers also can follow the curve out to the Grand Stair and up to the esplanade and the baseball stadium. Retail shops are tucked in throughout the space.

Poetry

There's romance in travelling on ferries through a body of water such as New York Harbour. Riders feel a calming effect while enjoying the opportunity for quiet reflection. To enhance this experience, there should be some poetry behind a terminal building's design. The design should fold extra meaning or layer an iconic element into a pragmatic solution.

At the St George Terminal, a soaring 25 metre (84 foot) tall, 106 metre (350 foot) long arched canopy supported by ten cantilevered columns faces Staten Island and crowns the building. Constructed of painted steel and with a shape inspired by the surrounding bridges, the arch is lit at night and acts as a powerful beacon for Staten Island.

Green Design

It is appropriate that the building, which serves as an educational tool and public example for transportation efficiency, has been designed to become America's first LEED (Leadership in Energy and Environmental Design)-certified intermodal transportation station.

"Green" features include an 1672 square metre (18,000 square foot) living roof installed over the central storage facility. Rainwater runoff from the parking lot is captured in a cistern. From there it is pumped up to irrigate the rooftop sod and plantings as necessary. The indigenous Staten Island plantings on the roof attract migratory Monarch butterflies. The softscaping also makes a symbolic contribution to New York City's heat island mitigation efforts.

Sustainable aspects include introducing oyster beds at the ferry slips, near the fuel pier, to help detoxify the water. A building overhang above the main waiting room acts as an attractive passive solar device that provides maximum shade in the summer while being angled to attract maximum warmth-providing sun in the winter. Photovoltaic louvres cut the terminal's energy use by 25 per cent. Other environmentally friendly features include waterless urinals, gas absorption chillers, electric vehicle charging stations, planting drought-tolerant trees, specifying structural steel that is 100 per cent recycled material, and using paving materials with recycled content.

Uninterrupted Service

The St George Intermodal Terminal took eight years to design and build, while the Whitehall Terminal was a 13-year project. Each effort required contributions from thousands of people representing dozens of different agencies, consultants, and contractors. Projects like this represent an enormous civic undertaking.

Phased construction ensured that the terminals each remained fully operational and experienced no service interruptions – no small task when serving 70,000 daily travellers. This requirement did, however, add to the schedule and budget of each project. When working in the central corridors, for example, construction workers literally had to stop what they were doing for five minutes every half hour and wait for arriving and departing passengers to pass through.

Future Trends

As with any major transport facility, security is an issue in water-based transport design. Rather than influencing the architecture, security features such as physical barriers and video surveillance must be integrated within the architecture. In the water-based transport facilities of the future, security will get even tighter. Ideally, all ferry terminals would become more intermodal and include cars. For now, however, that represents too much of a security risk in cities like New York.

About 650 square metres (7000 square feet) of additional destination restaurant and retail space was created in the St George Terminal. This provided a 30 per cent increase in retail development space and tripled the rent that the city had been collecting. In the future, we expect more revenue-generating retail spaces and amenities to be attached to these facilities.

4

Rail

204 Three Kinds of Flow
212 Moscow City Transport Terminal
216 King's Cross Station
224 Leuven Train Station
230 Stuttgart Central Station
234 Worb Train Shed
242 Central Station
248 Fulton Street Transit Center
254 Stratford International Station

Rail

Railway travel is currently the most environmentally friendly of transport types. Modern trains are fast and economical, carrying large cargoes of passengers and freight. They are fuel efficient and produce comparatively little pollution.

Their one drawback is the limitations of the track network. This has led to their decline in certain parts of the world including the USA, Canada and Australia, where automotive transport reigns. However, as we move into a more environmentally conscious era, the role of the railway is again high on the agenda, and Europe in particular is striding forward with a plethora of new rail-focused transport hubs.

This geographical bias is unsurprising, as railways were pioneered by the British. Following Stevenson's invention of the Rocket in 1825, and the opening of the Stockton and Darlington Railway, trains began to haul freight between stations at opposing ends of the Liverpool and Manchester Railway. Liverpool Road station in Manchester, a goods handling depot styled as a row of Georgian houses, is today part of the Museum of Science and Industry.

The British empire stretched across much of the globe in the 19th century and tracks were soon being laid as far afield as India, where in 1853 the Bombay to Thane railway opened. America was quick to follow the British example. Its preeminent engineers had visited the UK and in 1830 work began on the colossal undertaking to connect Baltimore with Ohio by rail. The line revitalized Baltimore as a port and provided a new outlet for the coal and iron industries, greatly accelerating Maryland's economic growth.

Railway buildings

With these new railways came station buildings. Humble at first, they soon grew in importance as the influence of the railways were realized. St Pancras Station in London, completed in 1877, was a massive column-free train shed designed by William Henry Barlow and R M Ordish. Its grand arches were a statement of intent, a built symbol of London's importance in a rapidly changing world. George Gilbert Scott's Gothic hotel, which sits in front of the station, added the decorated splendour and pomp of the 19th century.

It was this classical style that dominated station design the world over for fifty years or more. India's Victoria Station in Mumbai (completed in 1887), renamed Chhatrapati Shivaji Terminus, was designed in the Gothic style by Fredrick Stevens. The European Neo-Classical Pretoria Station in South Africa was the work of Englishman Herbert Baker. Even the architectural powerhouse of Italy took its lead on station design from the British, mainly because much of the money invested in railways came from the UK. The original Stazione Leopolda in Florence, built in the 1860s, takes many cues from the Trijunct station in Derby (1840) and Nine Elms in London (1838).

Far Left Works train shed by Smarch

Middle Fulton Street Transit Center, by Grimshaw Architects

Left top Leuven Station by Samyn and Partners

Left lower Stratford International Station by Rail Link Engineering

In more modern times architectural styles and cultural differences have played an important part in shaping station design. Dictators have also shaped our transport architecture: both Hitler and Mussolini promoted new challenging architectural styles. One such example is the Termini Station in Rome. Started before the Second World War by Angiolo Mazzoni, as part of Mussolini's Grand Plan, its stunning facade and colonnade were completed in 1950 by architects Montuori and Vitellozzi. This huge station, built in the clean lines of the Rationalist style is indicative of continental Europe's grasp of the Modernism at a time when the UK was struggling to find a new architectural voice.

Meanwhile, underground systems were being built in cities across the world and their stations reveal the variety and splendour of our architectural heritage. While London, and later New York, opted for the utilitarian approach, designing all stations to one basic blueprint, other European cities had some fun. Moscow's metro stations opened in 1935 as "palaces of the people" and feature ornate decoration, chandeliers and monumental columns. Alternatively, the Paris metro, inaugurated in 1900, is an Art Deco masterpiece.

On the other side of the world in Japan engineer Hideo Shima was the design force behind the next step in railway technology, in the form of elevated electric trains. The Skinkhansen railway first opened between Osaka and Tokyo in 1964. The electrically-powered trains running on level tracks – over 3000 bridges and through 67 tunnels – were unerringly punctual. They signalled a shift in the balance of knowledge in train and railway design from west to east, and the subsequent stations, such as those currently being completed by Makoto Sei Watanabe (page 204), are a world apart from Western designs.

Train design is currently evolving again, with the advancement of magnetic levitation technology and MagLev trains in both Japan and Germany. The Japanese MLX01 is capable of reaching speeds of 550 kilometres (344 miles) per hour and the first MagLev route now runs between Pudong Shanghai International Airport and the city's financial district.

Europe too is witnessing a full-scale revival of interest in railways. The two main factors are the completion of high speed links across the English Channel and a realization that mass transit is the way forward for energy conservation and environmental planning. While the car is still king in the USA, Europe's crowded roads and polluted cities are being dragged into the 21st century by environmentalists who are changing the way people think about travel.

Architects have a big role to play in this change. The station is the flag-bearer of the railway, and if it can be designed in a responsible and yet exciting way it will have a big effect on the public's perception of rail transport.

Three Kinds of Flow

DESIGN MAKOTO-SEI WATANABE
LOCATION JAPAN

Three kinds of flow is a study of form, fluidity, and movement at three railway sites. This extraordinary project uses a combination of conventional design and cutting-edge computer programmes to create three striking structures that attempt to define movement architecturally.

Shin-Minamata Station

Japan's Shinkansen high speed rail network has gradually expanded since its opening in 1964. It has now reached the southern island of Kyushu, serving the town of Minamata. Watanabe sees the design of the station as the distillation of one frozen moment in the trajectory of an object.

The roof and walls consist of a collection of rectangular pieces, apparently gliding past or into each other. Light deflects off the surfaces in ways that make the facade ripple and move. The design uses trial and error to find the "moment" at which the structure produced the best combination to keep out the rain, while allowing ventilation and confining train noise.

Kashiwanoha-Campus Station

This station takes its form from natural sciences due to its proximity to Tsukuba City's science buildings. Here, the architect united nature and science under the theme of "flow".

Using the regular patterns of stratified flow and irregular forms of turbulent flow, Watanabe developed glass-reinforced concrete sheets with wave-like surfaces. The peripheries of the screens are handled as if cut away – seemingly they would continue to expand if not trimmed to suit the requirements.

In reality, cost constraints limited the number of moulds made and so recursive shapes were designed that could be connected when reversed to provide adequate variation.

Kashiwa-Tanaka Station

The third design recalls the flow of the Tonegawa river. The station has three levels – a ground level concourse, a pedestrian deck, and the platforms above. The upper level is made up of a series of surfaces, some of which fold down to enclose part of the concourse. Slits in the surface accentuate movement while disguising rainwater collection gutters.

This vast steel structure has a unique quality of lightness, as do the two preceding stations. Watanabe has achieved a new "moving" aesthetic that assimilates perfectly with the raised rail transportation system.

Kashiwanoha-Campus Station

Kashiwanoha-Campus Station

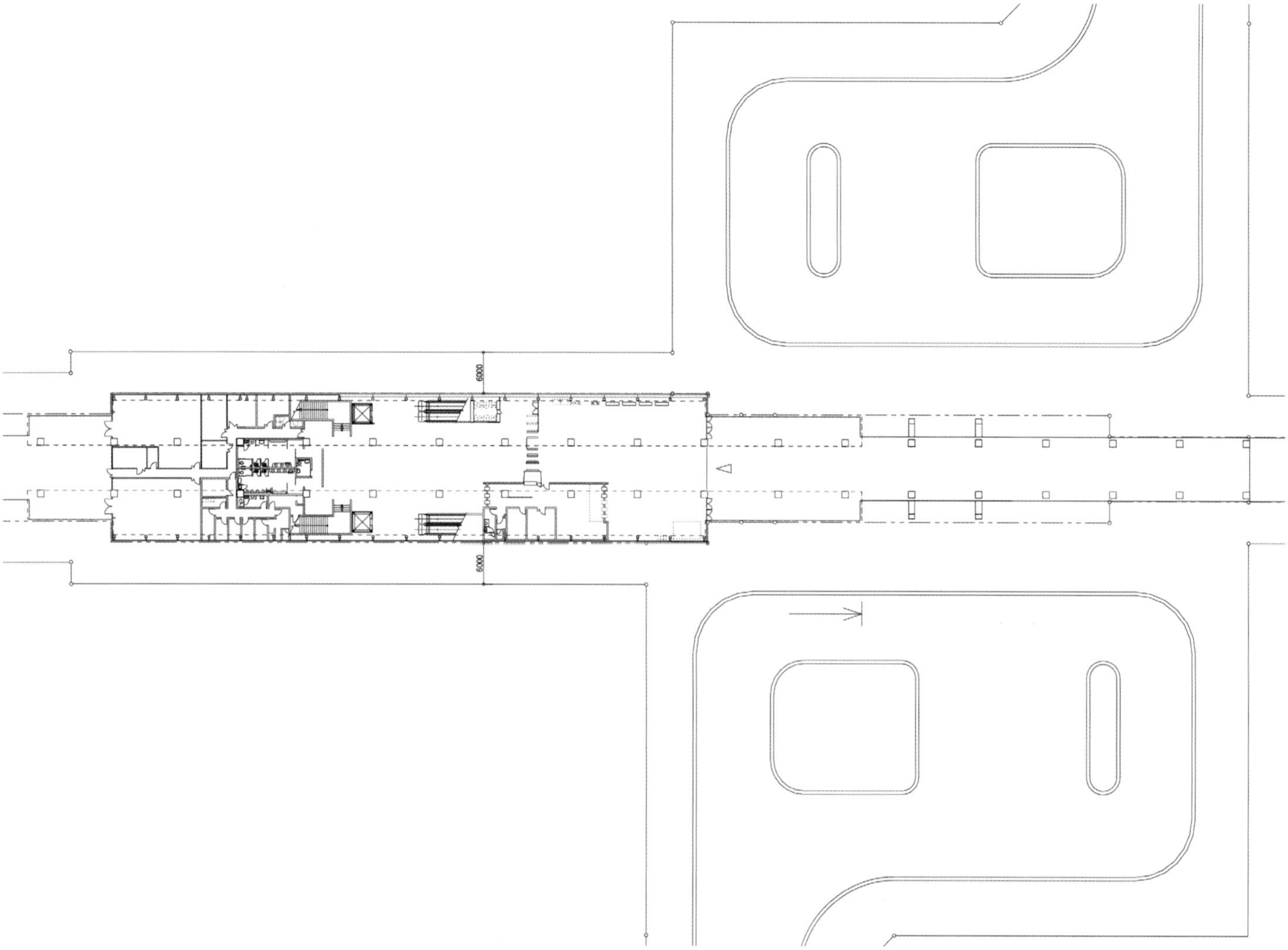

6000

6000

Plan view of site

Interior of facade with slit-like apertures

Waved facade with irregular apertures

The dramatic contrast of this station to its semi-rural surroundings is a testament to the architect's willingness to experiment and surprise. The irregular apertures in the facade accentuate horizontal movement, along with the wave form that almost begs to be continued the entire length of the track. Standing as a stark white block – but a block that seems to be speeding past at 100 miles per hour – the station design makes a place out of an otherwise purely functional train stop.

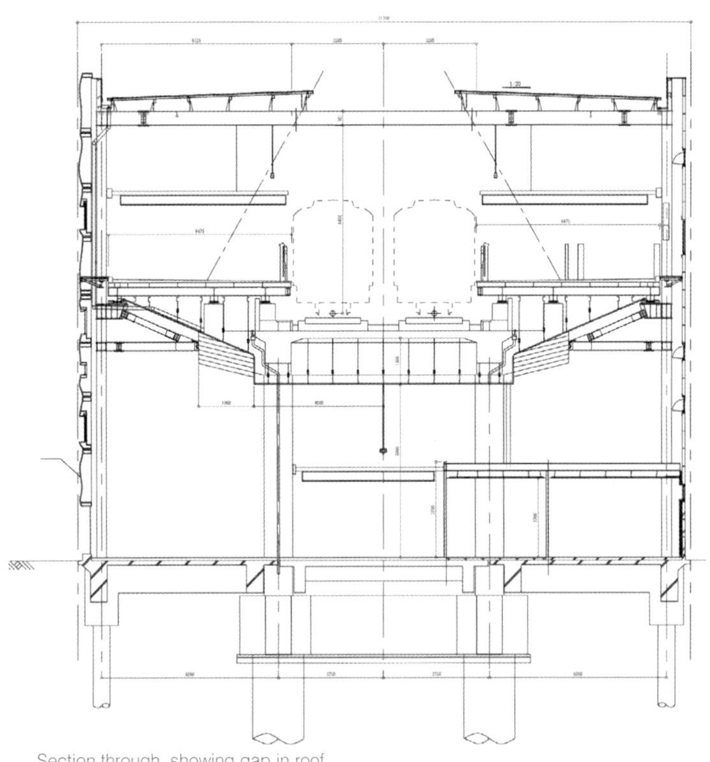

Section through, showing gap in roof

Shin-Minamata Station

Side elevation detailing facade

Injecting movement into a static object such as a station is a very difficult prospect. Here, at Shin-Minamata Station, the architect has opted to utilize thin planks and the space between them to present floating, immaterial aesthetic. Viewed from the exterior, one half of the facade seems to be emerging from the other, as if extending and moving off along the track. This technique could be replicated to further extend the station coverage and create an even greater sense of movement.

Internally, the façade allows in ample light

Visualization of the facade concept

Fixtures for the curved facade elements

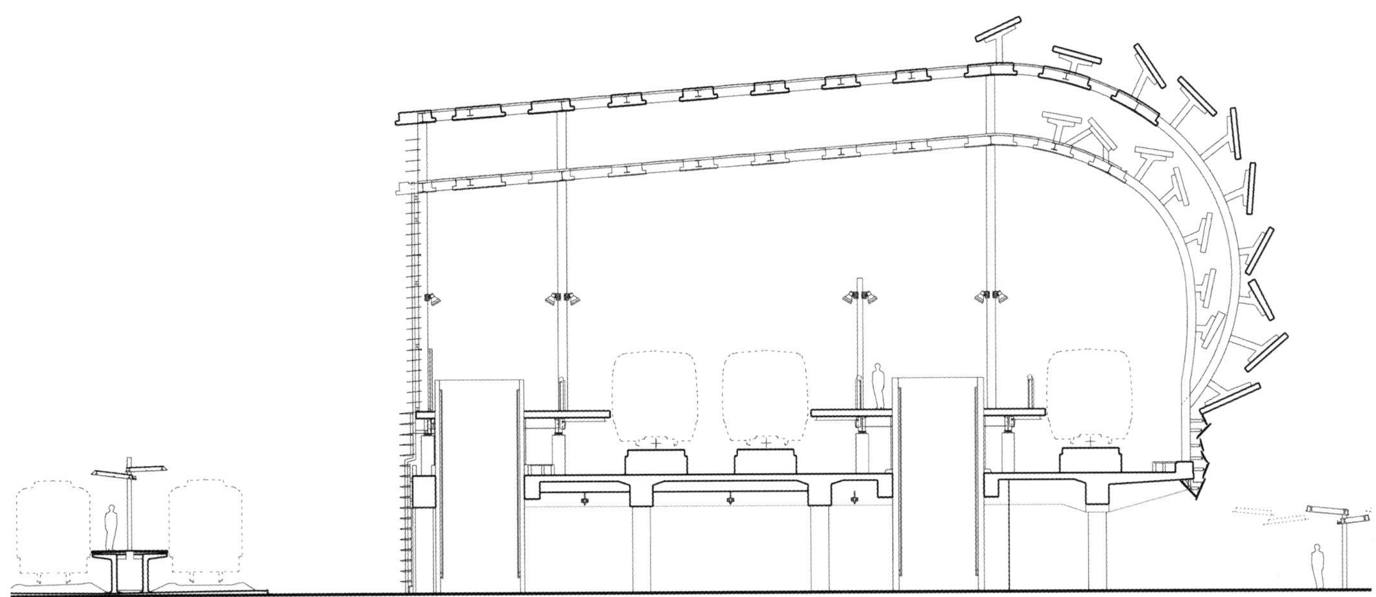

Section through showing facade positioning

Visualization emphasizing the drama of the design

Kashiwa-Tanaka Station

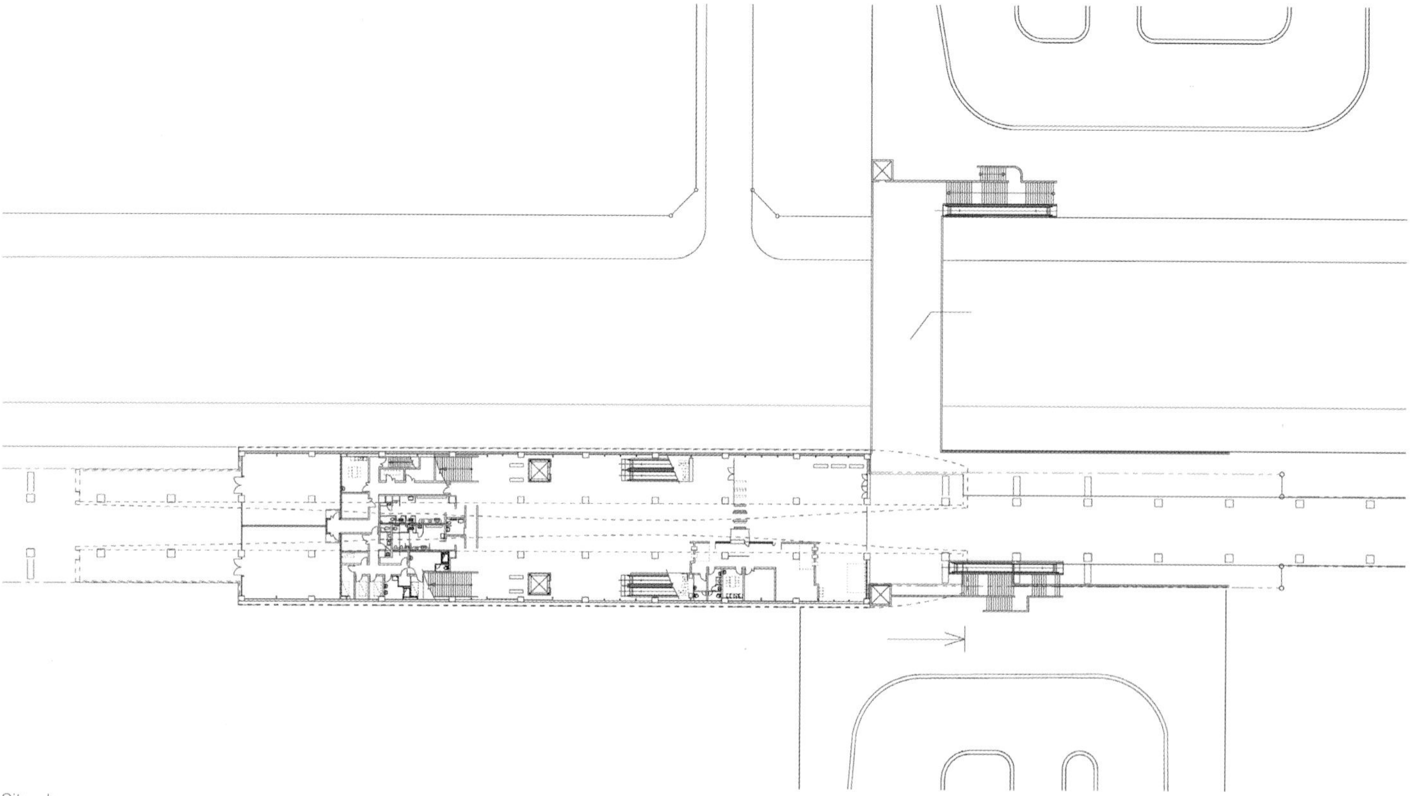

Site plan

The station hugs the track, similarly to a train

Elevation showing scale and height

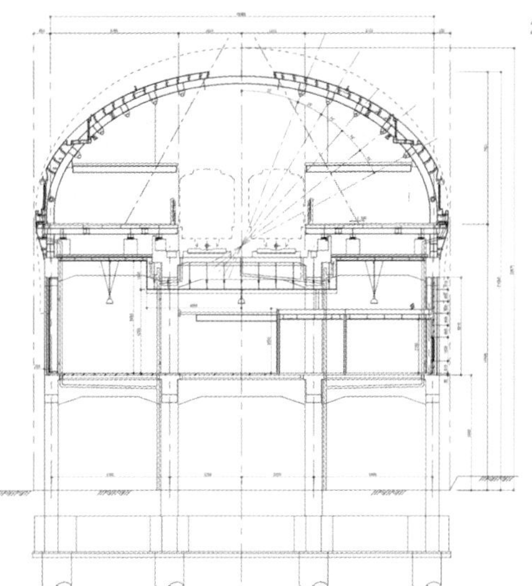

Section through with train positions marked

The reinforced concrete columns that support the tracks directly beneath Kashiwa-Tanaka Station are to be infilled with public facilities eventually. However, the simple albeit unusual design of the station itself, encased within its own pod, enables it to operate independently of works below. Eventually, a new plaza, to complement a planned agricultural park, and café will sit below the station.

Moscow City Transport Terminal

DESIGN BEHNISCH ARCHITEKTEN
LOCATION MOSCOW, RUSSIA

Commissioned to produce concept design proposals for a major new transport interchange with associated commercial development in Moscow, Behnisch Architekten has proposed a massive multi-storey scheme covering over 100 hectares (247 acres). The transport terminal is designed to provide efficient connections between the underground services of both the Moscow Metro and new Mini-Metro, linking them with public bus and tram services and the above ground high speed regional rail systems. Additionally, park and ride facilities and hire car franchises are also catered for.

With this array of transportation types, the scheme is of the scale and sophistication of the "landside" of many international airports – hire agencies, ticketing, check-in, baggage handling, lounges, catering facilities, and retail units all feature. However, the transport terminal itself is of a modest size compared to neighbouring buildings in the new Moscow City Development area that stretches out around the scheme. With this in mind, the architect has sought to provide the building with a sculptural identity with the addition of two distinctive skyscrapers. These will house headquarters for foreign businesses and the future home of Moscow's City Government, as well as serviced apartments, a fitness club, hotel, and host of retail and entertainment facilities.

Throughout the scheme, passive sustainable design and environmentally friendly development has been carefully considered. The main transport hall, which rises to a magnificent 50 metres (164 feet) in places, will be well lit with natural light even though it is below ground. Large funnels will direct light down and assist with ventilation and smoke exhaust. Externally, the orientation of the scheme means that the main office tower will shelter the site from the north, while southerly aspects will be opened up to take advantage of the sun's path. Road noise is masked by a double facade construction that incorporates sun shading. Ventilation will be naturally controlled and cooling to many parts of the building will be facilitated via a geothermal system, pumping water through the structure that has been cooled using ground or river water.

This monumental project stands as an example of intuitive and exciting development in a city that has for so long been neglected by innovative architects. Perhaps during the next few decades Moscow will be set on a path to become the truly modern metropolis that Russia deserves.

The interior, revealing retail and lower entrances to the interchange

REZEPTION
CINEM
Samsonite
DEPART
SIXT

Moscow City Development, with the transport terminal buildings in blue

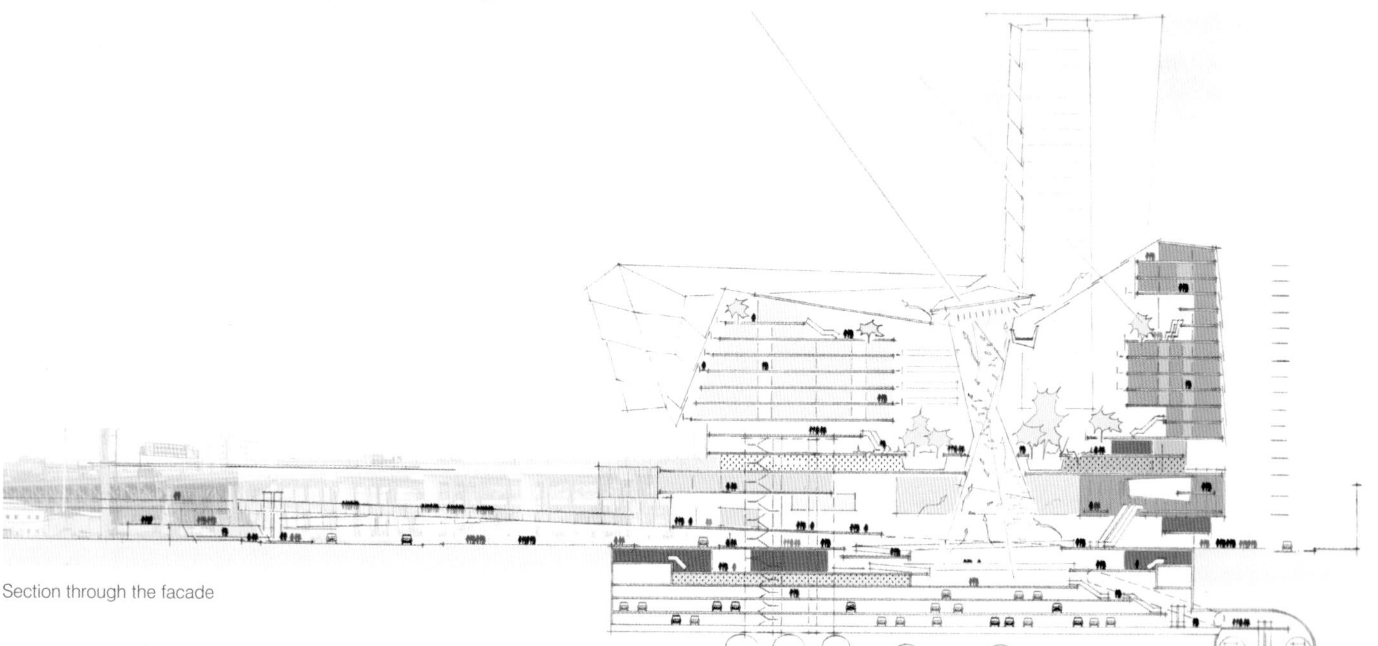

Section through the facade

Dwarfed by the Moscow City Development, the transport terminal and associated buildings is still a large undertaking. On the section shown to the left, underground train tunnels and taxi ranks can be seen to the right, while buses and overground trains enter from the left into the development. Above the transport terminal, light pours into the depths of the buildings via a large atrium that promotes reflected light. Parking is arranged on the lowest floors.

Model of the office towers

Aerial view of the office tower model

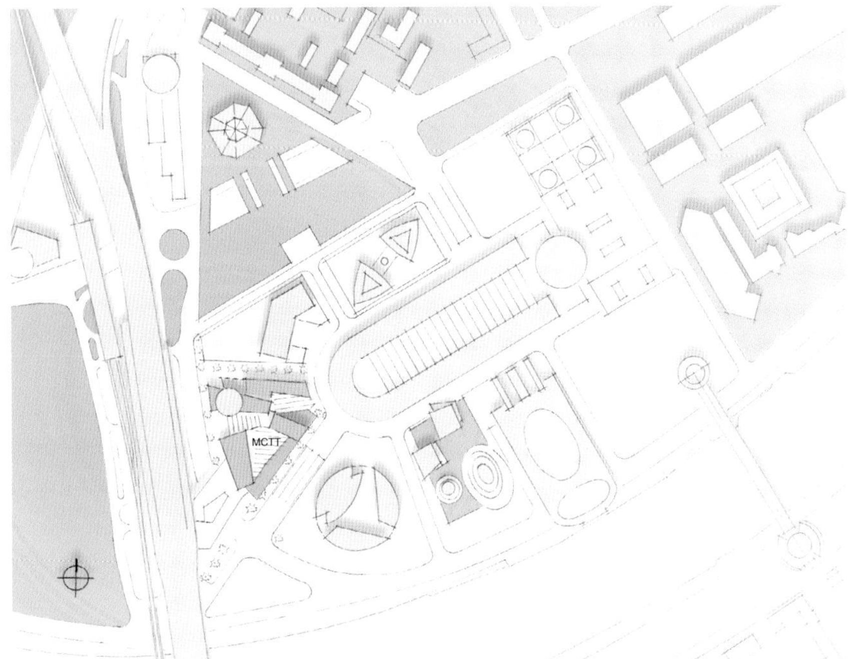

Masterplan of the Moscow City Development with terminal (MCTT)

King's Cross Station

DESIGN JOHN MCASLAN + PARTNERS
LOCATION LONDON, UK

Visualization of the refurbished station with new semi-circular western concourse

King's Cross is one of London's landmark stations, built as the city expanded in the mid-nineteenth century. Completed in 1852 by Lewis Cubitt, the design marked a departure from the decorated styles of the time, which can be seen in the adjacent Gothic Revival Great Northern Hotel at St Pancras Station, towards a more functional architecture. It is now one of Europe's busiest transport interchanges, processing an average of 50 million passengers annually through its mainline, Thameslink and Underground stations.

John McAslan + Partners was commissioned in 1998 to prepare a masterplan for the station and its surroundings. Passenger facilities at King's Cross have long been inadequate – ticket offices and shops are housed in a poor quality 1970s extension, and the surrounding area is run down and neglected. The project is due for completion in 2009, when the underground station directly below King's Cross will also have been completely refurbished and a new Channel Tunnel Rail Link arrives at the neighbouring St Pancras Station.

The aim of McAslan's scheme is to integrate King's Cross and St Pancras stations more effectively by creating a dynamic public realm. The key to the project is the removal of the 1970s extension and its replacement with a new western concourse featuring a dramatic glazed diagrid roof. This addition faces St Pancras Station and houses a new ticket hall and waiting area, which sits directly over the new underground ticketing hall. Its striking sculptural glazed structure will integrate neatly with the arched roof of the original station buildings and, in addition to a ticket hall, will feature passenger lounges, retail and catering units and escalators to the underground station.

When the 1970s southern concourse is removed, the great arched frontage of the 1852 station will be revealed again, announcing the station as the landmark that it once was. The area in front of it will be landscaped as a new public square. All the original train sheds will be extensively refurbished to present a new point of contrast to the refurbished Great Northern Hotel that sits above St Pancras Station.

The new station and its surroundings will create a vibrant multi-modal transport interchange for the King's Cross area. The £275 million project is the main driver for the regeneration of the entire area, from what was a seedy, deprived district into a new business, retail and leisure quarter and, via the Channel Tunnel Rail Link, high speed gateway to Europe.

 The revitalization of the station is long overdue. As one of the capital's busiest transport hubs, King's Cross' current arrivals and departures hall is a poor reflection of the grand rail infrastructure serving the city. The architect's new proposals will bring the station up to date, while also revealing the original historic building and creating a far enhanced public realm to the station front.

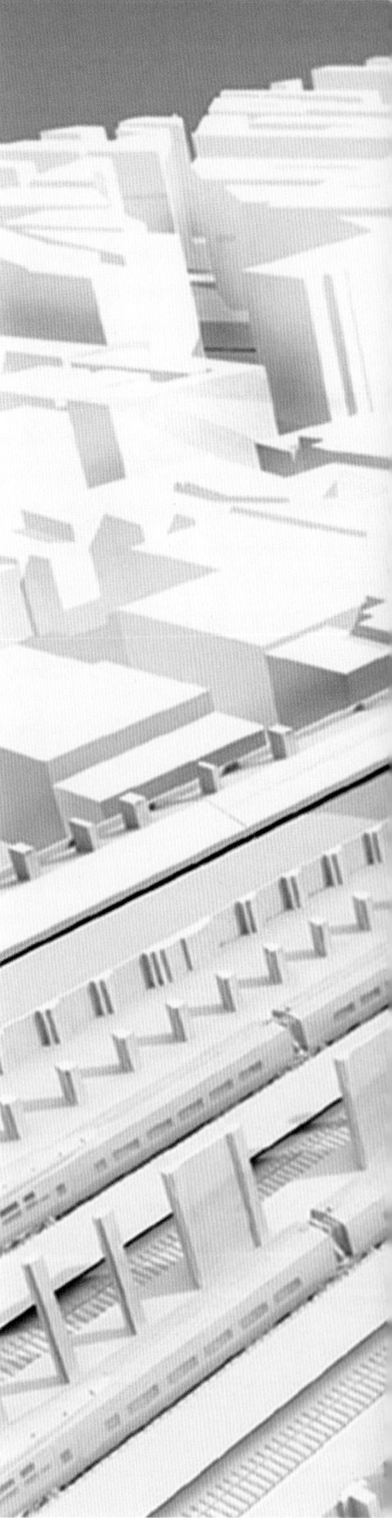

King's Cross and concourse between it and St Pancras Station

Cut-away of new concourse and tracks

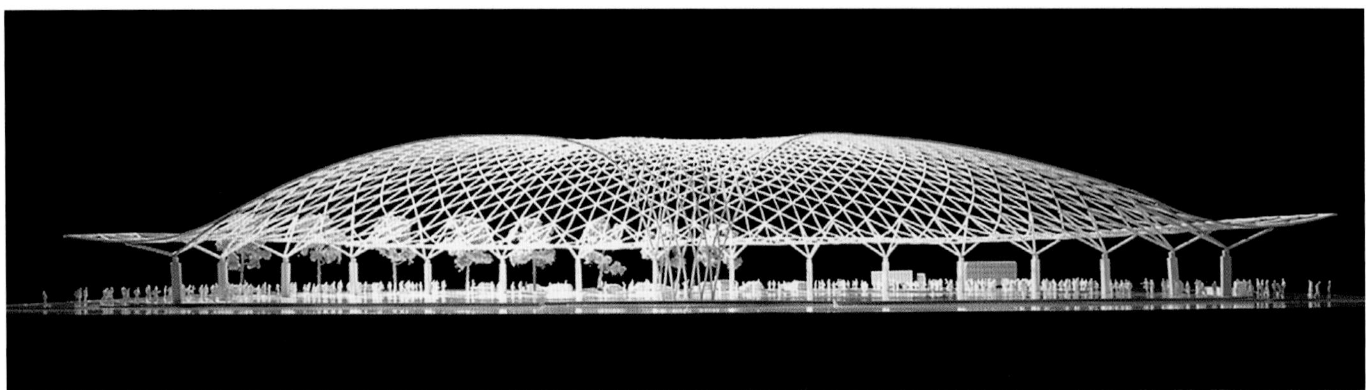

Model of the diagrid roof

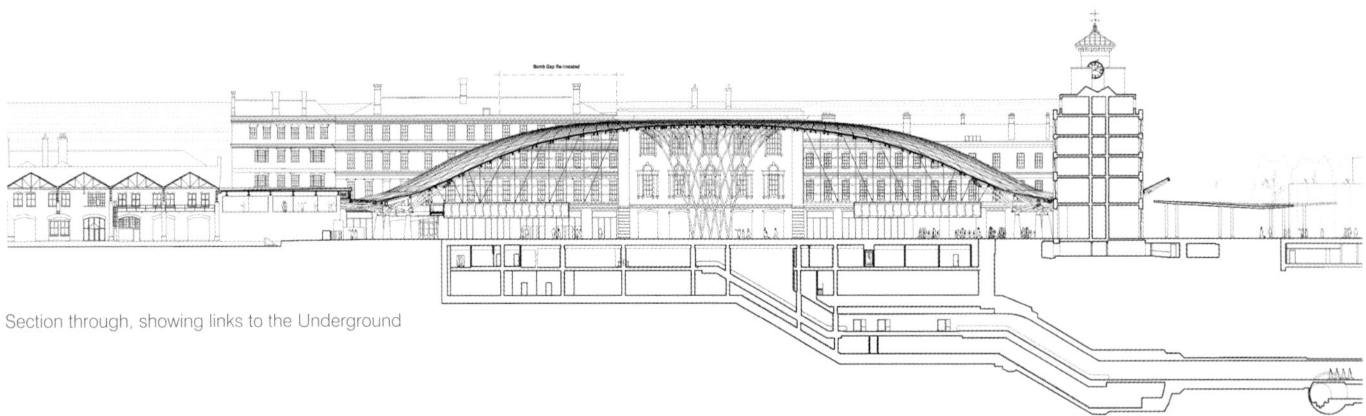

Section through, showing links to the Underground

McAslan's use of new architectural forms and techniques could have been offensive but instead they dovetail well with the historic elements of the station building. Clever interventions such as the grey colouring of the roof "tiles" on the western concourse, mirror those of the adjacent St Pancras train shed, while the visually impressive diagrid structure presents a new excitement to the station's architecture.

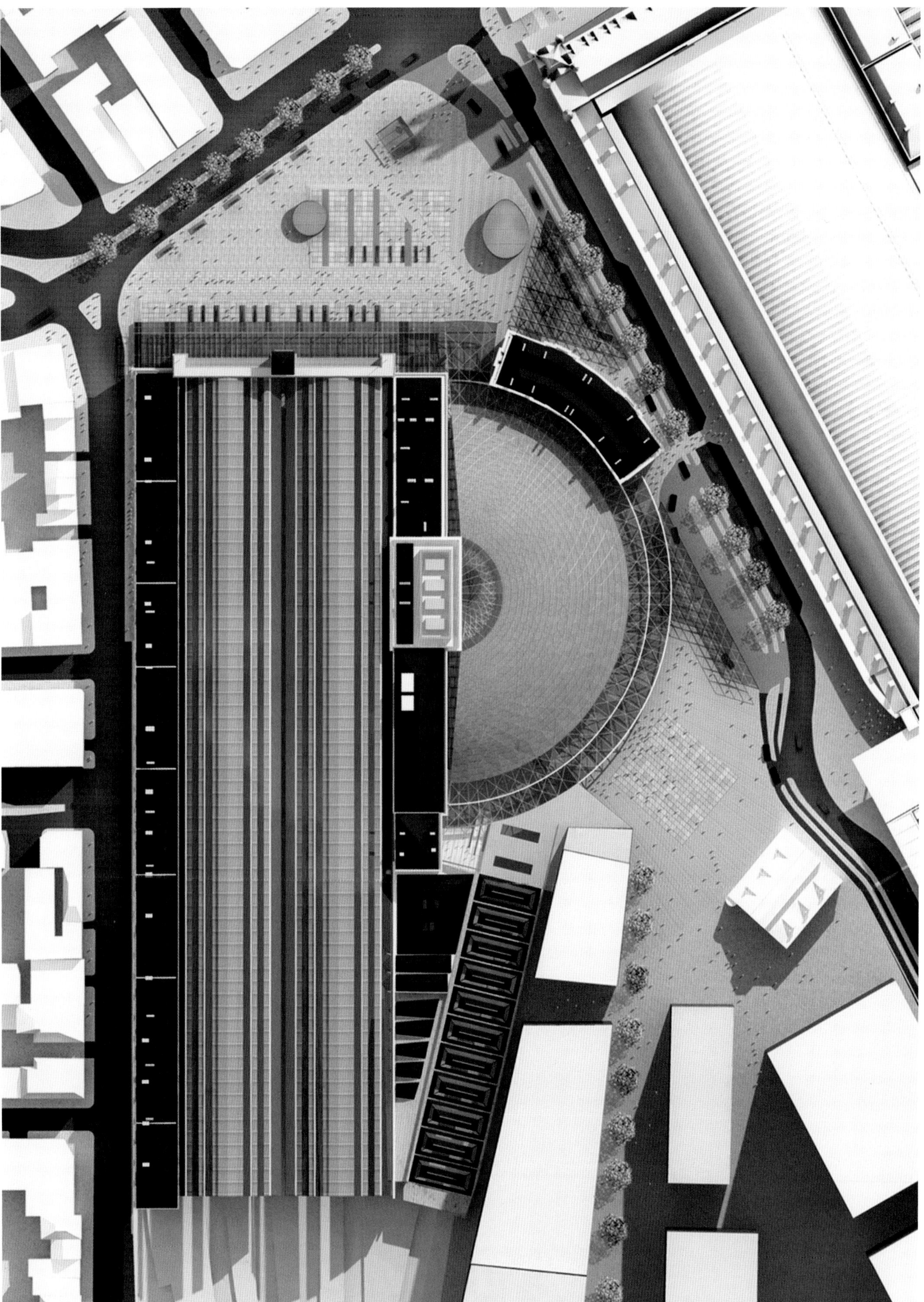

Plan view of the station

Interior of the western concourse

The monumental brick facade of the original station building is contrasted by the lightness of the new diagrid structure. A dramatic arrivals and departure space is created, far exceeding the current adhoc amenities in both grandeur and facilities. Here, travellers will also be able to access the underground via escalators, as well board overland trains within the main building through arches punched into the brick facade.

Leuven Train Station

DESIGN SAMYN AND PARTNERS
LOCATION LEUVEN, BELGIUM

The historic railway station at Leuven has been upgraded with the addition of a deftly designed hump-backed canopy that shrouds the multi-track platforms offering shelter from the elements. Designed by Belgian practice Samyn and Partners, the project was won in limited competition against the likes of Richard Rogers Partnership, Santiago Calatrava and Nicholas Grimshaw. It sees the tracks enveloped by the curvaceous steel and aluminium structure, punctuated by lift shaft lanterns.

This dramatic canopy also seeks to bring together two disjointed parts of the town situated on opposite sides of the tracks. It does this both symbolically and physically by bridging the train tracks that cut through the community and by providing an elevated covered pedestrian and cycle way and an underpass. Respecting the relationship with the surrounding urban environment, Samyn and Partners has created a low, track hugging design that does not present an overbearing presence to either the existing station or other buildings nearby. It is only when under the canopy that passengers will really appreciate the scale of the project.

The steel structure of the canopy rests on 25 tubular steel piles and an array of steel columns in groups of three or four depending upon the symmetry of forces. These columns also support the high voltage cables for the electrically powered locomotives. Springing from the piles, the primary structure of the canopy consists of twenty longitudinal parabolic twin steel arches. Lateral forces are transferred transversally by regularly spaced tie beams. Preformed steel decking, spanning between the arches, supports an insulation layer which is pressed between it and the aluminium roof cladding.

The roof cladding does not completely cover the station platforms. Between each longitudinal vault is a lens-shaped opening that allows in abundant natural light and encourages natural ventilation. Below this is a glass ceiling protecting passengers from the elements. The vault also helps to encase the noise of the locomotives within the confines of the station, minimizing disturbance to the surrounding area.

Spanning the platforms is the large pedestrian and cycle bridge. Split into two lanes, the timber-surfaced crossing is designed to be used not just by passengers but as a link between inner city Leuven and the suburb of Kessel-Lo. It provides a new, safe and convenient method of crossing the busy tracks, so uniting the disparate halves of the town.

A new canopy for an historic station

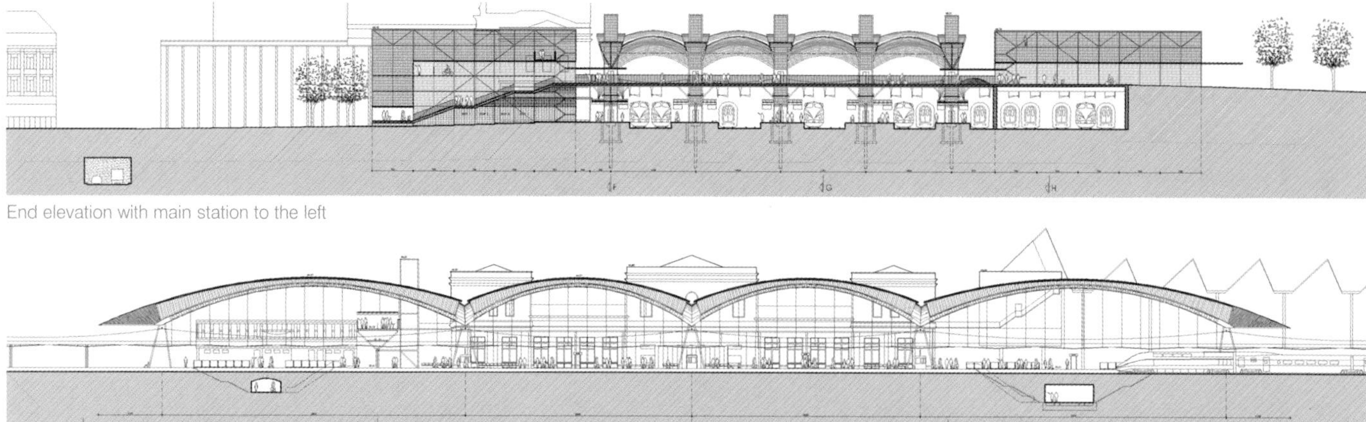

End elevation with main station to the left

Side elevation

One canopy spans each track

The intricacy of the canopy design sits well within the busy station environment. Cables and multi-legged columns intermingle with electrical power cables and stanchions. The design shelters the platforms while still allowing natural light and ventilation to filter through to ground level. Ultimately, it is an aesthetically pleasing addition to the station that combines functionality with architectural acumen.

Detail at a column apex

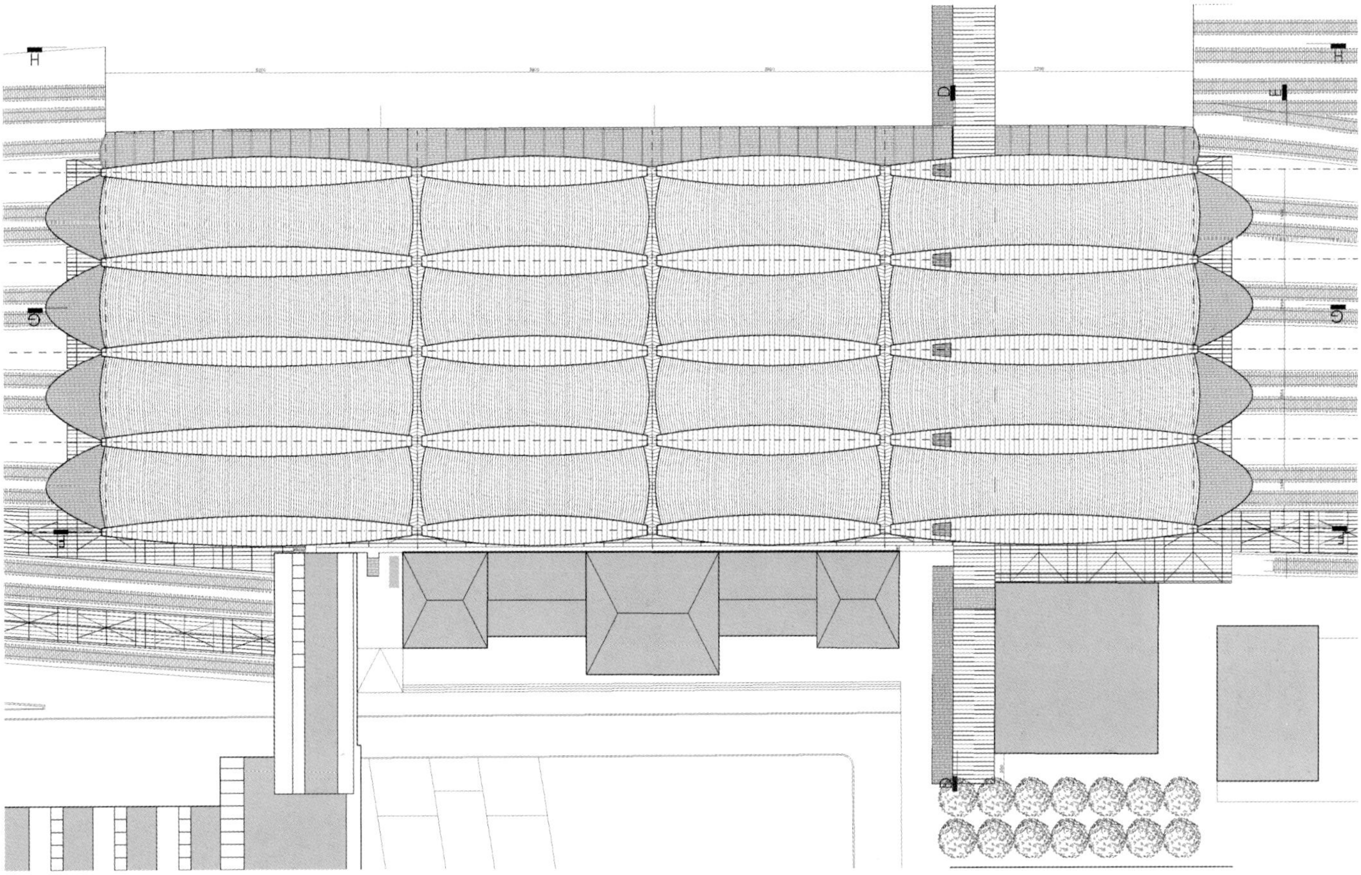

Plan view of the station

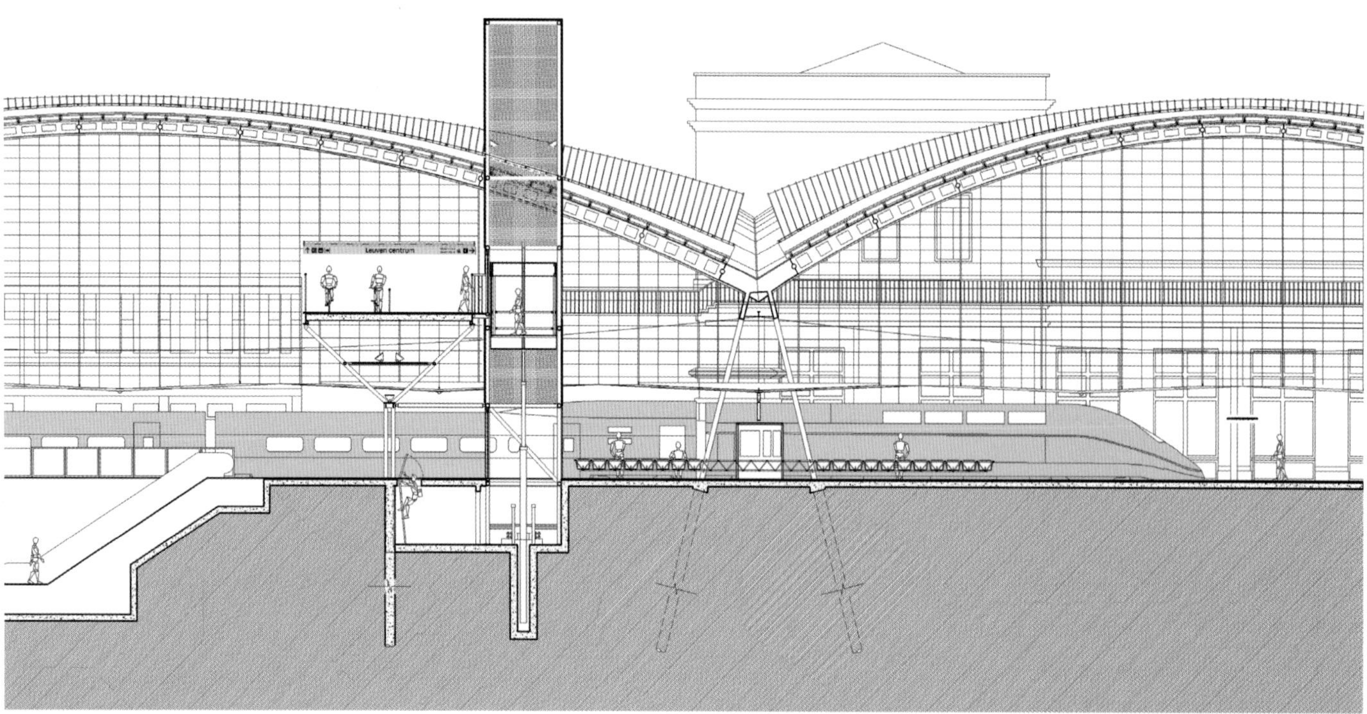

Sectional view showing the lifts and bridge

Computer rendering showing a lift and the bridge

The lightness in the way that the structure touches the ground is accentuated by the canopies which seem to be trying to lift off like "sheets in the wind". This delicacy is carried through to the pedestrian and cycle bridge that traverses the tracks, linking the two halves of the town. Its slender structure and glazed balustrades render it almost invisible against the backdrop of the canopy roofs and light wells. Other prominent features of the design include the large lanterns that penetrate the canopy roof. These are in fact glazed lift shafts that draw light down below the canopy as well as providing mid-platform access to the footbridge.

Canopy end cap with bridge in the background

View of the canopies under construction

Stuttgart Central Station

DESIGN INGENHOVEN ARCHITEKTEN
LOCATION STUTTGART, GERMANY

The "mega-project" to transform Stuttgart Station and a vast swathe of rail yards surrounding it has been rumbling along since 1994. This relatively sedate pace is, however, moving towards producing one of the most environmentally friendly rail transport hubs yet seen.

The reorganization of the original 1928 rail terminus by Paul Bonatz, from an end-of-the-line stop into a 21st century transport hub, involves moving all of the tracks some 12 metres (39 feet) underground and turning the platforms 90 degrees from their original orientation. This new subterranean station layout sits below a serene lawned park that becomes an extension to the Schlossgarten (castle garden) that has long been the "green heart" of Stuttgart.

The roof of the station has been designed by Ingenhoven Architekten, in collaboration with Frei Otto and Buro Happold. It is a vaulted concrete shell pierced by what the designers call "light eyes", protruding up into the new park. These elegant features allow both light and ventilation down into the station. The clever design sees them morph from delicate shell-like structures on the surface into load bearing columns below.

The illumination and ventilation that the light eyes offer is part of Ingenhoven's wider plan to make the station a zero-energy building, in which no heating, cooling, or mechanical ventilation will be used. This can be achieved due to the average year-round air temperature in the underground train tunnels. Remaining at a relatively constant 10 degrees Celsius, the tunnels and platform will experience only minor fluctuations in temperature. To combat any temperature changes in summer, air will flow from the tunnels to the platforms; while in winter the flow is reversed.

Heat build-up is further counteracted by convection, allowing hot air to escape through the grills in the light eyes which is accentuated by the Venturi effect of wind travelling over the roof. In winter, the surrounding mass will keep platform temperatures stable, as it does in the tunnels. Ingenhoven says: "Ecology, economy and technology are as much part of the new Central Station as are comfort and security."

The existing stone station from the 1920s is to be converted into a public meeting place with restaurants and shops, as well as continuing to serve as the station landmark. Within it, links will be made to the new station via large curved glass atria, which will signal the transition from old to new.

The overground park and "light eyes"

Section through the entrance canopy

Platform level view of columns and "light eyes"

Section showing underground platforms

Ground level plan showing entrances and light eyes

This delightful solution to achieving a city centre train terminal and formal park simultaneously provcs that both will benefit from intelligent architectural design. The station, whilst underground, will be well lit using daylight. The green space above is large enough to be enjoyed and aesthetically unusual due to the protruding sky lights and domed glazed entrances. The development links existing buildings on either side well: the absolute opposite of what would have happened if mainline tracks had been laid at ground level.

Worb Train Shed

DESIGN SMARCH
LOCATION WORB, SWITZERLAND

Winners of an architectural competition held by the Swiss Railway, Smarch, a firm set up by Beat Mathys and Ursula Stücheli, has created this exquisite "woven" structure, which is utilized simply as a train shed and carpark. Accommodating two trains, with space for 80 cars, as well as bicycle parking above, the building adds a new dimension to the rail station and creates a shimmering stainless steel addition to the small town of Worb, near Bern.

In essence, the building is a series of concrete columns that support a reinforced concrete slab for car parking. It is crowned with a shallow pitched steel and timber roof. The site is extremely constricted and curves in relation to the slow bend of the railway track.

Excitement is added by the building's "woven" facade, which is seen by some architectural commentators as a reinterpretation of Gottfried Semper's 19th century *Bekleidungstheorie*. This claimed that the archetypal patterns of wall coverings were derived originally from woven textiles, which human civilization had developed long before timber-framed and woven structures. The theory allowed Semper the license to persuade clients to incorporate intricate ornamentation into his building facades.

Smarch has taken this not altogether scientific theory and created a building that Semper would have been proud of. Polished stainless steel loops are placed around cylindrical concrete columns, spaced only three metres (10 feet) apart to produce a strong and yet aesthetically light structure.

One strip was installed each day and tightened into position around the concrete columns. In alternate spaces between the columns, the loops were clamped together to produce the undulation that creates the feeling that the building has been woven out of some giant space-age yarn.

The clamped stainless steel ribbons add rigidity and strength to the structure and produce a mesmerizing effect as light catches the polished surfaces. This in turn reduces the impact of the large building as it penetrates the town at close quarters with neighbouring buildings. This purely functional train shed could have been an unwelcome new eyesore for the small Swiss town. However, it is, in reality, a striking addition to Worb, and, one that makes arriving and departing seem like a mini adventure into a different otherworldly landscape.

A vision of speed caught in an instant

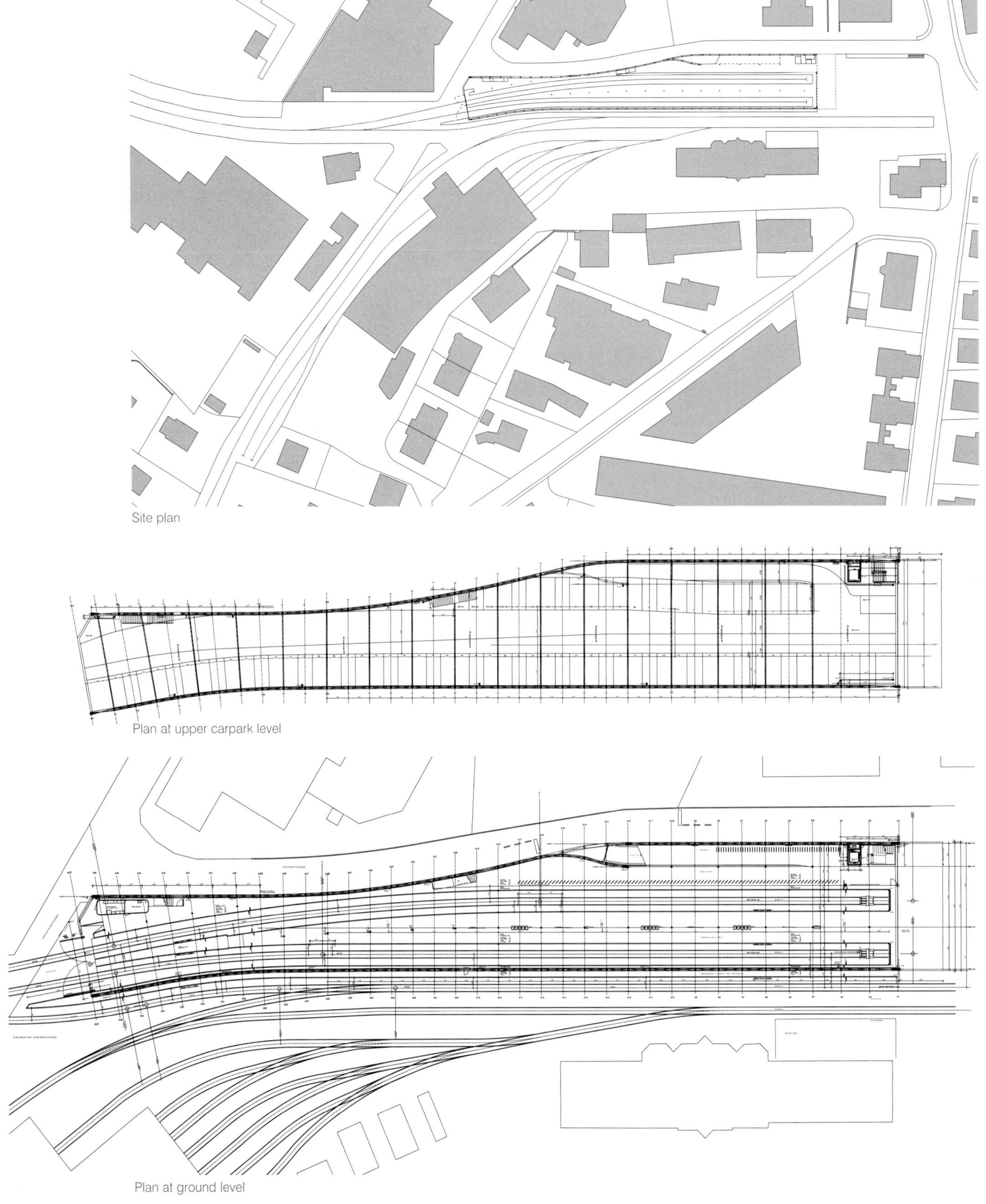

Site plan

Plan at upper carpark level

Plan at ground level

View of the locomotive entrance

The train shed at Worb is a wonderfully exciting piece of architectural design. It performs the dual function of covered carpark and locomotive stand-point and platform perfectly. Not an ounce of space has been wasted in the pursuit of aesthetic quality, and visitors can only be impressed by the building's straightforward appeal.

View of the platforms with the lluminated interior

Internally, the real and perceived weight of the concrete ceiling and carpark floor slab is offset by the transparency of the woven steel walls. Even though heavy concrete columns support the structure, they are lost in the delicate lines of the stainless steel facade. Artificial lighting adds an ethereal ambience to the space that features clean lines and considered solutions.

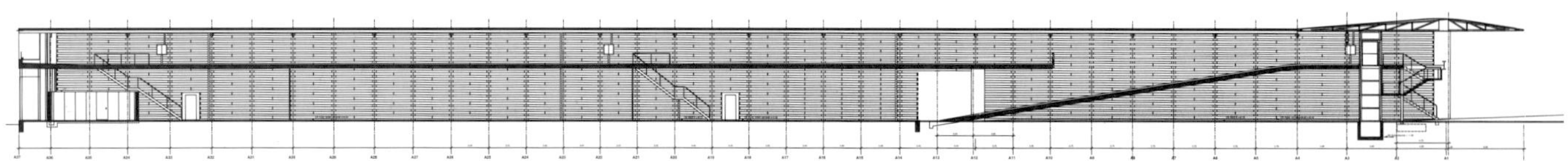

Side elevation

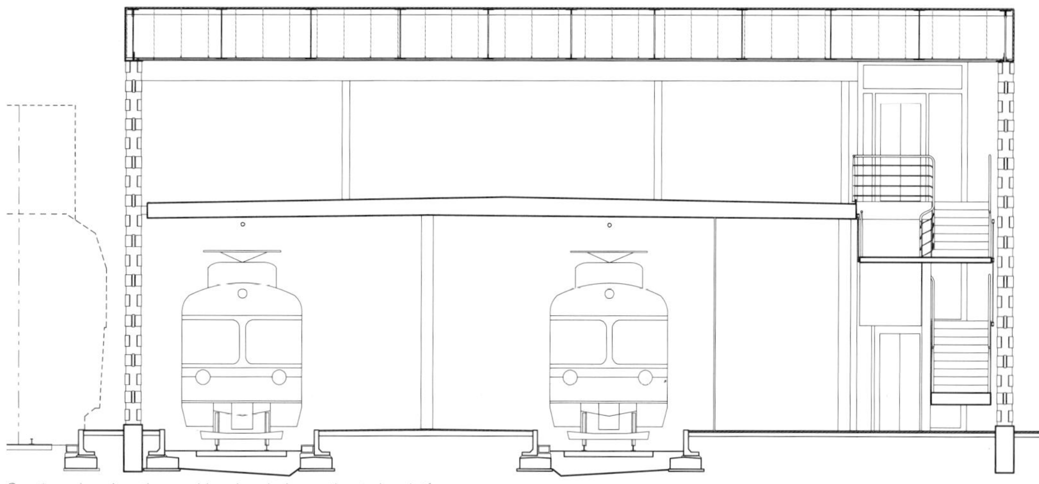

Section showing the parking level above the train platforms

Facade detail at column

While the stainless steel facade looks like it is woven around the concrete columns, on closer inspection the bands are simply clamped at the mid point between each column, creating an undulating effect. The waves of stainless steel banding combine perfectly with the slow curve of the building to enhance the sense of movement in the facade, the overall effect being inspiring whilst alluding to the nature of the shed's primary use.

Facade detail at band overlap

The simple beauty of the steel weaving

Central Station

DESIGN BRT ARCHITEKTEN
LOCATION DORTMUND, GERMANY

The regeneration and new building for Dortmund's main railway station was awarded to Hamburg-based architect, Bothe Richter Teherani (BRT) following an open competition. The practice's distinctive design moves away from the traditional rectilinear approach, favouring instead a transport hub, retail, and entertainment centre that is circular in plan.

The reason for this departure is, according to the architect, to better create the multi-theme centre required by the client. BRT's response encompasses three aspects: creating a link from the deprived north of the city to the well frequented retail centre in the south; bringing shopping and cultural destinations into the building; and producing an efficient hub for local, national and international rail services.

The resulting design is an eight-storey building – from entry and retail at street level to a 240 metre (785 foot) diameter "floating nightclub" under the roof canopy. Viewed as an organism by its creators, the semi-transparent apparition sits directly over the rail tracks. Its facade is solid to the north and across most of the roofscape but features large glazed elements on the roof and looking out over the city centre to the south.

Internally, the station is dominated by an entrance hall that rises up through all levels to form a dramatic atrium. This space, directly behind the glazed facade, allows light to flood into the building, illuminating a plethora of shopping, cultural and entertainment establishments. The hall narrows into an elongated lozenge and continues at full height through the centre of the building to link the prosperous south with the less frequented north of the city with a bustling retail promenade.

Entrance to the train platforms is on level two, where column-free construction and curvaceous ceilings bring pace and glamour to the travel experience. Beneath this, on level one, is a taxi rank and loading for the retail and entertainment outlets on levels three to eight. A large pedestrian ramp pushes out from the glazed southerly elevation to link the building with the city centre and tempt shoppers to venture further north.

Within the heart of this industrial metropolis, Central Station provides a dynamic new destination for both day and night. Its design is unorthodox in form but in keeping with the multi-use requirements of so many public buildings today. The unusual circular form is a symbol of vigorous regeneration and modernity for one of Germany's lesser-known cities.

Space-age transport architecture

DB
BAHNHOF DORTMUND
DB

Aerial view of the hub

Railway stations do not get any more dramatic than this. Dortmund will think that an alien spacecraft has crash landed smack in the middle of it when BRT Architekten's Central Station becomes a reality. The unusual design is all the more amazing as it hovers over multiple rail lines. On an urban regeneration level, the station will connect two disparate parts of the city drawing people from both sides into a common space.

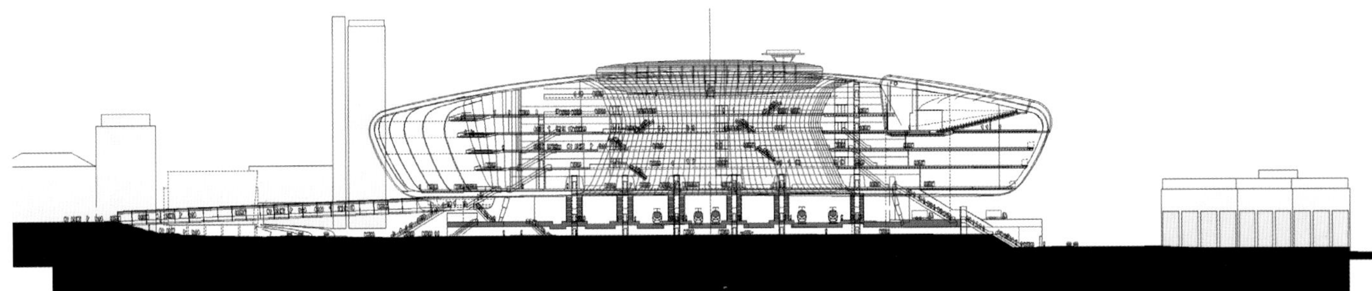

Section showing the central atrium side-on

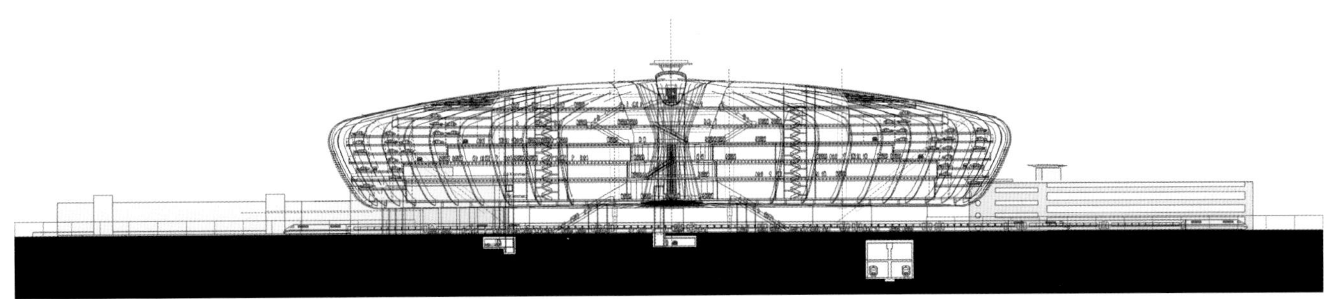

Section showing the end view of atrium

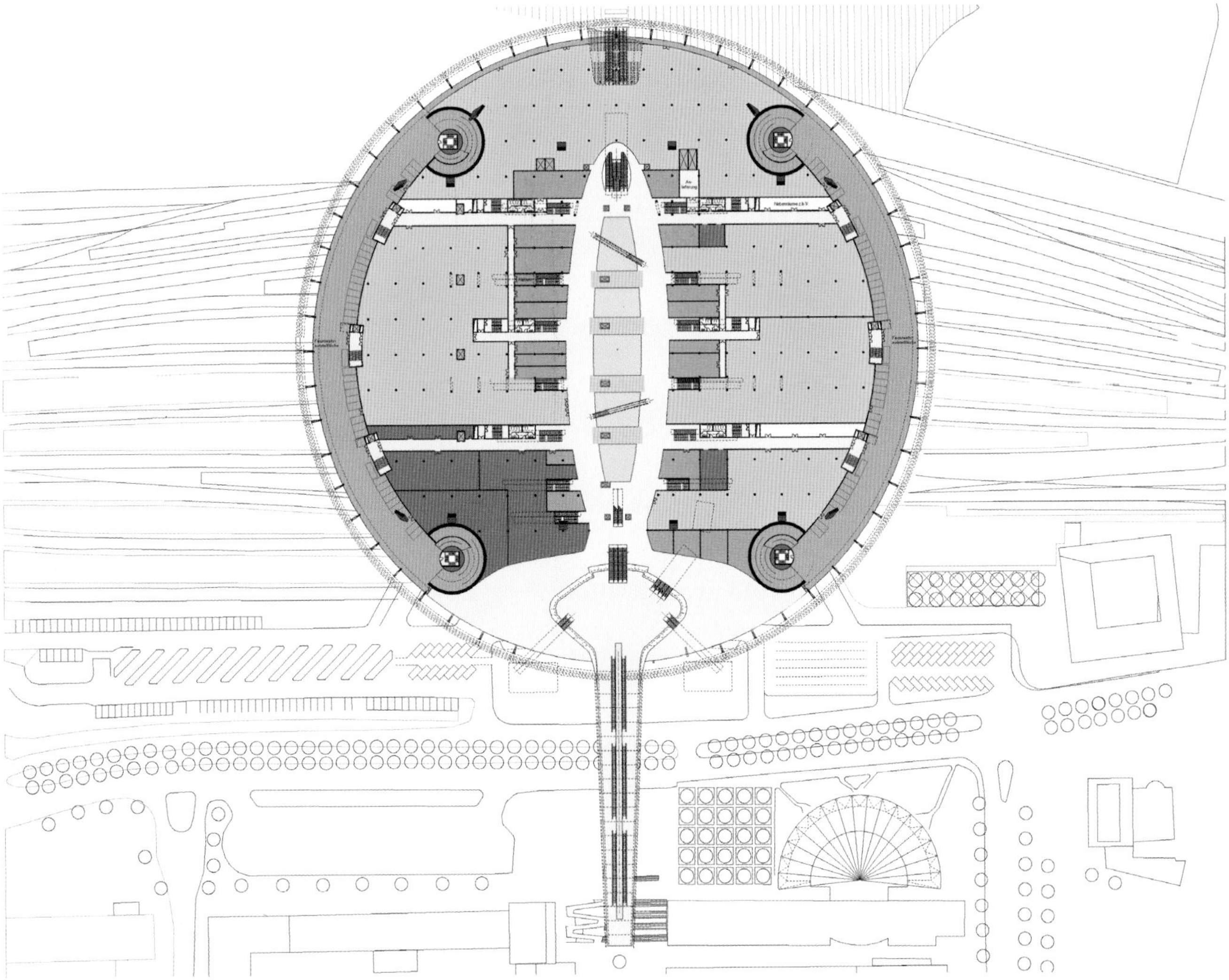

Plan showing the entrance hall and elliptical atrium

Internally, the station is dominated by two vast spaces, the entrance hall and the main atrium. Both rise the full height of the building and are designed to be busy spaces filled with retail outlets, cafés and restaurants. The facade of the entrance hall is fully glazed allowing natural light to flood into the building, even to platform level, where more spacious architectural design presents travellers with a high impact entrance to the city.

View of the large internal entrance hall

View of the enormous central atrium

Fulton Street Transit Center

DESIGN GRIMSHAW
LOCATION NEW YORK, USA

The Fulton Street transit complex is one of the busiest underground interchanges on the New York City subway system, handling up to 275,000 passengers per day. Its six existing stations were built at separate intervals, spanning a 30-year period at the start of the 20th century. There was no official works programme and the lines were operated independently of and in competition with each other, so there was no real incentive to make interconnection easy.

This ad hoc construction has led to the underground stations being connected by a maze of dark narrow corridors, multiple staircases and ramps. Add to this the considerable increase in passenger traffic, and the Fulton Street complex is in dire need of reorganization.

Engineer Arup is the lead consultant on the US $750 million project, which will streamline the existing underground network, providing improved connectivity between the subway lines converging at the Fulton Street corridor. Grimshaw is the architect of the Transit Center hub building located directly above the busiest subway intersection. Featuring a 34 metre (112 feet) high tapered dome, it acts as a beacon to commuters and houses the new entrance to the subway.

Clad in high performance translucent glass, the triangulated steel structure supports a filigree metal inner skin designed in conjunction with artist James Carpenter. This landmark structure funnels daylight deep into the subterranean concourses below street level. Surrounding the dome, a 15 metre (49 feet) high glazed entrance pavilion provides a street frontage onto Fulton Street and Broadway, also housing retail and restaurants.

The Metropolitan Transportation Authority's Environmental Impact Statement identified the need for wide-reaching street and subway pedestrian improvements, including full accessibility for people with disabilities. This called for the rationalizing of surface access points, the new station entrance building, a new pedestrian concourse under Dey Street, linking Fulton Street with the World Trade Center site and additional rationalized connections between the existing underground stations. The project will play a large part in the revitalization of Lower Manhattan as a centre for commercial, residential, and cultural activity.

The eye-catching new subway entrance

LeCirque
Orchid

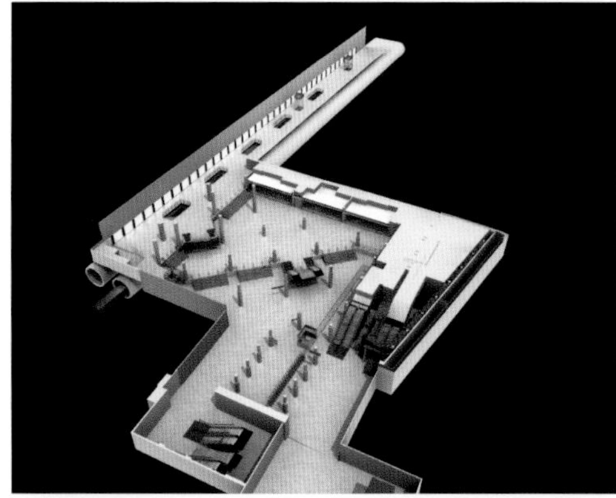

Lower basement level

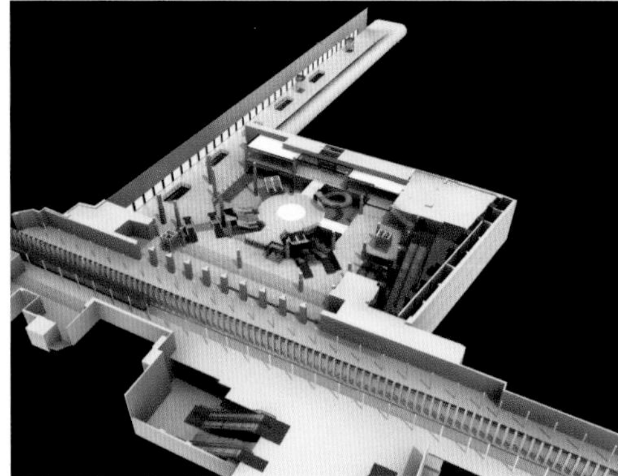

Basement ticketing and access to lower level

Structural cone visualization

The Transit Center has a strong visual presence at street level. Its delicate glazed cone acts both as a marker and light funnel, allowing daylight down through the ground floor and into the subway, via a large circular atrium with multiple escalator access points. Surrounding the cone, another "lightweight" structure, again constructed in glass, contains retail outlets and vendors, thus allowing the lower levels to be focused on transport related activities.

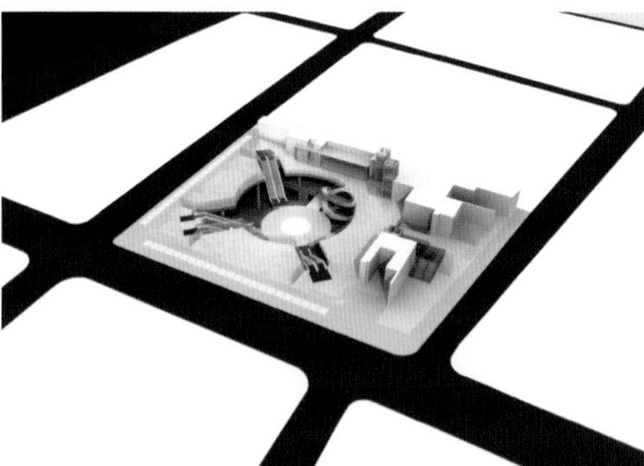

Ground level

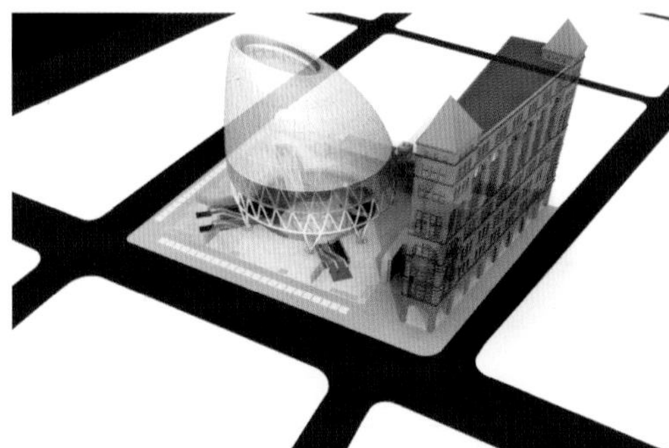

Ground level with cone and Corbin Building

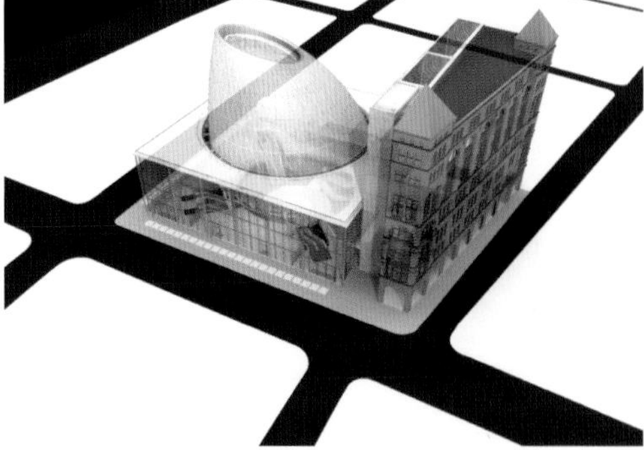

Ground level with glazed facade

Model illustrating the Transit Center and Corbin Building

Scale model of the scheme

Grimshaw's architecture is indicative of the High-tech Movement and it is surprising how well it sits next to historic structures such as the Corbin Building on John Street, one of the city's first skyscrapers (details of which can be seen to the right). Together the buildings present exemplary examples of architecture old and new, while also combining to present multiple entrances to the new transit centre in the heart of New York. In addition to enhancing commuter journeys, the completed Transit Center will also serve many of the expected tourist vistors to the World Trade Center Memorial and other cultural buildings.

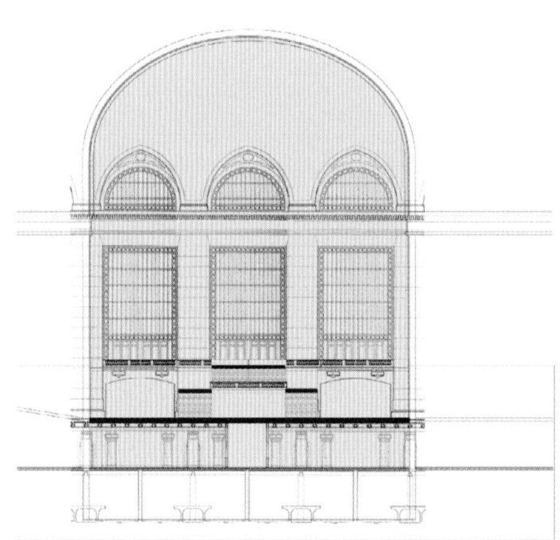

Corbin Building ground level detail

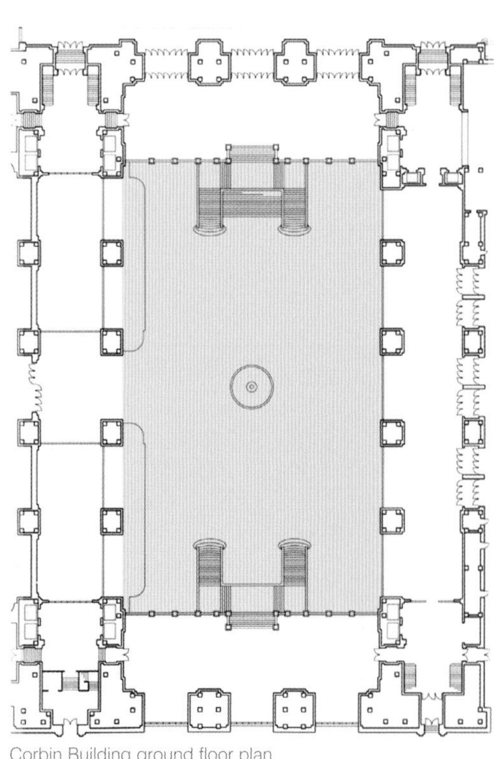

Corbin Building ground floor plan

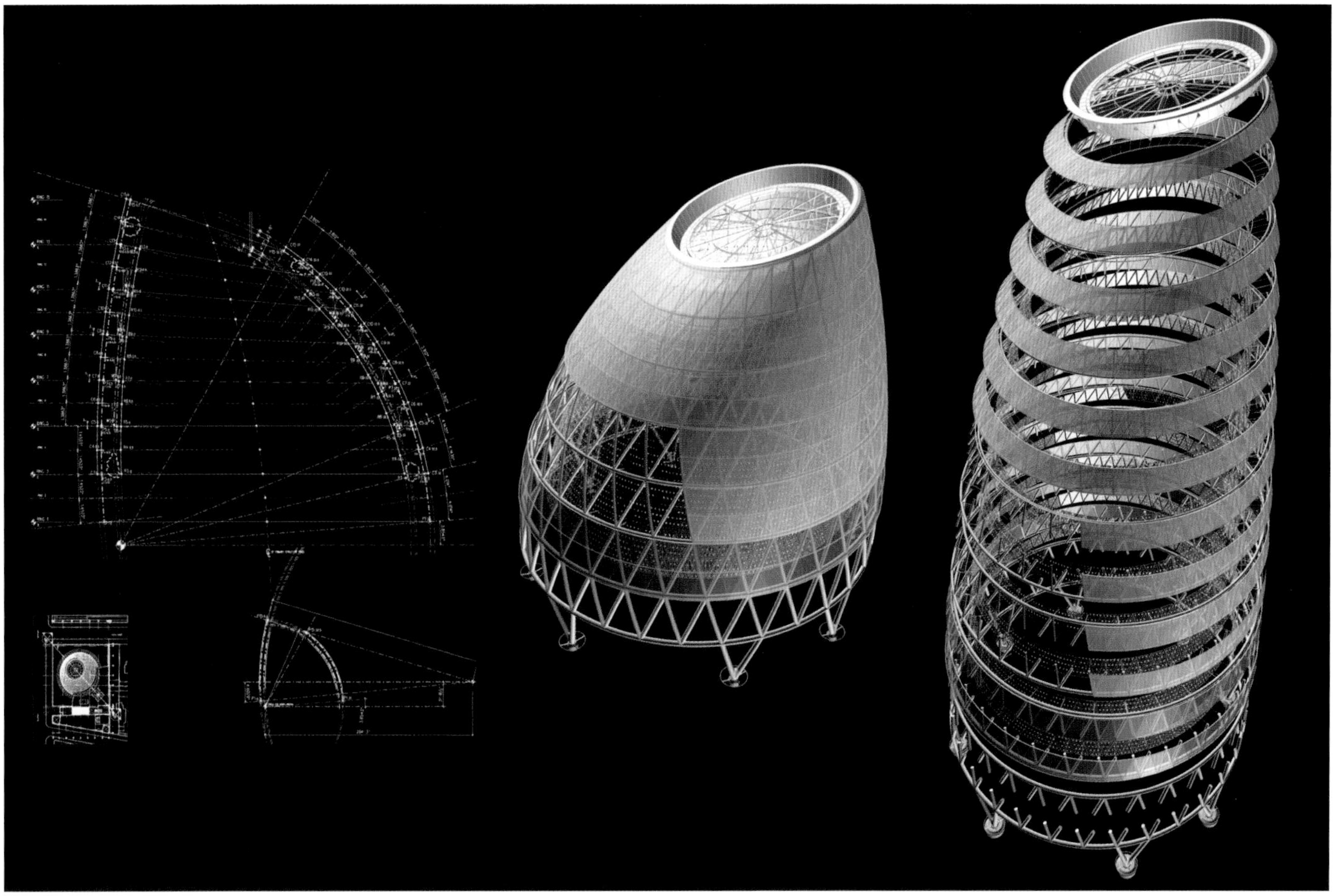

Details of cone design

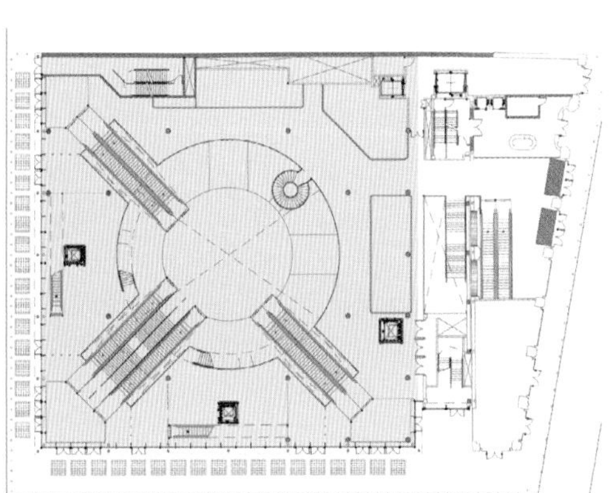

Ground floor plan

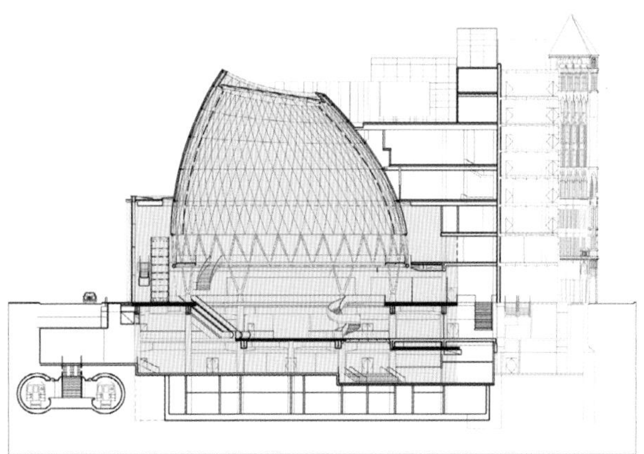

Section through the project

Stratford International Station

DESIGN RAIL LINK ENGINEERING
LOCATION LONDON, UK

International rail stations are common in continental Europe, as many lines cross numerous borders. However in the UK there are only two international rail terminals until now, at Waterloo in London and Ashford in Kent. This is changing rapidly with the arrival of the completed Channel Tunnel Rail Link (CTRL).

Government approval for the CTRL was granted in 1996 and work started immediately on a plan which would link London with mainland Europe as never before. Arup's rail network plan identified the quickest route into London, through its eastern fringes, and developed a concept that integrated both domestic trains with the new international rail link.

Part of this plan was the design and construction of Stratford International Station, which is an integral element within the vast regeneration of east London and the development of Stratford City – a part of the UK capital that will become synonymous with the 2012 Olympic Games.

The new station will provide a high speed rail link to the continent, as well as catering for domestic journeys throughout the south-east of the UK. Its form, designed by Rail Link Engineering for CTRL, is that of an elevated bridge, providing access to station facilities from both sides of the tracks.

The main concourse has been conceived as a public space at the heart of the local community with retail outlets and a café. The departure lounge and immigration points are accessed from both ends of the bridge and converge on a central portal with views to all areas of the station. A central atrium provides access to ground level platforms.

The translucent roof "levitates" above the station and cantilevers to provide shelter for the pick-up and set-down points to either side. Perimeter facades fold up to provide a diaphanous skin that projects beyond the roof plane so that at night the whole station will glow.

At track level, two international platforms are situated at the outer edges of the station, while two domestic platforms are located as central islands. A mezzanine level houses staff areas and accommodation for customs, immigration and the police. Plant areas are located at ground level at the bridge's perimeter for easy servicing and maintenance.

This disused brownfield site has now been transformed into a rail link that will process 2.8 million passengers each year and be the main point of entry into the UK for continental Europeans visiting the 2012 Olympics.

The main pavilion above track level

One of the first key buildings to be completed as part of London's bid for the 2012 Olympic Games, the station will play an important role in transferring athletes and spectators from central London to the main arena. Its clean simple lines mirror those of the Stratford City underground link. Both transport links form an important part of the regeneration of east London. The station is due for completion in mid 2006, with track work continuing until 2009.

Aerial view of the model

360-degree interior image during construction

Section showing the transparent roof lozenge

Internal circulation during construction

The drama of the station is dependent upon the flow of natural light to platform level. This is achieved via the large central atrium, where escalators descend from ticketing halls and retail concessions to both high-speed rail links and local services. The roof of this atrium is a transparent element, designed to "float" over the structure, illuminating both ground and platform levels. At night it will glow with light from the building's interior.

Environmental Rail Building Design

Oliver Lowenstein

Oliver Lowenstein is a green cultural theorist and writer. He has written widely on contemporary sustainable architecture and design, ecological art and craft, and new media and music. Much of this appears in the green cultural review journal Lowenstein runs, *Fourth Door Review*.

Albeit thin on the ground, ecological design is beginning to be integrated into travel buildings, adding another dimension to our understanding of sustainable transport, and providing a living example of environmental synergy in action. However, there is a long way to go in the development of environmentally friendly buildings, as is also true of the entire transport network.

While governments and the private consortiums that own the transportation networks try to convince the wider population that rail travel is "an effective, reliable and environmentally necessary mode of transport", in the UK at least, the reality is far different. In recent years, the railway network has come close to collapse due to poor winter weather planning, an historical lack of maintenance and numerous well reported accidents. The combination has spelt disaster for rail companies: people migrated away from rail travel, forcing them into the Catch 22 situation of having to cancel services and increase ticket prices. The majority of the public now suffers from a sense of injustice at the hands of the rail operators and has a gross lack of confidence in the reliability of rail travel.

However, like it or not, railways have long been heralded as the most environmental form of medium and long distance transport. Trains convey hundreds of people while cars can transport only a handful at the very most. The cumulative environmental benefits of trains as key to the future of any integrated transport systems outweighs their costs, and compared to private automobiles, whether run on non-fossil fuels or not, public transport is still the most rational long-term environmental choice.

Now, in the UK, a small proportion of the general public is slowly coming round to see railways as an environmental choice. And, while climate change may bring temporary chaos to the railways each year, it has underscored the seriousness of thinking about long term transport networks which credibly face the challenge of resource and energy efficiencies required to balance environmental factors such as carbon emissions.

With significant investment being poured back into the railways there seems at least some hope that the environmental dimension of railways will move increasingly to the foreground of planning and strategic thinking. But what has this got to do with buildings? In this context, the built environment in all its guises – although most visibly in the buildings that service the travelling public – is a part of the equation. Here, it seems the sustainable architecture, buildings, and materials nexus may find a unique opportunity. By pursuing the integration of sustainability into stations and other building projects, the dual-win environmental synergy of sustainable travel modes alongside an environmentally sensitive infrastructure reinforces the positive message that environmental thinking, when applied to whole systems, can be significantly more effective than in isolation. Not only this but if the psychological attractiveness of transit nodes, stations, and so on, were also integrated as part of a sustainable approach, this could have far-reaching effects for the choices members of the public make when travelling.

Building More Wisely

Rail stations, and the other myriad parts of the transport building infrastructure, are not a particularly glamorous part of the architectural world. While this book highlights some of the newest, best architectural designs, most passenger terminals are mundane affairs. Airports are the one major exception, the glamour of flying somehow exerting its influence on the building designs. These largest of transport nodes lead the pecking order, whereas bus stations and even more so the humble bus-shelter are at the other end of the spectrum – mostly ignored by architects and media alike.

A prolific range of showcase examples regarding the modest application of sustainable practice to the transport infrastructure is yet to be produced. As far as railways are concerned, in Britain and the USA there are the high-profile projects such as Nicholas Grimshaw's Waterloo Eurostar extension, or the same architect's designs for New York's Fulton Street Interchange, but these have been framed within the vocabulary of "hi-ecotech". In the UK, those with influence are now waking up to their environmental responsibilities, but for the most part the USA is simply ploughing on regardless. However, in the near future President Bush may even become more receptive to the sustainability dimension of buildings, following concerted pressure from a growing number of US States. And this new dimension may well offer an opening for forward-looking architects and building and construction companies.

However, continental Europe has gone some way to embrace the environmental mantle and a range of examples does exist. Although some work originates from the resource efficiency paradigm of lightweight materials, others demonstrate that there are projects that fuse the concerns of using natural and local materials, low energy use, and an aesthetic in sympathy with the environmentally conscious building movement.

The Norwegian Model

Although hardly known outside its native Norway, one of the most ambitious European transport building projects of the 1990s was the Gardemoen Airport which opened in late 1998, 32 kilometres (20 miles) north of Norway's capital, Oslo. As part of this, a new rail link was built from the city-centre station out to Gardemoen. At the initial planning stage, ten years earlier, sustainability was singled out as a priority for the later planning, design and tendering processes. By March 1995 research into suitable materials was being concluded using what the lead architect, Jan Ellef Soyland, describes as a top-down pragmatic rather than an "ideal" approach. It is this type of approach to sustainable design that least sends the client fleeing with the cheque book, while still encouraging a step towards a change in attitudes to transport building design.

During the run-up period to project commencement, the design research team on Gardemoen Airport carried out extensive research on materials, setting up an in-house data-base. For the airport as a whole there was a decision early in its planning to use exposed matt finish on surfaces and easily sourced natural materials including stone, wood and metal. Due to limited environmental materials information, both tests and analyses on all materials were carried out in-house, in collaboration with the Danish-Norwegian company Hjellnes-Cowi. As a result some products were dropped, primarily those connected to health hazards or allergic reactions and emissions (including the release of poison in potential fire situations, for example through PVC and CCA impregnated timber). Restrictions were also put in place on the use of rainforest timbers.

Another significant part of the evaluation of materials was around issues of their installation, either mechanically or chemically. Glues and surface treatments were subject to these evaluations, which engendered a systems approach of viewing the complex use of materials, installation and treatment as a whole. (Refer to appendix 2 for the criteria for evaluating materials.)

The project, although centred on the airport, also included the design and landscaping of the new railway to Oslo. Along with the Oslo and Gardemoen terminals, three new stations were built on the route – Lillestrom, Eidsvoll, and Asker stations. All these buildings were subject to the same environmental criteria set by the main airport. As such, they were and, unfortunately due to the slow uptake of sustainable ideals, still are models of sustainable design.

The first two stations, Lillestrom and Eidsvoll, were designed by the veteran Norwegian transport architect Arne Henriksen. The environmental project stipulation aided the design choice of natural materials – slate and wood – for both of his stations. He sees the environmental provision as setting a benchmark for their integration into the Norwegian transit building infrastructure.

Lillestrom is a medium-sized station in a town of the same description, on the Norwegian scale of things. The handsome feel of the platforms and their canopy shelters is entirely due to their simplicity of design and use of materials. They are constructed from laminated timber, glass and steel. Beyond the entrance hallway the slate flooring underpass links to the four platforms and the two sides of the railway-spliced town, bringing life and a local material connection for these separate parts of the town. The limited palette of natural materials is a simple and yet immensely effective method of designing sustainably: high-tech is not necessarily high environmental design.

Eidsvoll is an altogether smaller country station, at the end of the line, beyond the airport. Once again the station canopies are constructed from wood – a strikingly visual contrast to that of the ubiquitous use of man-made materials in modern British station shelter structures. But this use of locally sourced natural materials serves two agendas – it "builds" the station's attractiveness, as everyone likes the look and texture of wood, while also making use of readily available and inexpensive products.

The wood used in the laminated timber beams is pine grown in Norwegian managed forests from the region of east Norway (Østland), which encompasses Oslo. The wood used on the walls is birch plywood from Finland. No chemical treatment has been applied to either the timber beams, or the plywood walls. Instead they are treated with BioSafe oil, which contains no non-organic compounds or other additives. Other wood, the interior floor for example, is treated with a vegetable-based soap. Not only does it use sustainable materials but their calculated embodied energy is kept to a minimum too.

The slate was sourced from the Gudbrandsdalen region. The material's beauty as a building stone has long been prized, as it is filled with 50 to 75 millimetre (2 to 3 inch) long black amphibole crystals. This slate was also used at the Gardemoen Airport. The concrete used on the project is treated with multiple coats of a water-based paint at an approximate ratio of 20 per cent paint, and 80 per cent water.

For both airport and railway link the environmental criteria were organized around the available natural resources; the extent of transportation (energy consumption); energy consumption and working environment under production; the working environment under construction; environmental influence during use/emissions (eg the indoor climate); waste and reuse under construction and future demolishing; available environmental declaration; recipes of ingredients for important materials; and lifecycle analyses/ lifecycle costs.

Gardemoen airport is a flagship project for Norway, and the strategic, political and prestige reasons for including environmental issues in the design brief ought not to be overlooked. However, that is not to say that these projects embody perfect sustainable design. The significant limits of Gardemoen's environmentalism are clear as well. Consider the ubiquitous use of glass at the airport and the newly redesigned Oslo station site, which can hardly be claimed as an environmental feature as far as lighting and heating is concerned, especially in a country which spends so many winter hours in darkness. And, if environmentalists wanted to really question the validity of the project they can simply cite the point that airports encourage the most unsustainable of travel options, which in itself needs to be drastically reduced.

That said, the airport, with its wave-form roof and massive beam structures high above the passengers crossing the central atrium, is an impressively striking building. As is the whole transport system into Oslo that supplements it. As the third largest project in Europe at the time of its building in the mid-90s, the inclusion of environmental research and design as part of its brief gives it a benchmark quality for other transport infrastructure programmes and projects.

A German Solution

A smaller, more modest though equally interesting example of the integration of sustainabilty with transit systems can be found on the outskirts south-east of Stuttgart in southern Germany. As the result of the planning of a new local tramway (route U7), a competition to design four new stations was held. The new Ruhbank tramway runs through the local Waldau forests, so for the proposed station in these woods, at Degerloch, the competition stipulated a design which used local woods as a central feature.

The winning result, designed by the Stuttgart practice Jakob and Bluth, optimizes the integration of wood, glass and metal. Apart from the tramway platform and structure on the lower level, the transit interchange also features a bus station on the upper secondary level. The buildings use larch for structural columns and spruce for the canopies and sheltering. Larch was used for its longevity, and in part for its natural preservative qualities. Where the wood isn't exposed, the larch has been left untreated, lessening the requirement for additional preservation substances. Where it was required, low-impact boron preservative has replaced the heavily toxic copper chrome arsenic – outlawed for the last decade in Germany. A glazed roof sits atop the columns and the spruce is used for the canopies and shelters.

Overall the balance between all three materials was calculated to economically optimize the quantity of each of them so that no excess material was required. This so-called "Minimalismus" approach is statutory in Germany and Austria, which results both in the absence of left over cut-offs or other materials, and as an almost coincidental by-product, brings an aesthetic elegance to the design. The minimization of waste materials is a lesson still to be properly learned in the UK and the USA, where on-site waste can often account for 10 per cent of material costs. This method, rather than the other way round, where the aesthetics determine the choice and use of materials, is a growing trend in architecture and one that should be promoted in the search for more economical architecture.

As with many new projects, sustainability issues find their way into the brief because they are architecturally relevant rather than for puritanical environmental reasons. And this German project, again, is a pragmatic approach where a station has been designed that also closely fits the criteria of the sustainable building perspective. From these two projects emerge contrasting examples of how environmental building practices are synergizing with modern railway and transit systems. In so doing they are forming the beginnings of a new synthesis and alliance between ecologically sensitive modes of transport and the leading edges of building and design. However, on a wider scale, ecologically sustainable construction needs more investment and incentives from both public and private sectors if we are to convert the car-loving masses back onto the public transport system.

The dream of railways realizing something of their promise as "environmentally necessary modes of transport" is still in its infancy. The solutions put forward here are not globally applicable and each new project, dependent on its location, size and complexity, will encounter different environmental problems and solutions, but the innovative and aesthetically pleasing design ideals that created them are easily transferable. Couple this with local knowledge both of materials and public aspirations and sustainable railway and transport architecture can make a difference.

Appendix 1

This piece highlights projects that have utilized "natural" materials. There are of course many other approaches, which can be described as sustainable, depending on the definitions of sustainable one decides to follow. Another that could be mentioned here is a research project occuring in Holland at present. Adriaan Beukers, author of "Lightness: the inevitable renaissance of lightweight materials", and his research team at the technical Delft University of Technology have undertaken extensive research into ultra-lightweight fibre-based materials with reference to transport. For details of this part of their research see Eric Tempelman's book *Sustainable Transport and Advanced Materials*.

Appendix 2

The Gardemoen Airport project subjected each building material suggested by the design team to an evaluation using the following criteria: the kind of use and location the materials are meant for; quantity required; how the materials are installed (mechanically or chemically); dimensions required; architectonic and aesthetic properties (surface /colour); functionality; safety in use and in life; fire protection qualities; acoustic qualities; ease of cleaning and maintenance; environmental and ecological qualities; lifecycle analyses and lifecycle costs; alternative materials available.

Contact Details

Details set in roman refer to the architect; those set in *italics* refer to the photographer

AIR

Barajas Airport
Richard Rogers Partnership
www.rrp.co.uk
+44 (0) 207 385 1235
Amparo Garrido
+ 34 915 211 513
ampi@amparogarrido.com

Beijing Airport
Foster and partners
www.fosterandpartners.com
+44 (0) 207 738 0455

Philadelphia International Airport
Kohn Pedersen Fox
www.kpf.com
+1 212 977 6500
Alan Karchmer
+1 202.244.7511
ak@alankarchmer.com
Woodruff/Brown
+1 860.232.8977
woodruffbrown@yahoo.com
Keystone Aerial Surveys, Inc.
+1 215.464.2889
info@keystoneaerialsurveys.com
Advanced Media Design (AMD)
+1 401.475.6533
jon@amdrendering.com

Virgin Club House
Sharples Holden Pasquarelli
www.shoparc.com
+1 212 889 9005
Seong Kwon
shkwon@earthlink.net
+1 212 786 1024
Virgin Atlantic Airways

Bankok International Airport
Murphy Jahn
www.murphyjahn.com
+1 312 427 7300
Model shots: Keith Palmer
Construction: Carl D'Silva (Murphy Jahn)

Tianjin Binhai Airport
Kohn Pedersen Fox
www.kpf.com
+1 212 977 6500
Hayes Davidson
+44 207 262 4100
www.hayesdavidson.com

Ben Gurion International Airport
Moshe Safdie & Associates
www.msafdie.com
+1 617 629 2100
Alan Karchmer
www.alankarchmer.com
+1 914 698 4060

ROAD

Vauxhall Cross Interchange
Arup Associates
www.arup.com/associates
+44 (0) 207 755 5555
Christian Richters
+49 251 27 74 47
chrichters@aol.com

Burda Car Park
Ingenhoven und Partner
www.ingenhoven-overdiek.de
+49 211 3010 101
H.G. Esch
+49 (0)2248 4455-07
www.hgesch.de

Whale Jaw Bus Station
NIO Architecten
www.nio.nl
+31 (0)104122318
Hans Pattist
+ 31 180-59 98 33

Multi-storey Bike Park
VMX Architects
www.vmxarchitects.nl
+ 31(0)20.6761211
Jeroen Musch
www.jeroenmusch.nl
+31 (0) 650 241 662

Border Station
Ross Barney & Jankowski Architects
www.rbjarchitects.com
+1 312 832 0601

Cockpit and Barrier
ONL
www.oosterhuis.nl
+31 (0)10 244 70 39

Munich Central Station
Auer & Weber Architekten
+49 711 268 404 0
www.auer-weber.de

Underground Car Park
Szyszkowitz & Kowalski
www.szy-kow.at
+43 316 32 7575
Angelo Kaunat
+43 (676) 604 36 11
www.kaunat.com/
Hasso Hohmann

Molndal Commuter Station
Wingardh Arkitekt
www.wingardh.se
+46 (0)31 743 70 00
Ulf Celander
+4631-775 29 78
ulf@ulfcelander.se

Boxhill Interchange
McGauran Soon Architects
+61 3 9670 1800
mgs@mcgauransoon.com.au

Cycle Station
Oliver Lowenstein
fourthdoor@pavilion.co.uk
Architecture Ensemble
+44 (0) 207 278 7064
John Franklin
+44 (0) 7976 726 002

WATER
Yokohama Ferry Terminal
Foreign Office Architects
www.f-o-a.net
+44 (0) 7033 9800
Satora Mishima
James Haig Streeter
haigstreeterj@edaw.co.uk

Ship Naviduct
Zwarts & Jansma Architects
www.zja.nl
info@zja.nl
Zwarts & Jansma Architects
www.zja.nl
info@zja.nl

DFDS Terminal
3X Nielsen
www.3xn.dk
+45 8731 4848
Adam Mørk
+45 35858160
adam@adammork.dk

Salerno Ferry Terminal
Zaha Hadid Architects
www.zaha-hadid.com
+44 (0) 20 7253 5147

Leith Ferry Terminal
Jessam Al Jawad
jessam_aljawad@hotmail.com

Vlieland
DAAD
www.daad.nl
+31 (0) 593 582 450
Christian de Bruyie
+31 (0)75 622 73 65
www.studiochristiaandebruijne.nl

Falkirk (Wheel) Boat Lift
RMJM
www.rmjm.com
+44 (0)20 7549 8900
Matt Laver
www.mattlaver.com
+44 (0)131 664 4212

St George Terminal
HOK
www.hok.com
+1 212 741 1200
Adrian Wilson
+1 212 729-7077
www.interiorphotography.net

Whitehall Terminal
Frederic Schwartz Architects
www.schwartzarch.com
+1 212 741 3021
Jody Kivort
jkivort@hotmail.com
+1 917 676 0365

RAIL
Shinkhansen Stations
Makoto Sei Watanabe
www.makoto-architect.com
Makoto Sei Watanabe

Moscow City Transport Terminal
Behnisch Architekten
www.behnisch.com
+49-711-6077 20

Kings Cross Redevelopment
John McAslan + Partners
www.mcaslan.co.uk
+44 (0) 207 727 2663

Leuven Station
Samyn & Partners
www.samynandpartners.com
+32 2374 9060
Guido Coolens
+32 3238 7410
Samyn & Partners

Stuttgart Station
Ingenhoven Architekten
www.ingenhoven-overdiek.de
+49 211 3010 101
Holger Knauf
+49 (0)211 775502
www.holgerknauf.de

Worb Train Shed
Smarch
www.smarch.ch
+41 31 312 9600
Beat Mathys (Smarch)
Jantscher
+41 793 414 810
www.jantscher.ch

Dortmund CTRL
BRT Architekten
www.brt.de
+49 4024 8420

Fulton Street Interchange
Grimshaw Architects
www.grimshaw-architects.com
+44 (0) 207 291 4141
Esto/ Jock Pottle
www.esto.com
+1 914 698 4060

Stratford International Station
Rail Link Engineering
www.ctrl.co.uk Spheroview
www.spheroview.com
+44 (0) 1892 546 020

Bibliography

The majority of the research for this book was conducted through industry knowledge and contacts as well as the internet. Key sources were:

World Architecture, The Builder Group
Architectural Review, EMAP
RIBA Journal, CMP Information
Architects Journal, EMAP
Architectural Record, McGraw Hill
Arkitektur, Arkitektur Förlag AB
A+U, Japan Architect
Blueprint, Wilmington
Building, CMP Information
Light magazine, Wilmington
Monitor, Bleispa
Materia, Materia
Tectonica, ATC Ediciones
Arup Journal, Arup
Building Design, CMP Information
Canadian Architect, Business Information Group
De Architect, SDU
Frame, Frame
Indesign, Indesign Publishing
The Guardian
The New York Times
The Times
The Observer
The Independent

Books

The Airport Book: From Landing Field to Modern Terminal
Martin Greif, Main Street Press, Mayflower Books 1989
Planning and Design of Airports
Robert Horonjeff and Francis McKelvy, McGraw Hill Book Company 1983
Building for Air Travel : Architecture and Design for Commercial Aviation
John Zukowsky, The Art Institute of Chicago, 1996
New York
Susanna Sirefan, Ellipsis, 2001
New York
Will Jones, Carlton Publishing Group, 2002
Contemporary World Architecture
Hugh Pearman, Phaidon, 1998

Websites

Hudsonriver.com
Ruralroads.org
inventorsabout.com
wikipedia.org
irfca.org
greatbuildings.com
railcentre.co.uk
railwaysarchive.co.uk
britainexpress.com
canaljunction.com
canals.org
tamu.edu
sciencemuseum.org.uk
allstar.fiu.edu

Index

Page numbers in *italics* refer to picture captions

acoustic barriers *65,* 100–7
air terminals 10
  lighting 32
  passenger circulation 32
  retail design 14–15
  featured buildings:
    International Terminal, Philadelphia Airport, Pennsylvania, USA *11, 19,* 32–7
    Terminal 1, Changi Airport, Singapore 14
    Terminal Five, Heathrow Airport, London, UK 19
    Terminal One, Charles de Gaulle Airport, Paris, France 18, *56*
    TWA Terminal, New York, USA 18
Airbus A380 19
airports 10
  colour 20, 28, 48
  environment-friendly building 28
  lighting 14, 28, 38
  passenger circulation 13, 15, 20, 42, 48, 52
  passenger lounges 19, 38
  retail design 12–15, 18
  viewing areas 20, *35,* 48, 52
  featured buildings:
    Bangkok International Airport, Bangkok, Thailand 18, 42–7
    Barajas Airport, Madrid, Spain 20–7
    Beijing Capital International Airport, Beijing, China 19, 28–31
    Ben Gurion International Airport, Tel Aviv, Israel *9,* 52–7
    Chek Lap Kok Airport, Hong Kong 13, 14, 28
    Dulles Airport, Washington, USA 18
    Gardemoen Airport, Oslo, Norway 261, 262, 263
    Gatwick Airport, London, UK 10, 13
    Heathrow Airport, London, UK 19
    La Guardia Airport, New York, USA 10
    Stansted Airport, Essex, UK 18, 28
    Sydney Airport, Sydney, Australia 13
    Tempelhof Airport, Berlin, Germany 10, 18, 19
    Tianjin Binhai International Airport, Tianjin, China 48–51
    Vancouver Airport, Vancouver, Canada 13
    Virgin Atlantic Upper Class Lounge, JFK Airport, New York, USA 19, 38–41
  see also air terminals
Al Jawad, Jessam 139, 162–9
Alsop & Stormer 139
Andreu, Paul 18, *56*
The Architecture Ensemble 128–31
"Art in Architecture" projects 94
Arup Associates *132*
Beijing Capital International Airport, Beijing, China 28
Box Hill Transport Interchange, Melbourne, Australia 124
Falkirk Wheel, Falkirk, Scotland 174
Fulton Street Transit Center, New York, USA 248
Stratford International Station, London, UK 254
Vauxhall Cross Interchange, London, UK *11, 65,* 66–73
Auer + Weber Architekten 108–11
Australia
  Box Hill Transport Interchange, Melbourne, Australia 65
  Sydney Airport, Sydney 13
Austria: Underground Parking Garage, Graz 64, *65,* 112–17

Baker, Herbert 202
Balijon, Lodewijk 148
Bangkok International Airport, Bangkok, Thailand 18, 42–7
Barajas Airport, Madrid, Spain 20–7
Barlow, William Henry 10, 202
Behnisch Architekten 212–15
Beijing Capital International Airport, Beijing, China 19, 28–31
Belgium: Leuven Station, Leuven *203,* 224–9
Ben Gurion International Airport, Tel Aviv, Israel *9,* 52–7
Bonatz, Peter 230
Border Station, Sault St. Marie, Michigan, USA 94–9
Box Hill Transport Interchange, Melbourne, Australia 65, 124–7
Briare Canal, France 138
BRT Architekten 242–7
Burda Media Park car park, Offenburg, Germany 65, 74–9
Buro Happold 230
bus stations
  colour 118
  lighting 108
  viewing areas 108, 118
  featured buildings:
    Central Bus Station, Munich, Germany 65, 108–11
    Mölndal Commuter Station, Mölndal, Sweden 118–23
    The Whale Jaw Bus Station, Hoofddorp, Netherlands *9,* 80–7
  see also tramway stations; transport interchanges
Butterley Engineering 174

Canada: Vancouver Airport, Vancouver 13
Canal du Midi, France 138
canals and canal engineering
  boat lifts 138, 174–81
  history of 8, 9, 138, 174
  locks 9, 138, *139,* 148–51
  featured buildings:
    Falkirk Wheel, Falkirk, Scotland 138,174–81
    Naviduct Lock Complex, Enkhuizen, Netherlands 138, *139,* 148–51
car parks 64, 65
  colour 112
  lighting 66, 112
  featured buildings:
    Burda Media Park car park, Offenburg, Germany 65, 74–9
    Underground Parking Garage, Graz, Austria 64, *65,* 112–17
    Worb Train Shed, Worb, Switzerland 234
car showrooms: Cockpit, A2 Highway, Utrecht, Netherlands 100–7
Carpenter, James 248
cars 8, 60, 64, 65
Central Bus Station, Munich, Germany 65, 108–11
Central Station, Dortmund, Germany 242–7
Channel Tunnel Rail Link (CTRL) 216, 254
Chek Lap Kok Airport, Hong Kong 13, 14, 28
Chiao Wei-yo 9, 138
China
  canals and locks 9, 138
  featured buildings:
    Beijing Capital International Airport, Beijing 19, 28–31
    Tianjin Binhai International Airport, Tianjin 48–51
colour 20, 28, 48, 88, 112, 118
Cubitt, Lewis 216
cycle parks
  colour 88

environment-friendly building 128
featured buildings:
Cycle Parking Garage, Amsterdam, Netherlands 65, 88–93
Cycle Station project, UK 64, 128–31
Worb Train Shed, Worb, Switzerland 234
cycles and cycling 64, 88, *90*

DAAD Architecten *11, 139,* 170–3
Darius 1, emperor of Persia 8, 138
Denmark: DFDS Terminal, Copenhagen 139, 152–7
DFDS Terminal, Copenhagen, Denmark 139, 152–7
Drucker, Kenneth *196*
Dulles Airport, Washington, USA 18

Eidsvoll Station, Eidsvoll, Norway 261, 262
engineering in transport architecture 132–5
Engler, Paul and Klaus 18
the environment
environmental problems
climate change 64, *90,* 128
emissions 8, 28, 59, 64, 261
fossil fuel use 64, 128
pollution 8, 11, 59, 65, 128, 139, 202, 203
smog 8, 64
traffic congestion 59, 64, 65, 128, 139
waste 28, 263
environment-friendly building 260–3
choice of materials 261, 262, 263
energy saving measures 11, 28, 42, 190, *192,* 199, 230
living roofs 94, 182, 197, 199
photovoltaic panels 66, 128, 190, *192,* 199
prefabricated construction 28
see also sustainable design

Falkirk Wheel, Falkirk, Scotland 138, 174–81
Ferry Landing Stage, Vlieland, Netherlands *11, 139,* 170–3
ferry terminals
lighting 152, 158, 182, 190, 197
passenger circulation 139, 140, 152, 158, 190
ventilation 158
viewing areas *167,* 182, 190, 197
featured buildings:
DFDS Terminal, Copenhagen, Denmark 139, 152–7
Ferry Landing Stage, Vlieland, Netherlands *11, 139,* 170–3
Hamburg Ferry Terminal, Hamburg, Germany 139
Leith Ferry Terminal, Leith, Scotland 139, 162–9
Nagasaki and Shichiruiko terminals, Japan 139
St George Ferry Terminal, New York, USA *9,* 182–9, 196, 197–9
Whitehall Ferry Terminal, New York, USA *11,* 190–5, 196, 198, 199
Yokohama International Port Terminal, Yokohama, Japan 139, 140–7
Maritime Terminal, Salerno, Italy 158–61
Foreign Office Architects (FOA) 139, 140–7
Foster & Partners 18, 19, 28–31
Fourth Door Research 128–31
France
canals and locks 138
metro system, Paris 203
Terminal One, Charles de Gaulle Airport, Paris 18, *56*
Frederic Schwartz Architects *11,* 190–5
Fulton Street Transit Center, New York, USA *203,* 248–53, 261

Gardemoen Airport, Oslo, Norway 261, 262, 263
Gatwick Airport, London, UK 10, 13
Germany
Car Park, Burda Media Park, Offenburg 65, 74–9
Central Bus Station, Munich 65, 108–11
Central Station, Dortmund 242–7
Hamburg Ferry Terminal, Hamburg 139
Stuttgart Central Station, Stuttgart *9,* 230–3
Tempelhof Airport, Berlin 10, 18, 19
tramway stations 262–3
Grimshaw Architects *203,* 248–53, 261

Hadid, Zaha 158–61
Hamburg Ferry Terminal, Hamburg, Germany 139
health issues 8, 11, 261
Heathrow Airport, London, UK 19
Hellmuth, Obata + Kassabaum (HOK) *9,* 182–9, *196*
Henriksen, Arne 261
history of transport 8–10, 64, 138–9, 202
Hjellnes-Cowi 261
Hoar Marlow & Lovett 10
Holm, David *12*
Hong Kong: Chek Lap Kok Airport 13, 14, 28

India: Victoria Station (Chhatrapati Shivaji Terminus), Mumbai 202
Ingenhoven Architekten *9,* 74–9, 230–3
integration in the landscape
border stations 94
bus stations 108
train stations and buildings 216, *220,* 224, 234
International Terminal, Philadelphia Airport, Pennsylvania, USA *11, 19,* 32–7
Israel: Ben Gurion International Airport, Tel Aviv *9,* 52–7
Italy
Maritime Terminal, Salerno 158–61
Stazione Leopolda, Florence 202
Termini Station, Rome 203

Jakob and Bluth 262
Japan
MLX01 (MagLev) train 203
Shinkhansen railway system 203, 204
featured buildings:
Kashiwa-Tanaka Station, Kashiwa 204, 210–11
Kashiwanoha-Campus Station, Kashiwa, Japan 204, 206–7
Nagasaki and Shichiruiko ferry terminals 139
Shin-Minamata Station, Minimata 204, 208–9
Yokohama International Port Terminal, Yokohama 139, 140–7
John McAslan + Partners 216–23
Johnson, Steve (Architecture Ensemble) 128

Karmi Architects 52
Karpowicz, Terry 94
Kashiwa-Tanaka Station, Kashiwa, Japan 204, 210–11
Kashiwanoha-Campus Station, Kashiwa, Japan 204, 206–7
King's Cross Station, London, UK 216–23
Kohn Pederson Fox (KPF) *11, 19,* 32–7, 48–51

La Guardia Airport, New York, USA 10
Lau, S.Y. *58*

Leith Ferry Terminal, Leith, Scotland 139, 162–9
Leonardo da Vinci 9, 138
Leuven Station, Leuven, Belgium *203,* 224–9
lighting
  airports and terminals 14, 28, 32, 38
  bus stations 108
  car parks 66, 112
  ferry terminals 152, 158, 182, 190, 197
  train stations 212, 224, 230, *238,* 242
Lillestrom Station, Lillestrom, Norway 261, 262
Lissar Eldar Architects 52
Liverpool Road Station, Manchester, UK 10, 202
Lowenstein, Oliver (Fourth Door Research) 64, 128, *260*

MagLev trains 203
Maritime Terminal, Salerno, Italy 158–61
Mathys, Beat (Smarch) 234
Mazzoni, Angiolo 203
McGauran Soon Architects (MGS) 124–7
Metro subway system, Bangkok, Thailand 58, 59–61
Metro system, Moscow, Russia 203, 212–15
MG Bennett 174
Michel, Eve *196*
MLX01 (MagLev) train, Japan 203
Mölndal Commuter Station, Mölndal, Sweden 118–23
Montuori and Vitellozzi 203
Moscow City Transport Terminal, Moscow, Russia 212–15
Moshe Safdie & Associates *9,* 52–7
Murphy Jahn Architects 19, 42–7

Nagasaki and Shichiruiko ferry terminals, Japan 139
National Cycle Network 64, 128, *131*
Naviduct Lock Complex, Enkhuizen, Netherlands 138, *139,* 148–51
Netherlands
  Cycle Parking Garage, Amsterdam 65, 88–93
  Ferry Landing Stage, Vlieland *11, 139,* 170–3
  Naviduct Lock Complex, Enkhuizen 138, *139,* 148–51
  Sound Barrier and Cockpit, A2 Highway, Utrecht *65,* 100–7
  The Whale Jaw Bus Station, Hoofddorp *9,* 80–7
Netherlands Airport Consultants (NACO) 48–51
NIO Architecten *9,* 80–7
Norway
  Eidsvoll Station, Eidsvoll 261, 262
  environment-friendly building 261–2
  Gardemoen Airport, Oslo 261, 262, 263
  Lillestrom Station, Lillestrom 261, 262

ONL *65,* 100–7
Oosterhuis, Kas (ONL) 100
Ordish, R. M. 202
Otto, Frei 230

parking *see* car parks; cycle parks
politics of public transport 58–61
ports 138–9 *see also* ferry terminals
Pretoria Station, Pretoria, South Africa 202
Prust, Richard *132*
public transport 64–5 *see also* bus stations

Rail Link Engineering *203,* 254–9
railways 9–10, 202, 203
regeneration 66, *168,* 216, *218,* 242, 248, 254
Richard Rogers Partnership 20–7
RMJM 138, 174–81
roads 9, 60, 61, 64, 100
"The Rocket" locomotive (Stevenson) 9, 202
Rogers, Richard 20
Ross Barney + Jankowski (RBJ) 94–9
Russia
  Metro system, Moscow 203, 212–15
  Moscow City Transport Terminal, Moscow 212–15

Saarinen, Eero 18
safety and security issues 11, 66, *71,* 112
Sagebiel, Ernst 10, 18
Samyn and Partners *203,* 224–9
Semper, Gottfried 234
Sharples Holden Pasquarelli (ShoP) 19, 38–41
Shima, Hideo 203
Shimatsu, Yoichi *58*
Shin-Minamata Station, Minimata, Japan 204, 208–9
Shinkhansen railway system, Japan 203, 204
Singapore: Terminal 1, Changi Airport 14
Skidmore Owings & Merrill 52
Skytrain system, Bangkok, Thailand 58, 59, 60
Smarch *203,* 234–41
Sound Barrier and Cockpit, A2 Highway, Utrecht, Netherlands *65,* 100–7
South Africa: Pretoria Station, Pretoria 202
Soyland, Jan Ellef 261
Spain: Barajas Airport, Madrid 20–7
St George Ferry Terminal, New York, USA *9,* 182–9, 196, 197–9
St Pancras Station, London, UK 10, 202, 216
Stansted Airport, Essex, UK 18, 28
Staten Island Ferry system, New York, USA 182, 190, 196
stations *see* bus stations; subways; train stations
Stazione Leopolda, Florence, Italy 202
Stevens, Frederick 10, 202
Stratford International Station, London, UK *203,* 254–9
Stücheli, Ursula (Smarch) 234
Stuttgart Central Station, Stuttgart, Germany *9,* 230–3
subways and stations
  in Bangkok, Thailand 58, 59–61
  in New York, USA 132, 133–5, 203, 248–53
  sustainable design 28, 94, 128, 182, 199, 212, 260–3 *see also* environment
Sweden: Mölndal Commuter Station, Mölndal 118–23
Switzerland: Train Shed, Worb *203,* 234–41
Sydney Airport, Sydney, Australia 13
Szyszkowitz + Kowalski 64, *65,* 112–17

Takamatsu, Shin 139
Tempelhof Airport, Berlin, Germany 10, 18, 19
Terminal 1, Changi Airport, Singapore 14
Terminal Five, Heathrow Airport, London, UK 19
Terminal One, Charles de Gaulle Airport, Paris, France 18, *56*
terminals *see* air terminals; ferry terminals
Termini Station, Rome, Italy 203
terrorism 8, 18, 58
Thailand
  transport in Bangkok 58–61
  Bangkok International Airport, Bangkok 18, 42–7
3XNielsen 139, 152–7
Tianjin Binhai International Airport, Tianjin, China 48–51

"Tom Thumb" locomotive (Cooper) 9–10, 202
TRA Architects *9,* 52–7
train stations and buildings
access 248
environment-friendly building 260–3
history of 10, 202
in Bangkok, Thailand 58, 59
lighting 212, 224, 230, *238,* 242
ventilation 212, 224, 230
featured buildings:
Central Station, Dortmund, Germany 242–7
Eidsvoll Station, Eidsvoll, Norway 261, 262
Fulton Street Transit Center, New York, USA *203,* 248–53, 261
Kashiwa-Tanaka Station, Kashiwa, Japan 204, 210–11
Kashiwanoha-Campus Station, Kashiwa, Japan 204, 206–7
King's Cross Station, London, UK 216–23
Leuven Station, Leuven, Belgium *203,* 224–9
Lillestrom Station, Lillestrom, Norway 261, 262
Liverpool Road Station, Manchester, UK 10, 202
Moscow City Transport Terminal, Moscow, Russia 212–15
Pretoria Station, Pretoria, South Africa 202
Shin-Minamata Station, Minimata, Japan 204, 208–9
St Pancras Station, London, UK 10, 202, 216
Stazione Leopolda, Florence, Italy 202
Stratford International Station, London, UK *203,* 254–9
Stuttgart Central Station, Stuttgart, Germany *9,* 230–3
Termini Station, Rome, Italy 203
Victoria Station (Chhatrapati Shivaji Terminus), Mumbai, India 10, 202
Worb Train Shed, Worb, Switzerland *203,* 234–41
see also transport interchanges
tramway stations 262–3
transport interchanges
Box Hill Transport Interchange, Melbourne, Australia 65, 124–7
King's Cross Station, London, UK 216–23
Moscow City Transport Terminal, Moscow, Russia 212–15
St George Ferry Terminal, New York, USA 198
Vauxhall Cross Interchange, London, UK *11, 65,* 66–73
Whitehall Ferry Terminal, New York, USA 198
TWA Terminal, New York, USA 18
2012 Olympic Games, London, UK 254, *256*

UK
Cycle Station project 64, 128–31
Falkirk Wheel, Falkirk, Scotland 138, 174–81
Gatwick Airport, London 10, 13
Heathrow Airport, London 19
King's Cross Station, London 216–23
Leith Ferry Terminal, Leith, Scotland 139, 162–9
Liverpool Road Station, Manchester 10, 202
St Pancras Station, London 10, 202, 216
Stansted Airport, Essex 18, 28
Stratford International Station, London *203,* 254–9
Terminal Five, Heathrow Airport, London 19
2012 Olympic Games, London 254, *256*
Vauxhall Cross Interchange, London *11, 65,* 66–73
underground and stations 66, 203, 216, *223*
Underground Parking Garage, Graz, Austria 64, *65,* 112–17
USA
border traffic 94
Staten Island Ferry system, New York 182, 190, 196
subways, New York 132, 133–5
water-based architecture, New York 196–9
featured buildings:
Border Station, Sault St. Marie, Michigan 94–9
Dulles Airport, Washington 18
Fulton Street Transit Center, New York *203,* 248–53, 261
International Terminal, Philadelphia Airport, Pennsylvania *11, 19,* 32–7
La Guardia Airport, New York 10
St George Ferry Terminal, New York *9,* 182–9, 196, 197–9
TWA Terminal, New York 18
Virgin Atlantic Upper Class Lounge, JFK Airport, New York 19, 38–41
Whitehall Ferry Terminal, New York *11,* 190–5, 196, 198, 199

Vancouver Airport, Vancouver, Canada 13
vandalism *71,* 80, *84*
Vauxhall Cross Interchange, London, UK *11, 65,* 66–73
ventilation 158, 212, 224, 230
Victoria Station (Chhatrapati Shivaji Terminus), Mumbai, India 10, 202
viewing areas
airports 20, *35,* 48, 52
bus stations 108, 118
ferry terminals *167,* 182, 190, 197
Virgin Atlantic Upper Class Lounge, JFK Airport, New York, USA 19, 38–41
VMX Architects 88–93

Watanabe, Makoto-Sei 203, 204–11
The Whale Jaw Bus Station, Hoofddorp, Netherlands *9,* 80–7
Whitehall Ferry Terminal, New York, USA *11,* 190–5, 196, 198, 199
Wingårdh Arkitektkontor 118–23
Worb Train Shed, Worb, Switzerland *203,* 234–41

Yokohama International Port Terminal, Yokohama, Japan 139, 140–7

Zwarts & Jansma Architects 138, *139,* 148–51

Acknowledgments

Picture credits

Cover: Arup Associates/Christian Richters; **Back cover**: NIO Architecten/Hans Pattist, RMJM/Matt Laver, Wingardh Arkitektkontor/Ulf Celander, Kohn Pedersen Fox/Woodruff Brown; **2** Wingardh Arkitektkontor/Ulf Celander; **4** Samyn & Partners/Coolens & Deleuil; **7** Richard Rogers Partnership/ Amparo Garrido; **8** NIO Architecten/Hans Pattist; **9** Samyn & Partners, Ingenhoven Architekten/Holger Knauf, Moshe Safdie & Associates/Alan Karchmer; **10** DAAD/Christian de Bruyie, Frederic Schwartz Architects, Arup Associates; **11** Kohn Pedersen Fox/Alan Karchmer; **16/17** Kohn Pedersen Fox/Woodruff Brown; **18** Foster and Partners; **19** Kohn Pedersen Fox, SHoP/Seong Kwon, Moshe Safdie & Associates/Alan Karchmer; **20-27** Richard Rogers Partnership/ Amparo Garrido; **28-31** Foster and Partners; **31-37** Pedersen Fox/Woodruff Brown, Alan Karchmer, Keystone Aerial Surveys, Advanced Media Design; **38-41** SHoP/Seong Kwon, Virgin Atlantic Airways; **42-47** Murphy Jahn; **48-51** Kohn Pedersen Fox/Hayes Davidson; **52-57** Moshe Safdie & Associates/Alan Karchmer; **62-63** Ingenhoven Architekten/H G Esch; **64** Arup Associates; **65** ONL, VMX Architects/Jeroen Musch, Szyszkowitz & Kowalski/Angelo Kaunat; **66-73** Arup Associates/Christian Richters; **74-79** Ingenhoven Architekten/H G Esch; **80-87** NIO Architecten/Hans Pattist; **88-93** VMX Architects/Jeroen Musch; **94-99** Ross Barney & Jankowski Architects; **100-107** ONL; **108-111** Auer & Weber Architekten; **112-117** Szyszkowitz & Kowalski/Angelo Kaunat; **118-123** Wingardh Arkitektkontor/Ulf Celander; **124-127** McGauran Soon Architects; **128-131** Fourth Door Research, Architecture Ensemble/John Franklin; **136-137** RMJM/Matt Laver; **138** 3X Nielsen/Adam Mork; **139** DAAD/Christian de Bruyie, Jessam Al Jawad, Zwarts & Jansma Architects; **140-147** Foreign Office Architects/ Satora Mishima, James Haig Streeter; **148-151** Zwarts & Jansma Architects; **152-157** 3X Nielsen/Adam Mork; **158-161** Zaha Hadid; **162-169** Jessam Al Jawad; **170-173** DAAD/Christian de Bruyie; **174-181** RMJM/Matt Laver; **182-189** HOK/Adrian Wilson; **190-195** Frederic Schwartz Architects/Jody Kivort; **200-201** Samyn & Partners; **202** Smarch/Thomas Jantscher; **203** Grimshaw Architects, Samyn & Partners, Rail Link Engineering/Spheroview; **204-211** Makoto Sei Watanabe; **212-215** Behnisch Architekten; **216-223** John McAslan + Partners; **224-229** Samyn & Partners/ Coolens & Deleuil; **230-233** Ingenhoven Architekten/Holger Knauf; **234-241** Smarch/Thomas Jantscher; **242-247** BRT Architekten; **248-253** Grimshaw Architects/Esto Jock Pottle; **254-259** Rail Link Engineering/Spheroview.

Author's acknowledgments

Thank you to everyone at publisher Mitchell Beazley for their vision, patience, and assistance in working with me to put this volume together. Thank you to all of the architects designing the great projects shown in these pages and to the photographers and image creators for the fabulous pictures you see. Finally, thank you to my wife Stephanie for putting up with me throughout this project. PS: cheers to Monkey and Jahn.